Abdul Aziz bin Sattam is Associate Professor of Islamic Policy (jurisprudence of governance) at Imam Muhammad ibn Saud Islamic University, Riyadh, Saudi Arabia, where he also obtained his doctorate in this subject. He acts as a consultant for a number of Saudi universities in developing curricula of Islamic law schools and the specialism of law in general. He has published widely on aspects of Islamic law, litigation and banking.

Muhammad A. S. Abdel Haleem is King Fahd Professor of Islamic Studies at the University of London, and Director of the Centre of Islamic Studies, SOAS. He is Editor in Chief of the *Journal of Qur'anic Studies*, and author of *The Qur'an: A New Translation* (2004) and *Understanding the Qur'an: Themes and Style* (I.B.Tauris, 2010).

LONDON ISLAMIC STUDIES

General Editor: Muhammad A. S. Abdel Haleem (King Fahd Professor of Islamic Studies, SOAS, University of London)

London Islamic Studies is a new and focused series dedicated to publishing, in English, the best international scholarship on topics, issues and debates centred on furthering understanding – particularly in the West – of Islam and the Muslim world. Such topics might include, though not be confined to, Islamic finance and economics; history, tradition and modernity; theology and ethics; education; science; gender issues; and the contexts, meanings and interpretations of the Sharia (Islamic law). While intended to be broad and inclusive in its coverage, accommodating a range of perspectives, the series aims in addition to bring exceptional academic scholarship from the Arab and Islamic lands to the wider attention of an English-speaking readership.

Sharīʿa and the Concept of Benefit

The Use and Function of *Maṣlaḥa* in Islamic Jurisprudence

Abdul Aziz bin Sattam

Foreword by
Muhammad A. S. Abdel Haleem

Published by I.B.Tauris in association with
the Centre of Islamic Studies, SOAS, The University of London

I.B.TAURIS
LONDON · NEW YORK

Published in 2015 by I.B.Tauris & Co Ltd
www.ibtauris.com

Distributed worldwide by I.B.Tauris & Co Ltd
Registered office: 6 Salem Road, London W2 4BU

ISBN: 978 1 78453 024 2
eISBN: 978 0 85773 659 8

London Islamic Studies 1

A full CIP record for this book is available from the British Library
A full CIP record is available from the Library of Congress

Library of Congress Catalog Card Number: available

Typeset by Free Range Book Design & Production Limited
Printed and bound by CPI Group (UK) Ltd, Croydon, CR0 4YY

MIX
Paper from responsible sources
FSC® C013604

CONTENTS

LIST OF ILLUSTRATIONS

LIST OF TABLES

FOREWORD

The basic purpose of legislation in Islam is to secure the welfare of society by promoting people's benefit or by protecting them against harm. The ways and means which bring benefit (*maṣlaḥa*) to people are endless. Benefit itself is not a fixed entity: something can be beneficial at one time and harmful at another and even at one and the same time it may be beneficial under certain circumstances but prove harmful under other circumstances, but consideration of *maṣlaḥa* is an essential tool for legislation. The need for *maṣlaḥa* stems from the following considerations:

1. The Sharīʿa in Islam is intended to be suitable for all times and places.
2. Texts, as the basic sources of Islam, are by the nature of things limited.
3. Human conditions and life circumstances are always evolving, bringing in new situations that require legislation.

Even from the time of the successors of the Prophet Muhammad, considerations of *maṣlaḥa* have been found to be important in justifying decisions made by rulers. For example, although there was nothing in the Qur'an or the traditions of the Prophet Muhammad to say the Qur'an should be collected in one volume, the first caliph, Abu Bakr (r. 632–4), decided, on grounds of *maṣlaḥa*, that the Qur'an should be collected in a volume to help preserve it instead of leaving it on sundry materials or relying solely on the memories of those who learnt it all or partly by heart. Similarly the second caliph, Umar (r. 634–44), set up administrative departments for the state and introduced the system of prisons. He also suspended the application of the penalty for theft at a time of famine. Throughout the centuries, *maṣlaḥa* has played a crucial role in legislation and the concept was elaborated by jurists along with other sources of Islamic law.

Conditions were set for the *maṣlaḥa* so that it is not left to any ruler's or other individual's whims or desires: the first condition is that it must be an actual *maṣlaḥa* that brings benefit and averts harm and does not exclude a *maṣlaḥa* with a greater benefit. Then it must not lead to a *mafsada* with equal or greater harm. Third, considerations of *maṣlaḥa* must not contradict a principle or a text established by the Qur'an or Traditions of the Prophet Muhammad, or the consensus of opinions of recognized legal authorities. Within these conditions, *maṣlaḥa* makes Islamic law capable of expanding all the time and meeting all sorts of new conditions and circumstances. It shows the dynamic nature of Islamic law. Muslim jurists have expended a vast amount of time and effort in defining *maṣlaḥa* and making sure it is not left open to corruption or misuse. The subject forms a major area of Islamic jurisprudence. There is a vast amount of material about it in Arabic but very little available in English. Hence the importance of this book written by Dr Abdul Aziz bin Sattam, a highly qualified scholar who has studied the subject in great depth and breadth in Arabic, relying on the most authoritative sources, and is now giving us the benefit of his knowledge and expertise in English, which is highly welcomed.

We are pleased, at the Centre of Islamic Studies, to see such an erudite book on *maṣlaḥa* in English and we find it a welcome addition to the series of books on Islam published for the Centre by I.B.Tauris. We commend it to all scholars and readers interested in Islamic law.

Muhammad A. S. Abdel Haleem
SOAS, University of London

INTRODUCTION

According to Islamic understanding, wise action is intended to secure benefit (*maṣlaḥa*) and avoid harm (*mafsada*) without violating the divine laws. As *maṣlaḥas* and *mafsadas* are changeable, the Sharīʿa rulings related to them also behave accordingly. Thus, Muslim scholars state that rulings change with the variation of time and circumstance. This is one example of the dynamic and comprehensive nature underpinning the system of the Islamic Sharīʿa. The Sharīʿa-approved *maṣlaḥa* works as an effective tool for adapting people's needs to the Sharīʿa in all circumstances, times and places.

In this work, the definition and function of *maṣlaḥa* will be closely analysed and explained. This will be achieved by first deconstructing it into its regulators, considerations and types of preferability, and then reassembling it into an integrated whole, thereby revealing to the reader how the system of *maṣlaḥa* affects the change of rulings.

Very little work has emerged in the English language that explains, from the Islamic perspective, how *maṣlaḥa*, as a tool of Islamic legal theory (*uṣūl al-fiqh*), operates in adapting human circumstances to the rulings of the Sharīʿa. At the same time, many of the Arabic works on *maṣlaḥa* have proven to be partial studies illustrated by lengthy examples. Some of these sources even consider *maṣlaḥa* as an aspect of evidence, especially when discussing the purposes of the Sharīʿa, rather than as an integrated system with specific characteristics.

This study intends to cover the topic by employing three primary approaches: description, analysis and synthesis. Description will be employed when exploring *maṣlaḥa* and its components, analysis when disassembling *maṣlaḥa* into its constituent parts and synthesis when reassembling it into an integrated system.

The Hypotheses

This study proposes that:

1. Wise action in Islam is based on a Sharīʿa-approved *maṣlaḥa*.
2. *Maṣlaḥa* is a distinct concept from benefit, but is interrelated with it in general and specific senses.
3. Sharīʿa-approved *maṣlaḥa* has a fixed criterion in Islamic jurisprudence as well as unlimited applications.
4. This fixed criterion of Sharīʿa-approved *maṣlaḥa* can be encapsulated in an integrated system and used as a tool for revealing the change of rulings according to type, degree and direction.

Chapter One

WHAT IS *MAṢLAḤA*?

1. The Definition of *Maṣlaḥa*: Linguistic and Terminological

The Arabic term *maṣlaḥa* (pl. *maṣāliḥ*) finds its root in the verbal noun *al-ṣalāḥ* (righteousness), which in turn is the antonym of *al-fasād* (corruption). Its primary signification is of 'benefit'. *Aṣlaḥa*, meaning to restore something after it has been corrupted, is a verbal form of the term.[1] Thus, in linguistic terms, the word *maṣlaḥa* may generally be applied in one of two ways. The first is to describe an object, or action, as 'being perfectly suitable for something'. For instance, a pen could be described as a *maṣlaḥa* when it is perfectly suitable for writing. The second, which is a figurative usage of the word *maṣlaḥa*, is to indicate an action as bringing benefit or preventing harm. For example, seeking knowledge is a *maṣlaḥa* in that it results in certain benefits.

The word *mafsada* is the antonym of *maṣlaḥa*, a factor that creates some limitations upon their joint usage. The terms cannot be jointly and concurrently employed to describe the same thing and to the same degree. Correspondingly they cannot be simultaneously removed from the description of something such that it is described as neither *maṣlaḥa* nor *mafsada* at the same time and to the same degree. As benefit is also the antonym of harm, the removal of harm is itself a *maṣlaḥa*.[2]

Istiṣlāḥ is to seek *maṣlaḥa*, while the verbal form *istaṣlaḥtu*, means 'I have sought what is beneficial.' According to al-Ghazālī (d. 505 AH), the original meaning of *maṣlaḥa* as a technical religious term is to secure a benefit or remove a harm. However, the medieval theologian saw an alternative meaning to be of a more particular relevance: that of the preservation of the Sharīʿa objectives. Al-Ghazālī states,

> The original meaning of *maṣlaḥa* is to secure benefit or prevent harm, but I do not imply this meaning. Indeed securing benefits and preventing harms are the objectives of the Creator [God] to achieve the interests of humankind as people's welfare lies in realising their objectives. However, what I mean by *maṣlaḥa* is preserving the Sharīʿa objectives.[3]

He then goes on to clarify that in his view the objectives of the Islamic Sharīʿa are five: preservation of religion, life, reason, offspring and property. Al-Ghazālī suggests that whatever assures the preservation of these five represents a *maṣlaḥa* and whatever fails to preserve them is a *mafsada*, the removal of which is a *maṣlaḥa* in itself.

Al-Ghazālī indicates that *maṣlaḥa* is of three types: *ḍarūriyyāt* (necessities), *ḥājjiyyāt* (needs) and *taḥsīniyyāt* (complements). He further explains that *maṣlaḥa* at both the levels of *ḥājjī* and *taḥsīnī* cannot be judged by the process of *istiṣlāḥ* alone, unless supported by an original textual precedent, otherwise legislation will be based on mere personal opinion. However, once supported by an original precedent, it becomes a *qiyās* (analogy). As for those classified as *ḍarūriyyāt* (necessities), al-Ghazālī asserts that *maṣlaḥa* must be reached through *ijtihād* (personal reasoning) made by a *mujtahid* (a scholar qualified to make *ijtihād*) but there is no need for the presence of an original precedent.

According to al-ʿIzz b. ʿAbd al-Salām (d. 660/1 AH),[4] *maṣlaḥa* is either the benefits and pleasures or their causes. As such, he classifies it into two categories: the first is the genuine literal form, that is the pleasures themselves. The second is allegorical, or the causes of such pleasures.[5] Ibn Taymiyya defines *maṣlaḥa* as 'the action that brings a preponderant benefit not declined by the Sharīʿa'.[6] Al-Lakhmī defines *maṣlaḥa* as 'the benefit that the All-Wise Legislator has intended for His servants: the preservation of their faith, life, intellect, offspring and property, according to a specific order'.[7] It would appear al-Lakhmī was influenced by al-Rāzī (d. 606 AH)[8] as we find the latter, in his work *al-Maḥṣūl*, defining *al-munāsib* (the suitable) as:

> What leads to what suits humankind either through attaining or retaining something. Attaining could be called 'bringing benefit' and retaining could be called 'removing harm', because the removal of what is intended to be retained is a harm and retaining it is a removal of a harm. Attaining and retaining could be either *maʿlūm* (certainly known) or *maẓnūn* (surmised) and in either case they could be either religious or temporal.[9]

As achieving a decision within the framework of the Sharīʿa is intended to achieve the greatest level of benefit, perhaps the most appropriate definition for *maṣlaḥa* in this study is as follows: 'The best option that achieves the optimum desired benefit, while avoiding contravention of the Sharīʿa.'

2. The Sharīʿa and Securing People's *Maṣlaḥas*

From the Islamic perspective, God created people and did not leave them without managing their affairs. Rather, He assisted them with His messengers and revealed to each His law (Sharīʿa), the obedience to which results in guidance away from the darkness of misguidance. The Qur'an, which is understood by Muslims to be God's word, indicates that such is the case with every Sharīʿa and that its application extends to all nations in all times, from the creation of Adam to the Day of Resurrection:

> We sent to you [Muḥammad] the Scripture with the truth, confirming the Scriptures that came before it and with final authority over them; so judge between them according to what God has sent down. Do not follow their whims, which deviate from the truth that has come to you. We have assigned a law and a path to each of you. If God had so willed, He would have made you one community, but He wanted to test you through that which He has given you. So race to do good; you will all return to God and He will make clear to you the matters you differed about.[10]

Islamically, Sharīʿa aims to secure and maximize benefits, preventing and minimizing harms in the best and fairest way possible and in avoidance of any contradiction or confusion. It is argued within Muslim discourse that its comprehensive and compact nature is such that for it to be the work of the Prophet, or indeed for him to have taken it from any other human being, is inconceivable; rather for them the book was asserted to be from God and the Prophet affirmed it as such. As the Qur'an states, 'No falsehood can touch it from any angle, a Revelation sent down from the Wise One, Worthy of All Praise.'[11]

The various texts falling under the Sharīʿa are not considered, within Islamic legal theory, to be contradictory to one another; rather they are considered part of a holistic corpus, dealing with different aspects of human existence. Each text deals with a certain issue in a way that achieves the *maṣlaḥa* for which it was revealed. Based on necessity, when a detailed text clashes with a general rule, or a general fundamental principle clashes with a general or specific objective, the detailed text should be excluded from the general rule and an exception should be made for the particular text from the general one. This is an acknowledged method of *ijtihād* (juristic reasoning) and an approach to evaluating between contradictory evidences. Ibn Taymiyya notes,

> The knowledge of correct and corrupt *qiyās* (analogy) is one of the noblest disciplines. This is known only to one who is well acquainted with the subtle meanings, objectives and innumerable merits of the Sharīʿa, together with what it includes of benefits for people in this life and in the Hereafter and what it contains of the utmost wisdom, overwhelming bounties and perfect justice.[12]

Muslim scholars, irrespective of their juristic school, unanimously argue[13] that the rulings of the Sharīʿa fully cover people's interests and cater for their realization. This is, according to them, regardless of whether these interests belong to necessities, needs or improvements and whether they are for people's worldly life or for the life to come, as described in the Qur'anic verse, 'Today I have perfected your religion for you, completed My blessing upon you and chosen Islam as your religion...'[14]

Contrary to the view of the Ẓāhirī school and al-Rāzī, the majority of jurists agree that the Sharīʿa rulings are motivated by the aim to secure and maximize *maslaḥa* and prevent and minimize *mafsada* for the people. Based on this general rule, scholars argued that analogy is a recognized source of evidence within the Sharīʿa. This agreement is reported by several Islamic legal theorists when dealing with the definition of the *ʿilla* (effective cause) and how to prove it through 'suitability'. An example is seen in al-Shāṭibī who said,

> That the Sharīʿas were revealed to achieve people's *maṣlaḥa* in both this life and the life to come is a claim that requires substantiation or refutation by evidence. However, it is not suitable to do so here. This is a subject of difference amongst scholars of *ʿilm al-kalām* (scholastic theology). Al-Rāzī claimed that God's rulings and actions are not dependent on any cause. He also claimed that Muʿtazilī scholars have agreed that God's rulings are driven by the cause of achieving *maṣlaḥa* for the people and that this is the preferred opinion of most of the late jurists. When he [al-Rāzī] was obliged to admit the existence of effective cause in the Sharīʿa rulings in his arguments in the discipline of Islamic legal theory (*uṣūl al-fiqh*), he interpreted the effective causes as the signs that indicate the rulings in particular, and there is no need to examine this issue [here].
>
> However, the approved opinion is that which we have induced from the Sharīʿa: that it is established to secure people's *maṣlaḥa*. Such induction cannot be challenged by al-Rāzī or others, for God Almighty says about sending His messengers, '[We sent] messengers as bringers of good tidings and warners so that mankind will have no argument against God after the messengers' and 'We have not sent you [O Muḥammad], except as a mercy to the worlds.' He also said, in numerous verses, about the origin of creation, 'And it is He who created the heavens and the earth in six days – and His Throne had been upon water – that He might test you as to which of you is best in deed'; 'And I did not create the jinn and mankind except to worship Me'; and '[He] who created death and life to test you [as to] which of you is best in deed.' Moreover, the causation of the details of rulings in the Qur'an and the Sunna is countless […] as induction testifies to that such as to give certain knowledge;

> we are thus certain that this consistently applies to all details of the Sharīʿa. Because of this, *qiyās* (analogy) and *ijtihād* are proven [as recognized means of arriving at Sharīʿa rulings], and therefore we should act upon what this dictates [i.e. that rulings are meant to secure people's *maṣlaḥa*].

Al-Shāṭibī also added:

> Generally speaking, other scholars agree with [Imām] Mālik that in the case of acts of worship, the basic rule is that there is no logical cause for them. Though there remain disagreements surrounding the details, scholars of the Muslim community agree upon that essential rule. An exception exists amongst the Ẓāhirīs who do not distinguish between acts of worship and everyday practices. In the latter's view, both do not require logical effective causes. Thus, they do not recognise the very concept of *maṣlaḥa*, let alone *al-maṣlaḥa al-mursala* (unrestricted benefit) [that is, benefit not based on specific injunctions].[15]

Abū al-Ḥasan al-Āmidī (d. 631 AH)[16] also addressed this topic when he commented, 'The effective cause of God's injunctions is people's *maṣlaḥa*, in that they were sanctioned in order to achieve the [lawful] interests of the people.'[17]

A third scholar to comment on this is al-Shanqīṭī (d. 1339 AH), who stated in his *Aḍwā' al-Bayān*,

> You should undoubtedly realize the certain fact that God sets injunctions for people's *maṣlaḥa*. His actions and legalizations are all enshrined in wisdom and interests that are designed to bring *maṣlaḥa* and prevent *mafsada*. Late scholastic theologians, imitating their early fellows, claim that God's actions do not depend on an effective cause. They base their claim on the assumption that having an effective cause as reason for action entails that perfection will not occur unless the purpose for which the action is done [which is the effective cause] is fully achieved, and [given that not all actions achieve their intended purposes] God is far exalted above that as this entails [when the effective cause is not achieved] imperfection. Of course, all of this is void

> and unnecessary as it is common knowledge in Islam that God Almighty is utterly self-sufficient and that all creatures are in absolute dire need of Him [...] He, the Almighty, sets rulings and actions to achieve the interests of people who are in need of Him, not to achieve a *maṣlaḥa* that He will benefit from; indeed He is far exalted above that.
>
> The claim of many Islamic legal theorists that the Sharīʿa effective causes are merely signs and indicators originates from invalid conjecture. Indeed, God issues rulings because of the effective causes containing the benefits needed by His servants, not by Himself. God the Almighty and His Messenger have stated that God issues rulings due to the wise benefits that these rulings achieve. The clearest phrase denoting this is, 'because of'. God says in the Qur'an, 'Because of this we have decreed such and such...' and the Prophet, peace be upon him, states [for example], 'Seeking permission is required (before entering into someone's dwelling) because of sight [that is in order for sight not to violate others' privacies].'[18]

According to Islamic understanding, the Divine Legislator has left no *maṣlaḥa* that may draw people near to Paradise, but He informed them of it and commanded it. And He left no *mafsada*, which may draw them nearer to Hell, but He informed them of it and declared it prohibited. Ibn Taymiyya stressed this, stating,

> The essential point is that the Islamic Sharīʿa does not neglect any *maṣlaḥa*. Rather, God has already completed the religion and perfected His bounty. The Prophet, peace be upon him, has not left a thing which may draw us nearer to Paradise without informing us about it. He left us on the clear way, illuminated by day and night alike; no one deviates from it but perishes.[19]

Furthermore, al-ʿIzz b. ʿAbd al-Salām noted, 'God sent the messengers and the scriptures in order to establish the *maṣlaḥa* and prevent the *mafsada* of this life and the life to come.'[20]

Islamically, this divine care for *maṣlaḥa* in individual rulings is not solely confined to those specific cases, rather it is general. The Islamic legal theorists (*Uṣūlīs*) confirm this fact in their maxim, 'What matters is the general applicability of the wordings not the peculiarity of the occasion.' In this context, al-Ṭūfī (d. 716 AH)[21] states, 'With regard to the Sharīʿa's care of them [i.e. *maṣlaḥas*], it cares for them generally and particularly.'[22]

Texts of Qur'an and the Prophetic Sunna dealing with injunctions explain the causes and benefits for which injunctions were legislated. Thus certain acts were legislated in order to secure the *maṣlaḥa* that they generate and others were banned in order to prevent the *mafsada* that they generate. This means that, '*maṣlaḥa* must be considered and *mafsada* must be prevented, as this is why injunctions were prescribed'.[23]

Analysing Muslim scholarly discourse reveals their agreement that the Islamic Sharīʿa has catered for *maṣlaḥa* in its injunctions and that divine laws and injunctions are meant to achieve *maṣlaḥa* 'out of the Divine Legislator's mercy and grace'. In other words, God's catering for people's *maṣlaḥa* is a bounty and mercy from Him. Ibn al-Qayyim (d. 751 AH) says,

> The Sharīʿa's foundations and structure revolves around positive results and achieving people's *maṣlaḥa* in this life and the life to come. All of it [the Sharīʿa] is justice, mercy, *maṣlaḥa* and wisdom. Whatever matter turns from justice, mercy, benefit or wisdom into the contrary will not be from the Sharīʿa, even if it is theoretically considered to be part of it.[24]

Al-Shāṭibī[25] said, 'The Sharīʿa illustrates what renders the people's affairs completely and perfectly commendable in this life and the life to come.'[26] Al-Ṭāhir b. ʿĀshūr[27] argues, 'We are certain that the entire corpus of the Sharīʿa has objectives and is imbued with wisdom and benefits.'[28]

Muslim legal theorists assert that there is evidence for this in the Qur'an, the Sunna, *ijmāʿ* (juristic consensus), induction and analogical reasoning.

2.1. Qur'anic Verses Related to the Concept of *Maṣlaḥa*

The Qur'an states, 'Indeed, God commands justice, doing good and generosity towards relatives and He forbids what is shameful, blameworthy, and oppressive. He teaches you, so that you may take heed.'[29] According to this verse, the Divine Legislator commands 'justice and doing good', because of the *maṣlaḥa* entailed, and He forbids 'what is shameful, blameworthy, and oppressive', because of the harm entailed. The command indicates obligation, while the forbiddance indicates prohibition.[30] Hence, the command to achieve justice and doing good is simultaneously a command to secure their *maṣlaḥa*, and the command to leave what is shameful, blameworthy, and oppressive is a command to avert their *mafsada*. In addition, the verse employs the Arabic definite article, '*al-*', in the two words: *al-ʿadl* (justice) and *al-iḥsān* (doing good), causing the meaning to extend to a comprehensive and universal application. This entails that all forms of *ʿadl* and all forms of *iḥsān* contain *maṣlaḥa* and, therefore, all of its forms are commanded. The verse also forbids what is shameful, blameworthy, and oppressive, which requires complete abandonment of all such acts at all times. The general prohibition here applies to all as the verse commands all addressees to observe its directives. All of this is further emphasized by using the second person plural to confirm the universality of the teachings. Thus the verse reads: 'He teaches you, so that you may take heed.'[31]

Undoubtedly, justice, good acts and generosity towards relatives are *maṣlaḥa*s while shameful, blameworthy and oppressive acts are *mafsada*s, therefore the argument here is that the Divine Legislator meant to achieve the former and prevent the latter. Indeed, doing good is entirely dependent upon securing *maṣlaḥa* and preventing *mafsada*, and improper action is fully dependent on securing *mafsada* and preventing *maṣlaḥa*. Reflecting on the above verse Al-ʿIzz b. ʿAbd al-Salām comments, 'This is the most comprehensive Qur'anic verse calling for all *maṣlaḥas* and warning against all *mafsadas*.'[32] He further explains that the commandment of justice and doing good covers everything, minor and major alike, as the Divine Legislator has not differentiated between what is small and what is large or between what is little and what is much,[33] a fact elaborated by the Qur'an: 'And whoever has done an atom's-weight of good will see it, and whoever has done an atom's-weight of evil will see it.'[34]

While mentioning the evidence on the concept of *maṣlaḥa*, al-Ṭūfī cited the following verses, 'O people, an admonition from your Lord has come to you, a healing for what is in [your] hearts, and guidance and mercy for the believers. Say [Prophet], "In God's grace and mercy let them rejoice: these are better than all they accumulate."'[35] He then elaborated upon it, explaining that, 'God cared to admonish you, O people, and His admonition has the greatest *maṣlaḥa* for you as it protects you from destruction and leads you to guidance.' This verse, al-Ṭūfī adds, describes the Qur'an as a 'healing' for the heart (from doubts and the like), which is a great *maṣlaḥa*. It also describes it as 'guidance and mercy', which is one of the greatest forms of *maṣlaḥa*. Additionally, 'God's grace and mercy', al-Ṭūfī asserts, bring nothing but abundant compassion. They are then asked to 'rejoice' in congratulatory terms. Both rejoicing and congratulation occur on the attainment of a great *maṣlaḥa*. In addition, al-Ṭūfī sees the aforementioned statement: 'In God's grace and mercy let them rejoice: these are better than all they accumulate', as an alternative means of expressing *maṣlaḥa*; what 'they accumulate' is among their *maṣlaḥas*, but the highest kind of *maṣlaḥa* is the best to be sought. Thus, in al-Ṭūfī's view, in these seven ways, the verses indicate God's care for the benefit of His people.[36]

Another Qur'anic evidence, which is seen to be relevant to the concept of *maṣlaḥa*, is, 'God wants ease for you, not hardship.'[37] Undoubtedly, 'ease' is in the interest and benefit of people, whilst 'hardship' is harm and mischief, since it leads to suffering and consequently to the inability to fulfil one's duties.[38] This is further confirmed by the verse, 'He has placed no hardship on you in your religion…'[39] indicating that the Muslim Ummah has been relieved from the burden of *ḥaraj* (extreme hardship). Among the verses that the Islamic legal theorists also quote as evidence in this regard are the following:

1. 'They ask you about [the property of] orphans: say, "It is good to set things right for them. If you combine their affairs with yours, remember they are your brothers and

sisters; God knows those who spoil things and those who improve them. Had He so willed, He could have made you vulnerable too; He is almighty and wise."'[40]

2. 'And do not corrupt the earth after it has been set right; call on Him fearing and hoping. The mercy of God is close to those who do good.'[41]
3. 'The people of Medina and the neighbouring desert Arabs should not have held back from following God's Messenger, nor should they have cared about themselves more than him. If ever they suffer any thirst, weariness, or hunger in God's cause, take any step that angers the disbelievers, or cause any harm to an enemy, a good deed is recorded in their favour on account of it; God never wastes the reward of those who do good.'[42]
4. 'Let harm be requited by an equal harm, though anyone who forgives and puts things right will have his reward from God Himself; He does not like those who do wrong.'[43]

2.2. *Ḥadīths* Related to the Concept of *Maṣlaḥa*

Numerous *ḥadīths* are cited as evidence for *maṣlaḥa.* Among them is the narration, 'There should be neither harm nor reciprocation of harm.'[44] The prohibition of harm, whether afflicted or reciprocated, is clearly a great *maṣlaḥa* upon people, thus clarifying the purpose behind such forms of Divine Legislation.[45]

A further example is seen in the Prophetic narration,

> Faith has some seventy branches, the highest of which is the declaration that there is no true god but Allah, and the lowest of which is the removal of what is harmful from the road. And modesty is a branch of faith.[46]

This *ḥadīth* indicates that the Sharīʿa rulings are aimed at securing *maṣlaḥa* for the people. The Prophet categorized the religion such that the highest level is the starting point of belief in Islam: the declaration of faith in one God (*al-tawḥīd*). Thereafter faith is extended downwards until it reaches its lowest level, which is 'the removal of what is harmful from the road'. Thus *maṣlaḥa*, in its broadest range, irrespective of the different kinds and benefits, has been included in the religion.[47]

Another *ḥadīth* cited in this regard is,

> On every person's joints (or bones or organs), there is *ṣadaqa* (charity) due every day the sun rises. Doing justice between two people is *ṣadaqa*, assisting a man to mount his animal or lifting up his belongings onto it is *ṣadaqa*, a good word is *ṣadaqa*, every step you take towards prayer is *ṣadaqa* and removing harmful things from roads is *ṣadaqa*.[48]

Here, the mentioned deeds are considered acts of *ṣadaqa* and the one who practises them is promised to be rewarded for the worldly and religious *maṣlaḥa* they bring to both their fellow human beings and themselves. The deeds mentioned are simply examples of the overarching purpose behind Sharīʿa rulings: to secure *maṣlaḥas*, prevent *mafsadas* or achieve both.

2.3. 'Consensus' (*Ijmāʿ*) Related to the Concept of *Maṣlaḥa*

It is reported that both the *Ṣaḥāba* (Companions of the Prophet) and their *Tābiʿūn* (Successors) were 'in agreement' that *maṣlaḥa* stands as a recognized principle in Islamic legislation. As such, many of their rulings were based upon this principle. Their frequency in considering *maṣlaḥa* when determining legislation is said to have met little opposition and led to the practice becoming widespread.

Indeed the lack of opposition and the prevalence of the practice is considered to constitute a consensus upon its use. Many scholars have reported on this consensus. Al-Āmidī observed,

> Rulings have been legislated for people's interests. The fact that they are made for objectives based on wisdom is proven by both consensus and reason. As the leading jurists unanimously agree, God's rulings are never free from wisdom or an objective.[49]

Similarly, al-Ṭūfī states, 'Regarding *ijmāʿ*, scholars, with a few unreliable exceptions from the stringent Ẓāhirī school, unanimously agree that rulings are justified by securing *maṣlaḥa* and preventing *mafsada*.'[50]

Mālik (d. 179 AH)[51] stood as the strongest proponent of *maṣlaḥa,* to the extent that he argued for the validity of *al-maṣāliḥ al-mursala* (unrestricted benefits). Indeed, he was not alone in this regard; it has been claimed that all scholars acknowledged the use of this kind of *maṣlaḥa*, including those who did not acknowledge *ijmāʿ* as a proof. Al-Futūḥī (d. 972 AH) is also recorded to have commented on this consensus, stating, 'There is a consensus on the fact that "deeds" are justified by wise reasons and *maṣlaḥas*.'[52]

Speaking on the evidence for consensus, Ramaḍān ʿAbd al-Wadūd argues that,

> In general, the sages agreed that, prior to the revelation of the Sharīʿa, *maṣlaḥa* was considered when issuing the rulings that organize the affairs of this life. Then the Sharīʿa confirmed their consensus and explained that *maṣlaḥa* is to be considered in legislation in order to establish a system of life for this world and in the deeds pertaining to the Hereafter. Thus, all of the Sharīʿa rulings serve both the religious and temporal interests of people in order to achieve their pleasure in this world and the Hereafter. All the scholars of the Sharīʿa are in agreement on this point.[53]

2.4. Induction (*Istiqrāʾ*) and *Maṣlaḥa*

The evidence here is induced from those passages of the Qur'an and Sunna containing explanations for the reasoning behind the Legislator's decrees within them. These reasons also revolve around securing *maṣlaḥas* and distancing *mafsadas* from the people. In addition, this approach seems to have been taken, Islamically, both as an indication and a call from the Divine Legislator to people of deduction to adopt the same methodology: linking rulings to their respective causes and establishing the relation between the causes and effects. By doing so, they too can achieve the Divine Legislator's objective of obtaining or complementing *maṣlaḥas* and preventing or minimizing *mafsadas*.[54]

2.5. Rational Evidence and *Maṣlaḥa*

Rational evidence indicates the importance of the maintenance of the universe in a balanced order and the regulation of human acts to prevent corruption or deterioration. This is possible only by securing *maṣlaḥa* and preventing *mafsada* in accordance with the prerequisites required for achieving either.[55]

Securing *maṣlaḥa* and preventing *mafsada* does not mean, however, following the mere dictations of human desire. This is due to the fact that both *maṣlaḥas* and *mafsadas* are usually relative, entailing that they change from situation to situation, time to time and person to person. For instance, food and drinks constitute an obvious benefit for people, but this is true only when there is a need to consume them, when they are appetizing, when they do not cause any immediate or eventual harm and when they are obtained in a manner that does not harm the consumer or anybody else. Hence, many benefits may prove harmful to some people, or may be benefits only in a specific time or situation and harmful in others. This is seen to indicate that the permissibility of *maṣlaḥas* and prohibition of *mafsadas* are for the continuity of life and not for the satisfaction of human desires. Otherwise, there would have been no harm in people following their own conflicting desires. The very fact that unrestricted following of one's desires does lead to harm indicates that neither *maṣlaḥa* nor *mafsada* are put in place for this purpose. People's aims do vary, even regarding the same thing. One person may benefit from achieving his or her purpose, while another may be harmed due to a conflicting aim. Hence, according to this understanding also, the Sharīʿa cannot be based on human desires, which are all too often contradictory, but rather on absolute *maṣlaḥa*, whether they stand in agreement with human desires or not.[56]

Muṣṭafā Zayd skilfully summarizes the evidence indicating the authority of *maṣlaḥa*, stating that,

> It has been undoubtedly established that the Legislator considered the *maṣlaḥa* in every kind of evidence. The Qur'an contains no verse in which at least one *maṣlaḥa* is not included. As for the *Sunna*, it

> explains the Qur'an, and the explainer takes the same ruling as that which it explains. When it comes to consensus, all reliable scholars – including those who do not consider consensus as a means of religious evidence – justify Sharīʿa rulings by securing the *maṣlaḥa*s and averting the *mafsada*s. As for reasoning, every person of sound intellect would believe that the objective of the rulings pertaining to transactions and customs in any law is to achieve people's interests...[57]

3. Origins of Worldly *Maṣlaḥas*

According to Islamic understanding, the rulings of the Sharīʿa cover all types of *maṣlaḥa* whether individual or collective, worldly or pertaining to the Hereafter. Hence, the Sharīʿa, within this discourse, is seen not to care for this life to the neglect of the life to come, nor does it care for the life to come to the neglect of this worldly life.

The Qur'an states, 'Seek the life to come by means of what God has granted you, but do not neglect your rightful share in this world.'[58] According to the Muslim understanding, God, the Creator, being the Most Knowledgeable of His creatures and their needs, has not asked them to wholly abandon their rightful share in this world for the sake of the Hereafter, despite the great difference in their relative value. Thus, the Sharīʿa maintains a balance between the various *maṣlaḥas*. To achieve this balance constitutes the essence of moderation and fairness, which are among the primary objectives of the Sharīʿa.[59]

Within classical Muslim understanding, all of the rulings pertaining to people are seen to be commonly related to acts of *taʿabbud* (religious devotion), albeit in various degrees. This includes the rulings dealing with everyday life and worldly transactions. A certain degree of commonality between the worldly interests and those of the Hereafter should be maintained. Hence, according to this understanding, not a single worldly *maṣlaḥa* exists which does not also include a right due to the Divine Legislator in a manner that leads man to simultaneously achieve the religious *maṣlaḥa* of that act. This is what al-Qarāfī referred to when he said, 'There is nothing of man's rights, but includes a right due to God.'[60]

Whilst appropriate deeds and striving to achieve *maṣlaḥas* needs to be done in this world, the *maṣlaḥa*, which is the fruit of these deeds and struggles, is not necessarily confined to this life. It may occur in one of three forms. The first is a *maṣlaḥa* that occurs in this world and in the Hereafter. The second is a *maṣlaḥa* that occurs in this world only but not in the Hereafter. This in turn is of two types: a worldly *maṣlaḥa* which has no reward in the Hereafter and a worldly *maṣlaḥa* which has a reward in the Hereafter.

The third form is a *maṣlaḥa* which occurs in the Hereafter only. This kind is seen to be 'the absolute form of worship'. An example normally given in this regard is that of the intercession of the Prophet for the believers, which reports affirm occurs on the Day of Resurrection only.[61]

According to Islamic understanding, *maṣlaḥas* of the Hereafter are incomparable with those of this world, as the former are deemed far superior and everlasting. By the same token, the *mafsadas* pertaining to the Hereafter are incomparable with those of the worldly life as the former are far worse and everlasting.[62] As a result, a person is not permitted to judge his deed as a *maṣlaḥa* based on its ostensible characteristics or worldly consequences until he becomes aware of its consequences in the Hereafter as well. This latter can be arrived at by contemplating religious textual evidences and the limits they designate.[63] The *maṣlaḥas* pertaining to the Hereafter are seen as the basis for the worldly benefits, and any *maṣlaḥa* in contradiction of its own basis is considered nullified and discarded. Hence, any worldly *maṣlaḥa* that contradicts a *maṣlaḥa* pertaining to the Hereafter is to be considered null and void. In this respect, al-Shāṭibī asserts that,

> The *maṣlaḥas* obtained and the *mafsadas* averted by the Sharīʿa are to be considered, in as far as they manage this life, to serve the life to come, but not to serve personal desires in obtaining their usual *maṣlaḥas* or averting usual *mafsadas*.[64]

As for those who 'follow only their own desires when seeking worldly *maṣlaḥas*, without lending due concern to the *maṣlaḥas* of the Hereafter', they are addressed in the Qur'anic verse,

> Those who desire [only] the life of this world with all its finery, We shall repay them in full in this life for their deeds; they will be given no less. But such people will have nothing in the Hereafter but the Fire: their work here will be fruitless and their deeds futile.[65]

As a result, what seems to be suggested here is that a reliance on worldly benefits to the neglect of their value in the Hereafter is to waste these *maṣlaḥas*. This seems to be re-emphasized within the Qur'anic text, such as in the verse, 'Those whose efforts in this world are misguided, while they think they are doing good work?'[66] and, 'There are some who pray, "Our Lord, give us good in this world," and they will have no share in the Hereafter.'[67]

Hence, textual references within the Qur'an and *ḥadīth* bring one to the conclusion that, while anything opposing the benefits of the Hereafter is futile and cannot represent a *maṣlaḥa*, similarly, *maṣlaḥa* exists in anything which agrees with the benefits of the Hereafter. This is even if it implies an apparent loss of worldly benefit, such as spending money in charity, or the occurrence of a worldly harm, such as defending a city under attack from aggressors.

Consequently, true worldly *maṣlaḥa* is that which leads to benefit in the Hereafter. The realization of *maṣlaḥas* cannot be a purely rational act, as the intellect cannot recognize the benefits of the Hereafter except through revelation.

4. The Role of Human Reasoning (*al-ʿAql*) and Revelation (*al-Naql*) in *Maṣlaḥa*

Human intellect can neither fully nor flawlessly recognize *maṣlaḥa.* What it sees at a specific time as a *maṣlaḥa* may not be seen as such at other times. Furthermore, what appears rationally to be a benefit may, from another perspective, appear rationally to be harmful. However, when the intellect (*al-ʿaql*) is guided by revelation (*al-naql*), the outcome is then deemed to be nearest to perfection. This section will explore this point further.

Muslim tradition understands that God has favoured all people with intellect and has required them to adhere to His laws. It is without question that intellect constitutes a supreme *maṣlaḥa*, a precious benefit and great advantage. Based on the existence of intellect, people become religiously responsible and accountable; intellect is therefore the basis for any religious commandment or prohibition. The attainment of religious and worldly *maṣlaḥas* relies on the directives of the Sharīʿa, which in turn is based on intellect.

To discuss intellect, we will consider three spheres that represent the sources of learning and knowledge. The first is the senses; this is the smallest as it does not extend beyond the arena of traceable sensations. The second is the realm of reason which is wider and more comprehensive than the first area, as it also comprises things beyond sensory perception. The final sphere is that of revelation, which is the most comprehensive, general and extensive of the three. These three spheres are neither separated from nor contradictory to one another. In fact, each leads to the next and provides the basis for it. At the same time, each higher arena dominates and controls the preceding one, correcting its grasp and guiding it.

Figure 1: The relationship between the senses, reason and revelation

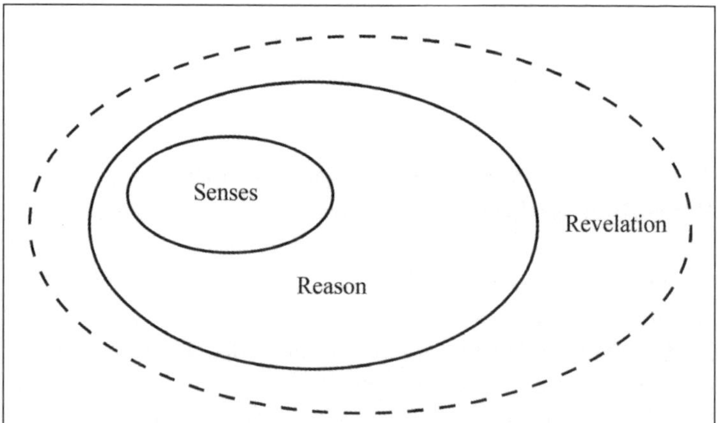

It is argued that no contradiction exists between the three spheres except in the minds of those who negate the existence of one of them and those who do not place them in their correct order. Furthermore, all intellectual and dogmatic nonconformities can be considered to be a result of the denial of one of the three circles, underestimating its significance as a means of comprehension, or misplacing it above or beneath another sphere. This is clearly explained in Figure 1.

The sphere of senses leads to the sphere of reason, which in turn leads to the sphere of revelation. This is because reason cannot exist in the absence of the senses, without which the former cannot function. Additionally, the absence of reason entails the inability to comprehend revelation and its commandments.[68]

When discussing the relation between reason and *maṣlaḥa*, al-ʿIzz b. ʿAbd al-Salām, al-Tabrīzī and al-Ṭūfī considered the partnership between reason and revelation to be fundamental. Ibn ʿAbd al-Salām comments in this context, 'Most of the *maṣlaḥas* and *mafsadas* of this world are known through reason, as are most of the divine laws.'[69] Al-Ghazālī states, '[Divine] legislation is intellect from without, while intellect is divine legislation from within; they support each other, rather they are united.'[70] It would appear that al-Ghazālī draws this statement, along with its preceding and proceeding statements, from al-Rāghib al-Aṣfahānī. The latter mentions the same idea in his book, *Tafṣīl al-Nashʾatayn wa Taḥṣīl al-Saʿādatayn*:

> The intellect resembles a torch, which did not light the oil. God says [in the Qur'an], 'God is the Light of the heavens and earth. His Light is like this: there is a niche, and in it a torch, the torch inside a glass, a glass like a glittering star, fuelled from a blessed olive tree from neither east nor west, whose oil almost gives light even when no fire touches it – light upon light – God guides whom He wills to his Light…'[71] It is God who guides. Indeed legislation is intellect from without, and intellect is legislation from within, they support each other, rather they are united…[72]

Al-ʿIzz b. ʿAbd al-Salām states,

> He who wants to know the suitabilities (*al-munāsabāt*), the *maṣlaḥas* and the *mafsadas*, both the preponderant and the less weighty, let him assume that the Sharīʿa has not been revealed and thus use his intellect to find the rulings. There would be hardly any ruling that is not included in that [general rule], except rulings of a purely worship-based nature whose benefits and harms have not been disclosed by God.[73]

Ibn ʿAbd al-Salām establishes the link between reason and the Sharīʿa, remarking,

> He who traces the objectives of the Sharīʿa in obtaining benefits and averting harms will reach the conclusion that a *maṣlaḥa* could not be ignored and a *mafsada* should not be approached, even in the absence of a textual evidence, consensus or specific analogy. Indeed, understanding the Sharīʿa itself necessitates that.[74]

According to al-Tabrīzī's school, which represents the majority of scholars, the text is, to differing degrees, the fulcrum for identifying the *maṣlaḥa*. From this there can be an expansion to include what the Sharīʿa approves as a means of evidence that is close to the text, such as *al-munāsib al-muʾaththir* (the effective suitable attribute) and *al-munāsib al-mulāʾim* (the appropriate suitable attribute). This circle then expands further to include *al-maṣāliḥ al-mursala* (unrestricted benefits), where there is no specific textual ruling. According to some Mālikī scholars, it would even be sufficient to include acts that do not contradict a specific Sharīʿa teaching and are granted general permissibility.

As for al-Ṭūfī, he considers the *maṣlaḥa* itself as the fulcrum, which can be gradually expanded according to rational beneficial interest, to the extent that it may block the text instead of being restricted by it. According to this opinion, *al-maṣlaḥa al-mulghāh* (the nullified benefit) could become *muʿtabara* (recognized). Although some commentary may give an alternative impression, al-Ṭūfī's view is contrary to the opinion of the majority of scholars. For instance, as has been mentioned, al-ʿIzz b. ʿAbd al-Salām argues for complete harmony between reason (*ʿaql*) and textual evidence (*naql*) with his statement concerning the judging of issues by intellect as if the Sharīʿa has not yet been revealed. However, this issue should be measured by the Sharīʿa's objectives, which are considered the highest aspired objectives of the intellect and the requirements of religious texts. Ultimately, it should be governed by the final outcomes that link worldly *maṣlaḥas* to their ensuing consequences in the Hereafter.

Additionally, the sphere of the intellect begins where that of the senses ends, and it is the intellect that links the details together, taking into consideration the respective reasons and causes. The first sphere (senses) is considered a premise to the second (reason), while the third (revelation) is like 'an ocean without shores', with only God possessing the knowledge of its limits. As a result, the intellect, as a limited entity, is seen to be incapable of matching revelation; it can only follow it and its guidance in recognizing truth.[75] Ibn ʿAbd al-Salām notes, 'How greedy are people in trying to know things which God has not made attainable; the more they contemplate and get keener [to know them] the more perplexed and oblivious they become.'[76] Thus, according to the above understanding, finding the *maṣlaḥa* is based on revealed religious teachings. Though the intellect serves as an indicator to the *maṣlaḥa*, the original basis of identifying it is revelation.

The overwhelming majority of scholars therefore agree that without the permission to use *qiyās* (analogy), it would not have been made permissible.[77] It has been stated that *maṣlaḥa* must be observed not because of an inherent quality in itself but because of the Legislator's commandment to do so. Hence, reason steps down and takes its position behind revelation, as al-Ghazālī observes:

> Indeed, reason provides a proof of the truthfulness of the Prophet. It then steps down and acknowledges that it accepts everything it receives from the Prophet concerning God and the Last Day. These are matters the mind cannot fathom through its own working, but cannot rule out either. Revelation may include something that the mind falls short of understanding. For example, the mind cannot conclude, on the basis of its own functioning, that the fulfilment of God's commandments is the cause of happiness in the life to

> come, or that sinful actions lead to a miserable fate. Yet, the mind cannot rule this out either. The mind, however, concludes that where a miracle proves the truthfulness of the one who brought it, then the latter must be truthful. Therefore, if he tells us this, our minds believe him through this process.[78]

Hence, what seems to be emphasized within the major trend of Muslim classical scholarship is the fact that despite the intellect's great impact and high standing as the essential prerequisite for assigning duties, it must be 'governed and led' by revelation. All of the worldly *maṣlaḥas* that the intellect appreciates are subject to what the revelation states. If they are consistent with revelation, then they are accepted, as only that which leads ultimately to *maṣlaḥa* in the life to come may be established as a *maṣlaḥa*. In other words, it is imperative that reason and revelation go hand in hand.

Al-Shāṭibī states,

> When revelation and reason go hand in hand in religious issues, this must be conditional on the revelation being the leader and reason the follower. That is to say, reason must confine its area of activity within the bounds drawn by revelation.[79]

Hence, the point emphasized here is that reason does not have the authority to render something obligatory or forbidden merely on the basis of assessing the *maṣlaḥa* and *mafsada*. It is the Divine Legislator alone who commands and prohibits. Hence, the criterion for determination is that of 'divine revelation'.[80]

Therefore, according to this understanding, cases that take place without reference to reason fall short, and statements that are contrary to reason are false. Ibn Taymiyya argues that prophets brought what the human mind may not fully comprehend, but they did not bring what the human mind knows to be impossible. Yet those who take reason to extremes issue rulings on certain matters and make them compulsory, permissible or forbidden on the basis of rational arguments that they wrongly believe to be true. By such arguments, they even contradict prophetic dicta. Similarly, on the other hand, those who discard reason entirely may accept certain falsities and engage in invalid situations and actions, disregarding the faculty of comprehension and critical thought 'with which God has favoured mankind'.[81]

Hence, according to this approach, securing *maṣlaḥa* and preventing *mafsada* cannot be determined by reason alone. Rather, both revelation and reason work hand in hand, so as not to let reason act independently from the Sharīʿa. This represents the main axis on which the Muslim classical approach relies in identifying *maṣlaḥas* and suggests that a Muslim jurist is required to fully understand the relation between revelation and reason. Ibn Taymiyya asserts, 'What authentic Sharīʿa evidence proves is consistent with what clear reason endorses.'[82] He also contends, 'A clear rational argument cannot be in conflict with an authentic revealed argument. It is not even possible for there to be conflict between true evidences, whether they are rational, revealed or a mixture of the two.'[83]

The central message within the classical Muslim approach to this subject is that there can be no contradiction between reason and revelation. The natural relationship between what is clear and what is authentic is that the authentic corrects the clear, and that the clear recognizes the authentic. If there is contradiction, it is an indication that the text is not authentic or the rational argument is unclear.

The argument made so far also seems to suggest that there is a 'natural' limit to the human mind. Ibn Taymiyya comments in reference to this,

> When a person who is well aware of the facts carefully considers what they say about their various branches of knowledge, that individual will find that they have no knowledge of information that is beyond their sphere. They only know what they call 'natural' and its related 'mathematical' sciences. Abstract mathematics, on the other hand, involves conclusions on the basis of abstract sums that do not exist in reality. When we carefully consider what they call 'metaphysical knowledge', we do not find in it knowledge of anything that exists in reality. These are only imagined things that their minds presume and are lacking in true existence.[84]

What Ibn Taymiyya emphasizes here is that not every abstract idea corresponds to something real, as a person may imagine something that has no real existence. Therefore, for him, to try to prove facts on the sole basis of abstract ideas is invalid. Hence, Ibn Taymiyya says,

> This shows their ignorance and that what they say is merely presumed mentally without having an actual reality. For example, if they are asked to give an example – and an example is only a partial prerequisite – they are unable to provide any, claiming that they are concerned only with comprehensive universal things. As they do so, they show that they are speaking without knowledge and referring to what they do not know to have any form of existence in reality. Indeed they are speaking about what has no substance in reality, and what is impossible to have such substance. When knowledge of existing matters is universal, its detailed facts will be established in reality.[85]

The Qur'anic text seems to be referring to this point when it emphasizes that many people seek *maṣlaḥas* that they believe they know. Yet when they secure them, they find them unlike what they thought or contrary to their desires. They may therefore begin arguing without knowledge, which will lead them to give precedence to their own views over revelation. In doing so, according to the Qur'anic discourse, they go beyond their intellectual limits and knowledge, and discard it by claiming that of which they have no knowledge. The Qur'an states,

> You have indeed argued about that of which you have some knowledge; why then do you argue about that of which you have no knowledge at all? Indeed, God knows, whereas you do not know.[86]

Also, 'Do not, then, compare anything with God. Indeed, God knows all, whereas you have no knowledge.'[87] To rely solely on reason independent of revelation is to neutralize reason and hold revelation inferior.

The outcome of the above understanding is that what is communicated via revelation leads to a *maṣlaḥa*. The human mind may agree with this, and where it does not it is maintained that human intellect falls short of understanding in such cases. Similarly, everything that revelation forbids is a *mafsada*, and the assessment of the human mind in relation to this is considered in like terms.

Thus, Islamically, the 'perfect' operation of *maṣlaḥa* requires a combination of clear reason and decisive revelation. When these two concur, the *maṣlaḥa* is secured and yields its beneficial effects both in this life and in the life to come.

Chapter Two

TYPES OF *MAṢLAḤA*

There are several types of *maṣlaḥa*: some are unanimously accepted, while others are subject to disagreement. This study is concerned with one type in particular, which is the *maṣlaḥa* that is recognized by the Sharīʿa, regardless of whether it is derived from a particular evidence (*dalīl khāṣṣ*), or from a general evidence (*dalīl ʿāmm*). In the first case, the *maṣlaḥa* is termed '*maṣlaḥa muʿtabara*' (recognized benefit) and in the second case, it is termed '*maṣlaḥa mursala*' (unrestricted benefit). This will be explained below.

1. The Recognized *Maṣlaḥa*

This is the *maṣlaḥa* that has been proven by a religious text (*naṣṣ*) or consensus of the scholars (*ijmāʿ*) through a relevant evidence (*dalīl*) on which a ruling can be based. Legal theorists (*uṣūliyyūn*) have termed it '*al-maṣlaḥa al-muʿtabara*' (recognized benefit) or '*al-munāsib al-muʿtabar*' (recognized suitable attribute). Scholars who accept analogy (*qiyās*) as a means of evidence agree that this type of *maṣlaḥa* can be used as a legal cause (*ʿilla*) and the basis for forming rulings.

This type includes all forms of *maṣlaḥas* for which rulings of the Sharīʿa have established, such as preserving intellect and preserving property. To preserve intellect, the Divine Legislator prohibited the consumption of alcohol and ordained punishment for those who drink it, while to preserve property the Divine Legislator forbade theft with its specific punishment.

Through this type of recognized *maṣlaḥa*, the concept of analogy as an evidence was introduced, for it is based on pondering the rulings of the Sharīʿa and understanding the purpose for which the Divine Legislator has ordained them, and applying that purpose to the new case for which a ruling is sought. Once such a purpose matches the new case, the initial incident's ruling is given to it by analogy.[1]

The adherence to this type of *maṣlaḥa* is seen within textual evidence as an obligation that must be upheld, whether the rationale for it is apparent to the subject of the law or not. The justification for this within textual evidence is the principle that everything brought by the Sharīʿa is a *maṣlaḥa* for mankind. In addition, one may like something, thinking that it is a *maṣlaḥa*, while in reality it is harmful. Likewise, one may dislike something, thinking that it is harmful, though it is better for oneself in this life and the life to come. The Qur'an states in Q. 2:216, 'You may dislike something although it is good for you, or like something although it is bad for you: God knows and you do not.'[2]

Ibn Taymiyya rephrases the above when he states,

> A believer should know that what he has been commanded to do [by the Sharīʿa] is a pure or preponderant *maṣlaḥa*, and what he has been forbidden from is a pure or preponderant *mafsada*. [He should also know that] God does not command people to do something out of any need for them, nor does He forbid any thing for them out of misery. Rather, He has commanded them to do what is good for them and forbade them from what is bad for them.[3]

2. The Nullified *Maṣlaḥa*

This is the *maṣlaḥa* that the Legislator has considered to be invalid. It consists of meanings that the Sharīʿa evidence indicates as null and void. Islamic legal theorists call this type '*al-maṣlaḥa al-mulghāha*' (nullified benefit) or '*al-munāsib al-mulghāh*' (nullified suitable attribute). Scholars agree that this type of *maṣlaḥa* cannot be used as causative evidence or as a basis for issuing rulings. This conclusion is justified classically by the suggestion that 'the Divine Legislator does not nullify a particular *maṣlaḥa* except when it leads to the loss of a greater *maṣlaḥa* or causes a greater *mafsada*'.[4]

Al-Shāṭibī says,

> There is no way to accept what the Sharīʿa has rejected, since *al-munāsaba* (suitability) alone does not determine the ruling; such would be the view of supporters of *al-taḥsīn al-ʿaqlī* (the doctrine that the Sharīʿa rulings can be arrived at by the unaided mind). Instead, when the effective cause for a ruling is clear and we understand from God that it is to be considered in arriving at rulings, only then do we accept it. The *maṣlaḥa*, in our understanding, is what brings benefit to humankind through securing benefit and preventing harm, in a way that the mind can never independently comprehend. If God does not approve this *maṣlaḥa* and nullifies it, then all Muslims agree that it is nullified.[5]

Therefore, according to this understanding, if a specific purpose is known to contradict the recognized objectives (*al-maqāṣid al-muʿtabara*) of the Sharīʿa, it is void, and will not be considered, as the Sharīʿa indicates its nullification.

An example of a *maṣlaḥa* nullified by the Divine Legislator within classical Islam is giving a brother and sister an equal share of inheritance. They are equal in terms of their creation, affiliation to parents, and the duty of kind familial relations. Yet it is argued that this *maṣlaḥa*, equality in inheritance, although appropriate, has been nullified by the Divine Legislator who made the female's share half that of the male brother (Q. 4:11). This is in order for their share of inheritance to correspond to their share of the social responsibility, as the male is required legally to provide for the family while the female is not.

3. The Unrestricted *Maṣlaḥa* (*Al-Maṣlaḥa al-Mursala*)

The unrestricted *maṣlaḥa* is the *maṣlaḥa* that has neither been acknowledged nor rejected by the Sharīʿa through a particular evidence from a text, consensus, or analogy. It is termed *mursala* (unrestricted) as it is not restricted by a particular proof that indicates it as either acknowledged or rejected.[6]

It is the suitable description for any ruling that the Divine Legislator has not shown to be acknowledged or nullified in any of the ways known to legal theorists (the *Uṣūlīs*). Hence, the Legislator is silent on such a ruling, neither acknowledging nor nullifying it. So this type of *maṣlaḥa* remains without textual consideration, or nullification, but is known to be an objective of the Divine Legislator through the indications drawn from the Qur'an and the Sunna, consensus, circumstantial evidence, or various other sources. Therefore, the unrestricted *maṣlaḥa* may be defined as follows: the suitable purpose that, though textually unreported, can be rationally considered to be the Divine Legislator's objective, as assigning a ruling to it would result in securing *maṣlaḥa* and preventing *mafsada*.[7]

Perhaps the most comprehensive definition for this type of *maṣlaḥa* is that adopted by al-Ghazālī, al-Shāṭibī, and Abū Zahra. From their work, the following can be extracted as a definition for the unrestricted *maṣlaḥa*: what appears to be a *maṣlaḥa* supported by a Sharīʿa objective in an incident that has no particular Sharīʿa indication as to whether it is acknowledged or rejected.[8] This definition has excluded both the imagined benefit (*al-maṣlaḥa al-mutawahhama*) and the strange benefit (*al-maṣlaḥa al-gharība*).[9] The latter can be rationally comprehended and is neither acknowledged nor rejected by the Sharīʿa, but is incoherent with the goals and objectives of the Sharīʿa. Therefore, it is excluded, along with the imagined *maṣlaḥa*. Equally, the definition has excluded the *maṣlaḥa* that is recognized (*muʿtabara*) or nullified (*mulghāh*) by a particular indicant in a text, consensus, or analogy. Therefore, the above definition is specific to the unrestricted *maṣlaḥa* only.[10]

Muslim legal theorists (the *Uṣūlīs*) use several terms as names for the unrestricted *maṣlaḥa*, which, to a great extent, revolve around the same or similar meanings: *al-istiṣlāḥ*, *al-ikhāla*, *al-istidlāl al-mursal*, and *al-munāsib al-mursal*.[11]

It is useful to define the *munāsib* in the context of the unrestricted *maṣlaḥa*. The *munāsib* is that which, once the ruling is based on certain features, results in a *maṣlaḥa* of the kind that the Divine Legislator wishes to be attained, or the prevention of a *mafsada* of the kind that the Divine Legislator wishes to be prevented. In other words, establishing a *maṣlaḥa* without this being indicated in a text is a *munāsib* that the Sharīʿa has neither acknowledged nor rejected.

In his *Sharḥ al-Rawḍa*, al-Ṭūfī says,

> The definition of *al-munāsib* is not agreed upon by the scholars. However, bringing the matter to a conclusion is very important as every kind of existence is based on it. In other words, nothing exists except in accordance with rational suitability (*al-munāsaba al-ʿaqliyya*). However, types of *munāsaba* vary in generality, specificity, hiddenness and clarity; the matter whose *munāsib* has been concealed is called *taʿabbudī* (worship-related), and that whose *munāsib* is apparent is called *muʿallal* (justifiable by *ʿilla* or effective cause).[12]

The term *munāsib* is derived from the Arabic word *nasab*, meaning kinship. Just as there must be a common link between individuals of the same kinship such as brothers, cousins and so on to be named as such, the same applies to the description of a *munāsib* that must be tied to its corresponding *maṣlaḥa* by a rational link. In other words, the *munāsib* description is that which can rationally lead to the intended *maṣlaḥa*.

Therefore, al-Ṭūfī asserts that a *munāsib* is that after which a *maṣlaḥa* is expected to come due to the rational link between the two. In other words, when the sound mind encounters the *munāsib* it is able to comprehend from it that it leads to the appropriate *maṣlaḥa*. For example, human reason realizes that the prohibition of intoxicants leads to the *maṣlaḥa* of protecting reason from disorder. Also, it is argued that 'sound' minds recognize that the prescribed retaliatory punishments (*qiṣāṣ)* are to achieve the *maṣlaḥa* of protecting life.

Al-Āmidī says,

> Abū Zayd defined the *munāsib* as that which when presented to the intellect is received with acceptance. Moreover, he deduced from this that it is not possible to use it as an argument in debate, without bearing in mind the possibility that the opponent could say, 'My intellect does not accept this, and the fact that others have accepted it is not an argument against me.' However, I say that this is not so, because if we look at the lowest level of *munāsib*, we find that minds immediately accept it.[13]

Al-Ṭūfī also mentions,

> We say that the *munāsib* is simply a clear, precise description which, by basing the ruling on it, leads by default to what is suitable to God's objective in achieving or maximizing a *maṣlaḥa*, or preventing or minimizing a *mafsada*; this applies in this life and the life to come in a way that can be so proven that only a prevaricator will deny it. In my opinion, this is the best definition that precisely describes the *munāsib* and achieves the essence of the *maṣlaḥa*. This applies to the examples of *qiṣāṣ*, and prohibition of alcohol as well as to the requirements for their perfection, such as requiring equality in *qiṣāṣ* and the prohibition of even small quantities of alcohol, since this leads to consuming larger quantities.[14]

The same principle applies to preventing *mafsadas*, such as prescribing retaliation in the case of intentional injury done to another, in order to prevent and minimize the *mafsada* of physically harming others. Another example is the case of killing the murderer as punishment and the execution of a large number of people who participated in the murder of one person. All of this is to minimize killing by deterring people from it.

Al-Qarāfī says,

> The *munāsib* is what comprises the attainment of a *maṣlaḥa* or the prevention of a *mafsada*. The former case is exemplified in the fact that possession of wealth is the effective cause (*ʿilla*) for levying the obligatory tax on wealth (*zakāh*), which benefits the poor [materially], as well as the rich [spiritually]. The latter case is exemplified in prohibiting the consumption of alcohol.[15]

Al-Nīlī remarks,

> The *munāsib* is that which, after establishing the ruling, leads to what people of sound minds judge as beneficial in this life and the Hereafter. In regard to this life, examples are the preservation of life and increase of wealth, while in regard to the Hereafter, examples are the attainment of rewards and the averting of punishment.[16]

A ruling is at times to attain a *maṣlaḥa*, to perfect it, or to perpetuate it. Furthermore, the *munāsib* is divided into levels. These are the necessity (*ḍarūrī*), need (*ḥājī*), and complement (*taḥsīnī*). These levels are prioritized in that order. In the case of conflict, the first has precedence, then the second, and then the third.[17]

Regarding the definition of *al-maṣlaḥa al-mursala*, al-Zarkashī (d. 794 AH)[18] defines it as, 'What is unknown, that is, what the Sharīʿa has neither acknowledged nor rejected. This is termed *al-maṣlaḥa al-mursala* or *al-istidlāl al-mursal*. The word *mursala* is used to indicate that it is neither acknowledged nor rejected.' Imām al-Ḥaramayn[19] (d. 478 AH) and Ibn al-Samʿānī called it *al-istidlāl*. In his *Al-Kāfī*, al-Khuwārizmī called it *al-istiṣlāḥ* and then said, '*Maṣlaḥa* aims at preserving God's objective of preventing *mafsada* from befalling people.'[20]

Al-Ghazālī asserts that the *maṣlaḥa mursala* exists when there is a meaning that rationally matches a ruling appropriate to it, while there is no agreed upon evidence from the Sharīʿa to testify to this. Ibn Burhān said that it is that which does not depend on basic (textual) evidence whether general or particular.[21]

Al-Shāṭibī defines it as developing a ruling on a matter for which there is no previous ruling and there is no supporting precedent. He says,

> However, such exercise comes within *ijtihād*, which is in accord with the general principles of the Sharīʿa, even if there is no specific principle to attest to it; this is called *maṣlaḥa mursala*. Everything of that kind which the righteous predecessors have brought to effect comes under this understanding, and is in no way contrary to any (Sharīʿa) objective.[22]

This establishes that such a matter is in harmony with the Divine Legislator's objectives. In another place, al-Shāṭibī indicates that the unrestricted *maṣlaḥa* is a matter on which there is no previous ruling, and there was nothing in the Prophet's era to require the introduction of such ruling. He says,

> When there is no likelihood that an action will [exist, so as to] require a ruling, but the action comes into existence later, then an additional

> ruling that conforms to the Sharīʿa's action in similar rulings is given to it. This is the unrestricted *maṣlaḥa* and it is one of the acted upon sources of Sharīʿa since it is based on the approved evidences of the Islamic Sharīʿa as detailed in the science of Islamic legal theory (*uṣūl al-fiqh*). Thus, it is not correct to classify the unrestricted *maṣlaḥa* as an innovation in religion (*bidʿa*).[23]

Based on the foregoing, the difference between the effective *maṣlaḥa* (*al-maṣlaḥa al-muʾaththira*) and the appropriate *maṣlaḥa* (*al-maṣlaḥa al-mulāʾima*), and the levels of suitability (*munāsaba*), as in Table 1, represent the difference between the recognized *maṣlaḥa (al-maṣlaḥa al-muʿtabara)*, and the unrestricted *maṣlaḥa* (*al-maṣlaḥa al-mursala*). As the table includes recognized kinds of *maṣlaḥas* only, it excludes what is metaphorically called the nullified *maṣlaḥa (al-maṣlaḥa al-mulghāh)*, which includes the imagined (*mutawahhama*) and strange (*gharīb*) *maṣlaḥa*.

Table 1: Kinds of *maṣlaḥa* recognition, strength and type, with examples

Type of the recognized *maṣlaḥa*	**Strength of the *maṣlaḥa***	**Type of recognition**		**Example**
Indicated by a particular evidence (*dalīl khāṣṣ*)	Effective *maṣlaḥa*	When the particular description is recognized, through a text or consensus, as matching the very same ruling.		Intoxication is the particular reason (*ʿilla*) for prohibition of alcohol. Another type of intoxication matches this *ʿilla*. Prohibition is the very same ruling. The *maṣlaḥa* is protecting reason.
Indicated by a general evidence (*dalīl ʿāmm*)	Appropriate *maṣlaḥa*	Highest level of suitability	When the particular description is recognized as matching the general type of ruling.	Young age is the particular *ʿilla* in establishing a father's guardianship (*wilāya*). Guardianship is the general type of ruling under which comes, for instance: guardianship over wealth, and guardianship over the child itself.

Type of the recognized *maṣlaḥa*	Strength of the *maṣlaḥa*	Type of recognition		Example
Indicated by a general evidence (*dalīl ʿāmm*)	Appropriate *maṣlaḥa*	Medium level of suitability	When the general description is recognized as matching the very same ruling.	The difficulty caused by rain is the *ʿilla* for the concession (*rukhṣa*) of combining two prayers at one time. Difficulty is the general *ʿilla*, as there are several types of difficulties. Combining two prayers at one time is the very same ruling.
		Lowest level of suitability	When the general description is recognized as matching the general type of ruling.	Premeditated criminal aggression is the *ʿilla* for *qiṣāṣ*. Premeditated criminal aggression is the general type of *ʿilla*, as aggression may cause injuries or take life. *Qiṣāṣ* is the general type of ruling that includes retaliation for injuries, or for a person's life.

Al-munāsib al-gharīb (the strange suitable) is the name given by scholars to the lowest level of suitability that occurs when the general type of description matches the general type of ruling. This also refers to the strange *maṣlaḥa*. This is the view of Ibn Qudāma in *al-Rawḍa* and al-Ṭūfi in *Sharḥ Mukhtaṣar al-Rawḍa*, as well as that of al-Āmidī and others. This is also the intended view when speaking about the lowest degree of suitability, unlike the view of some scholars that *al-munāsib al-gharīb* refers to the nullified *munāsib*. This latter view is held by al-Subkī (d. 771 AH) in *al-Jawāmiʿ* and followed by the author of *Marāqī al-Suʿūd* who stated that 'The strange (*munāsib*) has been nullified by God Almighty.'[24]

3.1. The Categories of the Unrestricted *Maṣlaḥa*

The unrestricted *maṣlaḥa* is of two categories: the first, which is subject to disagreement among jurists, is the one for which its suitability to the objectives and general rules of the Sharīʿa has been attested. The second category is that for which its conformity to the objectives and general trends of the Sharīʿa has not been attested.[25] Hence it is excluded from the dispute and is not considered within the category of unrestricted *maṣlaḥa*, even though some scholars have included it. This is what was termed strange (*gharīb*) by al-Ghazālī.[26]

4. Area of Agreement Regarding *Maṣlaḥa*

First, the recognized *maṣlaḥas* established by any form of recognition are not subject to disagreement; rather there is agreement in that they can be used in causation. These kinds of *maṣlaḥa* do not belong to the *mursala* type. Second, the types of *maṣlaḥa* that are proven by evidence as nullified cannot be used in causation by the agreement of scholars. They also, according to the agreement of the majority of scholars, do not belong to the *mursala* type.

5. Area of Disagreement Regarding the Unrestricted *Maṣlaḥa*

The unrestricted *maṣlaḥa*, which is subject to disagreement among Islamic legal theorists (*Uṣūlīs*), is that whose recognition or rejection has not been proven; the one that falls within the area of transactions (*muʿāmalāt*) not the area of acts of worship (*ʿibādāt*); and the one in which the rulings formed on its basis lead to a Sharīʿa objective known from general evidences. In transactions, the default ruling is permissibility (*ibāḥa*), unless a prohibition is expressed. Thus, rulings can be founded on *maṣlaḥa*. Another area of disagreement is whether or not the application of *maṣlaḥa* should be restricted to the necessary *maṣlaḥa* (*ḍarūriyya*), which is certain (*qaṭʿīyya*) and general (*kulliyya*), as reported by al-Ghazālī who allowed causation on this basis.[27]

The requirement that the *maṣlaḥa* must be necessary to be considered is subject to disagreement. This is because the *maṣlaḥas* of need (*ḥājiyya*), and that of complement (*taḥsīniyya*) are also required, and both are complementary to the *maṣlaḥa* of necessity, with overlap between them. Al-Shāṭibī says, ‘It is established that the complement [*maṣlaḥa*] serves that of need, and that of need serves that of necessity, yet it is the one of necessity that is the objective.'[28] The common link and overlap between these types of *maṣlaḥa* will be discussed when speaking about the consideration of importance in ranking *maṣlaḥas*.

As for the condition of certainty (*qaṭʿīyya*), it is often not required in the process of *ijtihād*, nor established in each individual instance; rather a preponderant surmise (*ẓanniyya*) is sufficient. Moreover, the existence of this in the majority, rather than all, of cases is sufficient. In this sense, al-Shāṭibī says,

> God's objective is to make people conform to the general rules and the habitual things normally occur in the majority of, rather than in all, cases and the Sharīʿa is established on this basis. Therefore, rules are constructed according to the normal generality rather than perfect universal generality from which no constituent may be absent. The fact that the Sharīʿa is established on this basis is clear. Do you not see that assigning duties is general? Yet, God made puberty a sign on this, which indicates the existence of reason being a basic prerequisite for assigning duties. Reason in this case is known to exist in the majority, though not in all people. This is not always the case and this is not perfectly reflected in all cases, as there are some people who have perfect reason well before they reach puberty, and there are others who lack sound reason after they reach puberty. However, in the majority of cases, puberty and sound reason are interrelated.
>
> Equally, God has permitted breaking the fast and shortening prayers during travel because of difficulty, although difficulty may be experienced in other areas, and may not always be felt in the case in travel. Despite this, God has not considered such exceptions, but has let the rule run its course. Other examples include establishing a minimum measurement (*niṣāb*) for a person to be considered wealthy, deciding criminal sentences based on the testimony of witnesses, accepting solitary reports (*āḥād*) and surmised analogy (*qiyās ẓannī*), as well as other cases whose outcomes may not be repeatable under similar conditions. In all of these cases the exceptions are few compared to the majority of cases. Thus, these rules are considered to be general in a normal, rather than all-inclusive sense. All duties are assigned according to this.[29]

It is clear that certainty and all-inclusive generality are not possible. Ibn al-Munīr states that Abū Ḥāmid al-Ghazālī's stipulation that *maṣlaḥa* must be certain is some sort of insistence on the unattainable; it is a request for what is not possible either from the customary or Sharīʿa point of view, as certainty in future happenings is unobtainable.

Concerning areas of disagreement, Islamic legal theorists (*Uṣūlīs*) hold two positions:

1. Whatever is called *maṣlaḥa*, whether proper or not, is an area of disagreement. The proper *maṣlaḥa* is what has a general origin (*aṣl kullī*) to which it can be assigned. The improper *maṣlaḥa* is the strange one which does not come under a general origin, but at the same time does not contradict the objectives of the Sharīʿa and does not violate a general rule, nor does it conflict with a general evidence (*dalīl kulli*).
2. Disagreement is only over the unrestricted *maṣlaḥa* that coheres with the general trends of the Sharīʿa. This is the one that has a general origin to which it can be assigned. In fact, all *maṣlaḥas* have a general origin to which they can be attributed, even if individual *maṣlaḥas* may vary in their distance from the general origin – some are far, others are even further.[30]

The second position is explained by Table 2:

Table 2: Areas of agreement and disagreement according to type of *maṣlaḥa*

***Maṣlaḥa* type**	**Correctness agreed on**	**Rejection agreed on**	**Correctness disagreed on**
Recognized *maṣlaḥa*	✓	X	X
Unrestricted *maṣlaḥa* in transactions (*muʿāmalāt*)	X	X	✓
Unrestricted *maṣlaḥa* in acts of worship (*ʿibādat*)	X	✓	X
Strange *maṣlaḥa*	X	✓	X
Nullified *maṣlaḥa*	X	✓	X

The disagreement among scholars lies in whether *maṣlaḥa* is an independent evidence or included within another type of evidence. However, all scholars state that the Sharīʿa is based on *maṣlaḥa*, and all leading scholars have based some sub-rulings on *maṣlaḥa*, even if they differed in the terminology they used. Thus, this should be a cause for agreement rather than disagreement. Yet, this is well known to be an area of disagreement among scholars of *uṣūl al-fiqh*.[31]

Table 3: Recognition of *maṣlaḥa* in the view of the four Sunnī Imāms

Name of Imām	Recognition of *maṣlaḥa*
Abū Ḥanīfa[32] (d. 150 AH)	One of the types of juristic preference (*istiḥsān*)
Mālik	An evidence independent of analogy (*qiyās*)
al-Shāfiʿī	One of the types of analogy (*qiyās*), if it is recognized
Aḥmad b. Ḥanbal[33] (d. 241 AH)	One of the types of analogy (*qiyās*)

The difference in opinion has resulted in four views representing four distinct schools (Table 3):[34]

1. Prohibition of upholding unrestricted *maṣlaḥa*. This is the view attributed to al-Shāfiʿī, al-Qāḍi Abū Bakr and his followers, and several other scholars. According to Imām al-Ḥaramayn, it is the view of some groups of scholastic theologians.
2. Unlimited permissibility (*jawāz muṭlaq*) of unrestricted *maṣlaha*. This is reported as the view of Mālik and an early opinion of al-Shāfiʿī. Imām al-Ḥaramayn and his fellows such as al-Qurṭubī, al-Qarāfī, and al-Abyārī criticized Mālik for this position. In his *Jannat al-Nāẓir*, al-Baghdādī says in defence of Mālik,

> There is no apparent disagreement between al-Shāfiʿī and Mālik about the issue of *maṣlaḥa*. Mālik says that if a *mujtahid* surveys the sources of the Sharīʿa, he will conclude that *maṣlaḥas*, in their whole and constituent

> parts, are cared for, and that there is no *maṣlaḥa* but it has been generally recognized. However, he excluded from this rule any *maṣlaḥa* that conflicted with any of the Sharīʿa principles. What the followers of al-Shāfiʿī have reported about him [al-Shāfiʿī's position on] the same issue does not exceed this statement [of Mālik], as there is nothing more specific than it, except acting upon a recognized *maṣlaḥa* based on a particular basic principle of the Sharīʿa. Yet, this is unlike their view of this lack of restriction. This clarifies that those who accept the unrecognized *maṣlaḥa* already accept the unrestricted *maṣlaḥa* introduced by Mālik, as there is no middle ground between the two perspectives.[35]

3. The third view may be considered as an improved restatement of the first view. This view is attributed by Imām al-Ḥaramayn to al-Shāfiʿī and the majority of Abū Ḥanīfa's followers. He said, 'They accept the unrestricted *maṣlaḥas* provided that they are in conformity with the recognized *maṣlaḥas* attested to by the Sharīʿa's basic principles.' This condition excludes such a *maṣlaḥa* from being of the *mursala* type, if its conformance to the Sharīʿa's principles is interpreted as suitability (*munāsaba*), because it then becomes one of the forms of analogy, as noted by al-Zarkashī and explored above.
4. The final view is the one chosen by al-Ghazālī and al-Bayḍāwī[36] (d. 685 AH) and their followers. They acknowledge *maṣlaḥa* only if it stems from necessity, and is certain and general. All three conditions must be fulfilled, otherwise it will not be considered, according to al-Zarkashī. This is originally the view of of Imām al-Ḥaramayn and thus al-Zarkashī's statement appears to be an interpretation of it.[37]

In conclusion, the preponderant opinion is to recognize the use of the unrestricted *maṣlaḥa* as evidence, provided that it is compatible with the Sharīʿa objectives and does not contradict a text or an established Sharīʿa rule. This is reported as the view of the majority of the Companions (*ṣaḥāba*) of the Prophet and their successors (*tābiʿūn*), the four Imāms: Abū Ḥanīfa, Mālik, al-Shāfiʿī and Aḥmad, and the majority of Muslim legal theorists. Hence, the unrestricted *maṣlaḥa* is seen by them as a rich resource for deducing and forming rulings on newly emerging issues. It is argued that the position of the opponents in this regard, the Ẓāhiriyya and Shiʿites, who deny analogy, was a 'later development', occurring after the consensus of the Companions was reached, and therefore their disagreement is not considered.[38]

6. The Difference between the Recognized *Maṣlaḥa* and the Unrestricted *Maṣlaḥa*

The difference is that the recognized *maṣlaḥa* is acknowledged and accepted by the Sharīʿa through a particular evidence whereas the unrestricted *maṣlaḥa* is neither acknowledged nor rejected by any particular evidence; rather it is attested to by the general principles and objectives of the Sharīʿa. In this way, the Sharīʿa attests to the general kind of *maṣlaḥa* as being accepted and included within its general objectives. This latter type of *maṣlaḥa* is the one called 'unrestricted' and the one subject to disagreement.[39] On this basis, removal of harm is a recognized *maṣlaḥa* to which a particular evidence has attested, namely the Prophetic *ḥadīth* that reads, 'There should neither be harm nor reciprocation of harm.'[40] An example is if a worker sold food that was stored in a refrigerator without the owner's permission due to fear that it would go bad following a power cut, intending to recover its value. That action would be allowable, since protecting its value is better than letting the food go bad. This is a *maṣlaḥa* that has been indicated by a general evidence, which is the Sharīʿa objective of preserving wealth. Thus, a *maṣlaḥa* is called *mursala* (unrestricted) when its recognition is indicated by a general evidence.

7. The Difference between the Nullified *Maṣlaḥa* and the Unrestricted *Maṣlaḥa*

The difference is that the nullified *maṣlaḥa* is rejected by the Sharīʿa through a particular indicant, while the unrestricted *maṣlaḥa* is neither acknowledged nor rejected by any particular indicant; rather the Sharīʿa has attested to and recognized such general types of *maṣlaḥas*.[41]

8. The Difference between the Strange *Maṣlaḥa* and the Unrestricted *Maṣlaḥa*

The strange *maṣlaḥa* and the unrestricted *maṣlaḥa* resemble each other in the fact that the Sharīʿa has neither acknowledged nor rejected them by any particular evidence. The difference is that the Sharīʿa has generally attested to and accepted the unrestricted type of *maṣlaḥa*, but has not done so with the strange type of *maṣlaḥa*.

9. Determining the Position of the Unrestricted *Maṣlaḥa*

The reason for clarifying the foregoing differences is to illustrate that both the unrestricted *maṣlaḥa* and the recognized *maṣlaḥa* share recognition by the Sharīʿa, yet with a difference in degree. The recognized *maṣlaḥa* that the Sharīʿa has indicated through specific evidence is stronger in recognition than the unrestricted one whose kind has been indicated as recognized only in general. These distinctions also demonstrate that both the nullified *maṣlaḥa* and the strange *maṣlaḥa* are rejected by the Sharīʿa, yet not to the same extent. The nullified *maṣlaḥa* which is rejected by a specific evidence is rejected more emphatically than the strange *maṣlaḥa* which is only rejected by the Sharīʿa in general.

It might be said that the unrestricted *maṣlaḥa* belongs, in a sense, to both the recognized and nullified, or strange categories of *maṣlaḥa*, which are agreed upon. This is because it could be argued that what the Sharīʿa, by its objectives and principles, has acknowledged as suitable through general agreement should be included with what it has accepted through particular evidence. By the same token, what neither conforms to the general trends of the Sharīʿa nor is attested to by its objectives could be claimed to be included in the nullified type.[42] If such a claim is made, the answer will be that this is true in as far as each *maṣlaḥa* is attributed to its type, but the differences in degree should be considered, as explained previously.

Figure 2: The relationship between types of *maṣlaḥa*

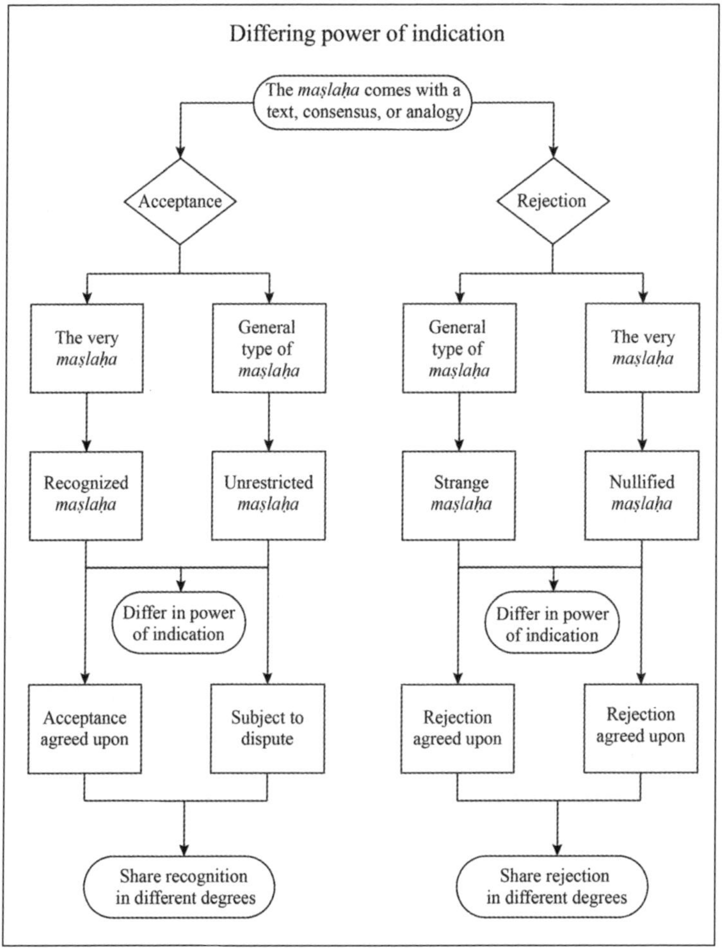

From Figure 2, it can be seen that *maṣlaḥa* is classified in one of three ways:

1. According to recognition or rejection. That is that *maṣlaḥa* is of two types: recognized or rejected.
2. According to recognition of *maṣlaḥa* itself, that is to say, there are three types of *maṣlaḥa*: recognition agreed upon, rejection agreed upon, and subject to dispute, which is the unrestricted *maṣlaḥa*.
3. According to the degree of recognition. This means that there are four types of *maṣlaḥa*: recognized, nullified, unrestricted and strange.

10. The Difference between Analogy and the Unrestricted *Maṣlaḥa*

1. What is established through analogy has had the ruling transferred from another incident, which is the root or original case whose ruling has been indicated by a text or consensus. On the other hand, the ruling of what is established through the unrestricted *maṣlaḥa* is not transferred from elsewhere; rather it is originally independent and not inferred from another case.
2. The evidence of what is established through analogy must be specific. This is the shared *ʿilla* that extends the ruling of the original case into the new case. Moreover, the *ʿilla* of the original case is established by text or consensus and not deduced from other cases. On the other hand, the evidence of what is established by the unrestricted *maṣlaḥa* is not specific. Instead it is a general principle approved by general objectives of the Sharīʿa. Thus the evidence of the unrestricted *maṣlaḥa* is the general objectives of the Sharīʿa, which in fact indicate meanings explained by al-Ghazālī as follows:

> The fact that these meanings constitute Sharīʿa objectives is known not by a single evidence, but by countless evidences

> from the Qur'an, the *Sunna*, circumstantial evidences, as well as various signs. This is why it was called unrestricted *maṣlaḥa*.[43]

In analogy, the original and new cases are brought together by a specific meaning indicated by a particular evidence. However, in the unrestricted *maṣlaḥa*, the meaning on which the ruling is formed is not indicated by a particular evidence, but by a set of general evidences and rules.[44]

3. In what is established by analogy, the new case shares the *ʿilla* for the ruling with the original case. By contrast, what is established through the unrestricted *maṣlaḥa* does not depend on something similar; rather it depends on the *maṣlaḥa*'s compatibility with the trends of the Sharīʿa and its conformance to its objectives, as there is no particular evidence to establish its recognition or rejection.

This does not negate the fact that both the unrestricted *maṣlaḥa* and analogy share the mutual goal of securing benefits and preventing harms, which is *maṣlaḥa* in the absolute sense. The ruling that is established through either of them is considered to be established through *ijtihāḍ*, and not through a text or consensus.[45]

11. The Difference between Juristic Preference (*Istiḥsān*) and the Unrestricted *Maṣlaḥa*

1. Juristic preference (*istiḥsān*) requires that the issue in which it is used to arrive at a ruling has other similar parallels for which a different ruling was given. As for *maṣlaḥa*, there are no similar parallels that have carried a ruling opposite to that indicated by the *maṣlaḥa* in that instance; rather the ruling is established by means of *maṣlaḥa* from the outset.
2. Juristic preference requires that the issue in question is excluded from the rulings on parallel issues and given a distinct ruling due to stronger evidence that requires so. In

contrast, *maṣlaḥa* does not require that the issue be excluded from the ruling on other parallels, nor be distinct in its ruling due to the existence of stronger evidence.

3. Ruling according to juristic preference may use an original case as a basis for conducting analogy. For this reason, the Ḥanafī scholars said that juristic preference is 'a hidden analogy measured against an apparent analogy for the strength of its *ʿilla*; in contrast to the unrestricted *maṣlaḥa* which does not have an original case to be measured against'.[46]
4. Juristic preference is more specific than the unrestricted *maṣlaḥa*, because it requires a less weighty opposing evidence (*marjūḥ*) over which juristic preference is given priority. In contrast, the unrestricted *maṣlaḥa* does not require opposition, and is therefore more general. Al-Qarāfī says,

> Juristic preference is more specific, because we require in it that there is a less weighty opposing evidence over which juristic preference is given preference. Therefore, we say: it is to discard an aspect of *ijtihād* in favour of a stronger one. On the other hand, the unrestricted *maṣlaḥa* does not require opposition, and is free of such a need.[47]

5. In his commentary on *al-Muwāfaqāt*, ʿAbd Allāh Draz stated,

> Both the unrestricted *maṣlaḥa* and juristic preference use a general original case as an evidence to extend a ruling to specific new cases. The difference between them is that the latter specifies a particular ruling by excluding it from a general evidence based on *maṣlaḥa*, while the former establishes a new evidence based on *maṣlaḥa* in cases where no particular evidence exists.[48]

Thus, the supporting evidence for juristic preference could be a text, consensus, *maṣlaḥa*, custom and so on. In addition, the ruling based on *maṣlaḥa* in juristic preference occurs only in some cases while the unrestricted *maṣlaḥa* is a general rule whose ruling applies to all similar forms and instances where no text or consensus exists, and there is no original case for which analogy can be used.[49]

12. The Difference between *Bidʿa* ('Innovation' in Religion) and the Unrestricted *Maṣlaḥa*

1. The unrestricted *maṣlaḥa* exists only in that with a meaning that can be rationally comprehended in detail. It is therefore found only in transactions (*muʿāmalāt*) and customary practices (*ʿādāt*), and does not exist in pure acts of worship. In contrast, *bidʿas* can be found only in acts of worship and not in other acts.[50]
2. The unrestricted *maṣlaḥas* will need to conform to the general trends of the Sharīʿa in general and not contradict any of its principles. In contrast, *bidʿas*, according to those who engage in them, have no restrictions or conditions.
3. The unrestricted *maṣlaḥa* is mostly used to achieve a necessary or needed matter in order to make things easy and remove hardship. Without this, hardship and restriction take place; it is known that needs are complementary to necessities and dependent upon them. However, *bidʿa* is different; as it is seen to mostly cause difficulty, and create hardship.
4. *Bidʿa*, unlike the unrestricted *maṣlaḥa*, is seen to 'demolish the principles and pillars of the Sharīʿa and contradict its objectives'. It is argued that if *bidʿa* gives an imagined impression of containing a *maṣlaḥa*, then such a *maṣlaḥa* is nullified and not recognized by the Sharīʿa, as has already been discussed previously.[51]

Table 4 explains the differences between *maṣlaḥa* and analogy, *maṣlaḥa* and juristic preference and *maṣlaḥa* and *bidʿa*.

Table 4: Comparison of types of *maṣlaḥa*, analogy, juristic preference, and *bidʿa*

Types of differences	**Areas of differences**						
	Recognized *maṣlaḥas*	**Unrestricted *maṣlaḥas***	**Strange *maṣlaḥas***	**Nullified *maṣlaḥas***	**Analogy**	**Juristic preference**	***Bidʿa***
Acceptance of this specific *maṣlaḥa* with particular evidence	✓	X	X	X	✓	X	X
Acceptance of its general type with general evidence	X	✓	X	X	X	X	X
Rejection of this specific *maṣlaḥa* with particular evidence	X	X	X	✓	X	X	✓
Rejection of its general type with general evidence	X	X	✓	X	X	X	✓
Shared *ʿilla*	X	X	X	X	✓	✓	X
Creation of a ruling without a precedent	✓	✓	X	X	X	X	X
Ruling established by *ijtihād*	X	✓	X	X	✓	✓	X
Ruling established by compliance with the Sharīʿa objectives	X	✓	X	X	X	X	X
Adds further hardship	X	X	X	✓	X	X	✓
Offers relief and removes hardship	✓	✓	X	X	✓	✓	X
Ruling based on removing hardship	X	X	X	X	X	✓	X
Occurs in acts of worship	✓	X	X	✓	✓	✓	✓
Occurs in customary acts	✓	✓	✓	✓	✓	✓	✓
Ruling restricted (specified) by evidence	✓	✓	X	✓	✓	✓	X
Ruling unrestricted by evidence	X	X	✓	X	X	X	✓
Ruling contradicts the Sharīʿa	X	X	✓	✓	X	X	✓
Ruling complements the Sharīʿa	✓	✓	X	X	✓	✓	X
Ruling is an exception from its parallels	X	X	X	X	X	✓	X

Giving a summary of differences aims to distinguish between the *maṣlaḥa*s in terms of type and degree on the one hand, and between *maṣlaḥa*s, analogy, juristic preference, and *bidʿa* on the other. The importance of this in making decisions of *maṣlaḥa* is that the more small differences are recognized and identified according to an accurate critierion, the more precise the estimation of *maṣlaḥa* is. This leads the decisions based on such a *maṣlaḥa* to be far-reaching and precisely achievable. The criterion used for decision making must start with the highest and finish at the lowest level of *maṣlaḥa*, as illustrated in Figure 3.

Figure 3: Levels of precedence between types of *maṣlaḥa*

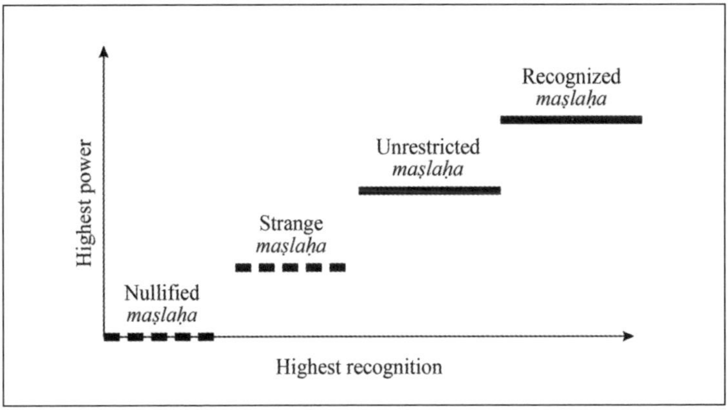

In the case of irreconcilable conflict, the recognized *maṣlaḥa* is given precedence over the unrestricted *maṣlaḥa*, the unrestricted *maṣlaḥa* is given precedence over the strange *maṣlaḥa*, and the strange *maṣlaḥa* is given precedence over the nullified *maṣlaḥa*.

Chapter Three

MAṢLAḤA REGULATORS: FUNCTION AND TYPES

Islamically speaking, no one should invent purposes, or even *maṣlaḥas* and *mafsadas* of his own accord. These are set by the Legislator, God the Wise.[1] Hence, according to this understanding, it is not the role of a human to set such purposes or *maṣlaḥas*. On the contrary, these are set by the Legislator and Muslims are duty bound to follow them[2] without adding to them.[3] The human role in this regard is to find and operate them within a set of regulators (*ḍawābiṭ*), which is the topic of this chapter.

1. Definition of 'Regulators'

The Arabic word for 'regulator' is *ḍābiṭ* (pl. *ḍawābiṭ*). It is derived from the root *ḍabṭ*, which refers linguistically to sticking to something so as to keep it under control. Al-Layth says:

> *Ḍabṭ* means sticking to something so as not to depart from it. The verb *ḍabaṭa* means to protect something with determination. If it is said, 'So and so is *ḍābiṭ*,' it means that he or she has a decisive approach, or are strong and powerful. In *al-Tahdhīb*, it means 'strong in action, power and body', while a person described as *aḍbaṭ* is someone who works with both hands.[4]

Ḍawābiṭ is the plural in the highest form, implying decisiveness, perfection and strength.[5] Terminologically, *ḍābiṭ* refers to what combines (and regulates) several branches of a main theme.[6]

2. Function of the Sharīʿa Regulators

The main function of the Sharīʿa regulators is to maintain moderation, which ensures justice, the primary purpose of its divine laws. Justice and moderation, in the Islamic understanding, ensure great rewards in the life to come and ample blessings in this present life. Every 'deviation' from moderation constitutes moving away from justice, as justice and moderation are closely interlinked, thus any 'deviation' from one is a 'deviation' from the other.

3. Procedural Definition of the Function of Regulators

Al-Ṭāhir b. ʿĀshūr says, 'Regulation means that a concept should have a certain limit which it neither exceeds nor falls short of, in a way that renders undoubted that part of the concept which can rightly be considered a religious objective.'[7]

Thus, regulators, or *ḍawābiṭ*, highlight the limits of Sharīʿa objectives that may be neither exceeded nor neglected. This means that these objectives are bound by certain regulators and limits to ensure that they remain in a state of moderation. This is a prominent feature of the Islamic Sharīʿa in all its spheres. Some writers and researchers call it 'moderation' or the 'balanced' way,[8] and al-Shāṭibī states, 'In all tasks it assigns, the Sharīʿa follows the middle, fairest way.'[9]

A basic assumption is that because people differ in their outlooks and their evaluation of things, if matters are left to their own views, they could be subject to excessiveness or negligence. Therefore, the Sharīʿa has established regulators for the *maṣlaḥas* set up for their benefit. Al-Shāṭibī says,

> Traditions, as well as many acts of worship, have a clear concept of regulating people's *maṣlaḥas*. If people were left to what they may determine, there would be no regulation and therefore no recourse to religious rules. When there are regulators, it is easier to follow the right course. Therefore, God has set certain limits and causes so that we may not go beyond them.[10]

Going beyond justice and moderation may take one of two forms. The first is 'excessiveness', which introduces an increase into something that is already essentially legitimate. Such an increase may be in the constants (unchangeable matters of the Sharīʿa) or in the variables (changeable matters), by adding additions to either, but not both, as they are mutually exclusive. New constants and variables simply cannot be added in the same situation, time and place. New additions can only be formed by transforming legitimate variables into constants or making legitimate constants variables.

The second form of going beyond justice is 'negligence', which means leaving out a portion of something that is already essentially legitimate. What is left out could be either legitimate constants or variables. The two cannot be combined. Constants and variables cannot be left out in the same situation at the same time and place. Legitimate constants can only be left out by making them variable, while leaving out the legitimate variable quality can only be done by treating it as a constant.

Therefore, according to this understanding, both 'excessiveness' and 'negligence' have the same quality in common, leading one away from justice and into injustice though they differ in their methods of doing so. In the case of excessiveness, the method is increase by means of introducing things that are seen to have 'no basis in the Sharīʿa'. In the case of negligence the means is leaving out religious aspects that are impermissible to disregard. Both excessiveness in constants, which occurs by introducing new constants that have no foundations in the Sharīʿa, and negligence in variables, which occurs by leaving out some essential variables, share the common ground of prohibiting what is lawful and forcing the rules of the Sharīʿa away from the lives of people. On the other hand, excessiveness in variables, in which new unfounded ones are introduced, and negligence in constants, in which some essential ones are left out, share the common ground of making lawful what is prohibited and taking people away from the rules of the Sharīʿa.

The process of 'abandoning moderation' through excessiveness or negligence and the steps leading to this are shown in Figure 4.

Figure 4: Abandoning moderation

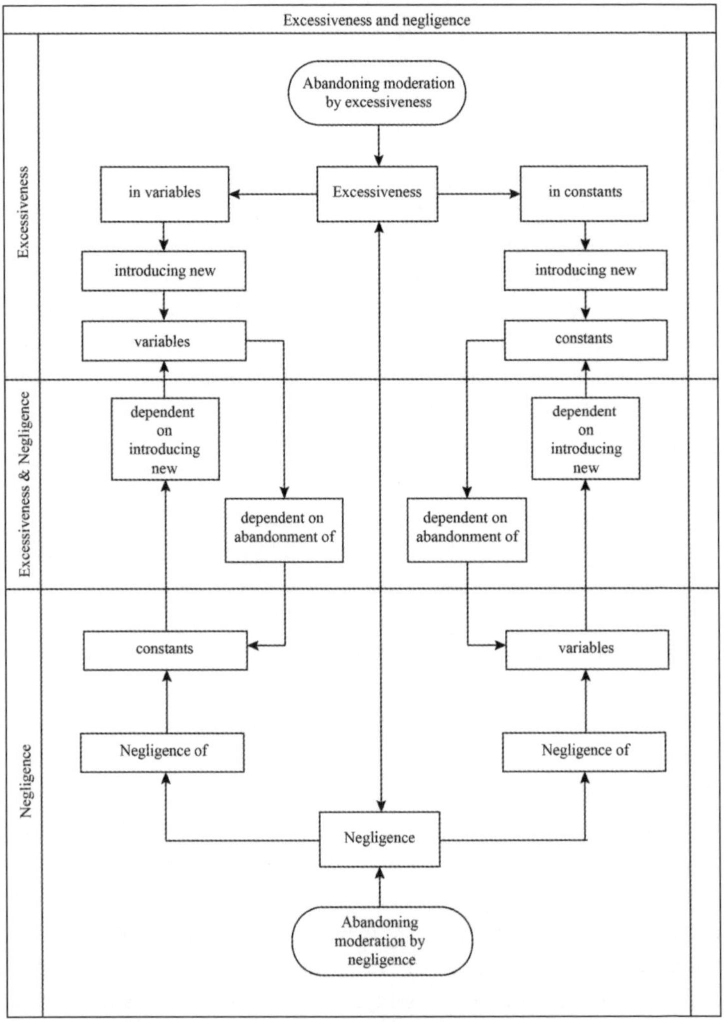

Generally speaking, Sharīʿa regulators aim to return people back to moderation. If they tend towards excessiveness and extremism, they are required to go back to ease and to abandon rigidity and hardship. If they lean towards negligence and indulgence, they are required to return back to adherence to the middle course. Al-Yūbī says,

> The main principles and the general fundamentals [of the Sharīʿa] must be constant so that individual cases and sub-issues can be referred to them in cases of ambiguity and dispute. The variable will thus be judged in accordance with the constant and will take its ruling. The reverse, judging the constant on the basis of the variable, must not be done, because this would render the constant into a variable. In such a case, important matters would change and regulators would be lost. In addition, values, moralities and fundamental principles would be left, constants would be discarded, and there would be nothing to serve as a foundation to build upon.[11]

The role of a certain regulator may differ according to what it seeks to regulate. It operates on constant rulings differently from variable ones, because the point of departure differs, as does the necessary work required to return matters to justice and moderation (Table 5).

Table 5: The Sharīʿa regulators in relation to constancy and comprehensiveness

Nature of the ruling	**Description of the method of dealing with the nature of the ruling**	**Result**	**Result description**
Constant rulings	Subjecting variables to constants without regulators makes the variable a constant, which deprives the Sharīʿa of its comprehensive nature.	Neglect of the Sharīʿa and pursuit of desires.	Excessiveness and extremism.
Constant rulings	Subjecting variables to constants within proper Islamic regulators does not change the variable into a constant. The Sharīʿa thus retains its comprehensive and constant nature.	Neglect of desires and following the Sharīʿa.	Justice and moderation.
Variable rulings	Subjecting a constant to a variable makes the constant a variable. Thus the Sharīʿa is deprived of its constant nature.	Neglect of the Sharīʿa and pursuit of desires.	Negligence and indulgence.

In short, all evidence in the Sharīʿa is made up of two premises. The first is theoretical and aims to achieve the goal of the *maṣlaḥa* in the decision approved by the Sharīʿa. The ruling here is not reached through deduction. The second is textual, being the Islamic ruling that represents the proof of the *maṣlaḥa* on which decisions are taken. This latter one is constant and will not change because the *maṣlaḥa* it aims to achieve cannot become a *mafsada*, nor can the *mafsada* it seeks to prevent become a *maṣlaḥa*. The former may be said to rely on traditions, practices, expertise and other changeable circumstances. Therefore, it changes when they change. However, the Sharīʿa ruling and the pursuit of the legitimate *maṣlaḥa* are seen to be constant: they do not change.[12]

The constant characteristic of the Sharīʿa makes it stable, able to accommodate differing events in time and place, as well as their changes. The Qur'an states, 'And We have sent the Scripture down to you [Prophet] explaining everything, and as guidance and mercy and good news to those who submit to God' (Q. 16:89). This is emphasized by al-Shāfiʿī in his book *Al-Risāla* when he states that whatever occurs to the subject of the law there will be in the Qur'an guidance for it.[13] This is so that Muslims can achieve *maṣlaḥas* without hardship and without losing the basis upon which they build their religious practices. Therefore, the function of regulators is to preserve stability by ensuring constancy and keeping it free of flaws. The same applies to the characteristic of comprehensiveness that aims to make the Sharīʿa easy and compassionate. Thus, Muslims will not find themselves in real difficulty because the Sharīʿa lives up to the changes in life, generating new rulings that apply to new human situations. It gives them flexibility, so that they find for every new occurrence in life a suitable ruling and for every variable based on a legitimate *maṣlaḥa*, a suitable ruling in the Sharīʿa that changes as the legitimate *maṣlaḥa* changes. This reflects what the textual evidence calls 'mercy' and 'ease': 'It was only as a mercy that We sent you [Prophet] to all people' (Q. 21:107); 'God wants ease for you, not hardship' (Q. 2:185).

Al-Būṭī says,

> You thus realize that the following regulators' relationship to *maṣlaḥa* is a relationship of revelation and nomination, not a relationship of exception and limitation. In other words, what is beyond these regulators does not fall within the framework of *maṣlaḥa*, even though some people may imagine it so.[14]

This means that whatever goes beyond the Islamic regulators of *maṣlaḥa* is unwarranted restriction and extremism that leads to harm and must not be followed. Hence, the Sharīʿa regulators are means to prevent excessiveness and negligence, and to maintain justice and moderation. They are the mainstay of the middle way that ensures freedom from hardship so that life may progress with ease and grace in matters of this world and the life to come.

Figure 5 shows the graph of this middle way:

Figure 5: *Maṣlaḥa* as moderation

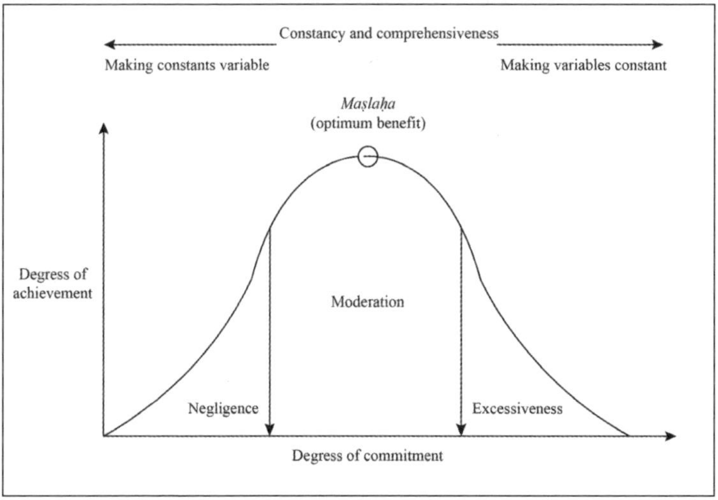

As can be clearly seen, moderation and steering a middle way is the objective of the regulators. The term *al-wasaṭiyya*, which means 'moderation or middle way', is much used these days though in different ways. It has been coined to highlight the concept that represents an essential characteristic of the Islamic Ummah, derived from Qur'anic texts: 'And thus We have made you [believers] into a middle Ummah (best community) so that you may bear witness [to the truth] before others and so that the Messenger may bear witness [to it] before you…' (Q. 2:143).

Ibn Taymiyya says, 'It has already been stated that this divine religion is a middle way between those who are excessive and those who are negligent. Whatever order God has given His servants, Satan tries to impede it in either of two ways: excessiveness or negligence. Satan does not mind which way is successful.'[15] Hence, the one who follows the middle way is seen to belong to the 'worthy, fair group' that follows a middle way between two extremes. They neither accept excessiveness and extremism, nor indulgence and negligence. This is their characteristic in faith, morality and behaviour.[16] The middle way does not mean mixing truth and falsehood, as this suggests mere compromise and making concessions before even knowing the right course from the wrong one. The right course is seen to be the one that ensures justice and moderation in accordance with the Sharīʿa. This may be understood from the *ḥadīth* narrated by Anas who said, 'The Prophet (peace be upon him) drew a number of lines. He said, "This line is a person's hope, and this is his day of death. As he is in between he is overtaken by the closer line."'[17] It is also the import of the Qur'anic verse that says, 'And this is My path, leading straight, so follow it, and do not follow other ways: they will lead you away from it. This is what He commands you to do, so that you may become righteous' (Q. 6:153).

Some of those who speak about the middle way nowadays seem to suggest pursuing a middle course between what is consistent with the Sharīʿa and what is inconsistent with it. This is actually negligence in as much as one takes up of what is wrong so as to mix it with what is right.

As such, it is impossible to avoid excessiveness and negligence except by adopting the middle way represented by what the Divine Legislator has commanded because it is only this middle way that ensures justice and moderation. Such justice and moderation are the objectives of the regulators established by the Sharīʿa. In achieving the Sharīʿa-approved *maṣlaḥas*, the regulators ensure the preservation of justice and moderation and prevent excessiveness and negligence.

4. *Maṣlaḥa* Regulators

4.1. Regulator No. 1: The *maṣlaḥa* must not contradict the texts of the Sharīʿa

When a *mujtahid* (a scholar who exercises *ijtihād*, or personal reasoning, to arrive at rulings) knows that a certain *maṣlaḥa* is not contrary to the Sharīʿa, his knowledge may have one of three degrees of import. The highest is knowledge of agreement between the two. The middle degree is knowledge that there is no contradiction and the lowest is the absence of knowledge about any contradiction.

Knowledge of agreement between the *maṣlaḥa* and the Sharīʿa is the highest degree of non-contradiction. All Sharīʿa-approved *maṣlaḥas* which have Sharīʿa-accepted evidence, whether through a clear text, the unanimity of scholars, or analogy are included among the *maṣlaḥas* that are known to be in agreement with the Sharīʿa through that evidence.

Knowledge of no conflict is the middle degree of non-contradiction. *Maṣlaḥas* that are not directly indicated by textual evidence yet have several pieces of evidence, such as Sharīʿa objectives and jurisprudential rules, confirming their desirability, are considered Sharīʿa-approved *maṣlaḥas*. They are known, through examination of such evidence, to not be in contradiction with the Sharīʿa.

Non-knowledge of conflict is the lowest degree of non-contradiction. *Maṣlaḥas* that are not known to conflict with the Sharīʿa, because they belong to the genus of what the Divine Legislator normally brings about, are, therefore, also Sharīʿa-approved. Ibn Taymiyya describes these as actions that secure clear *maṣlaḥas*, while there is nothing in the Sharīʿa to prevent it. However, he asserts that this is the subject of a famous disagreement among scholars. Some jurists call such a benefit *maṣlaḥa mursala*, others call it *raʾy*, while a third group associate it with *istiḥsān*.[18]

This controversy among scholars may have led them to ignore some important *maṣlaḥas*. Ibn Taymiyya describes this as follows: 'Many of them have ignored types of *maṣlaḥa* which should be upheld simply because, "the Sharīʿa has not given a verdict on them." Thus, they allowed some duties or recommended actions to be left undone and some prohibited reprehensible actions to be committed, though the Sharīʿa may have given a verdict in this regard of which the scholar is unaware.'[19]

A person may be confused about the degrees of non-contradiction, assuming that the difference between them is one of type, rather than degree. This may lead him to disregard the lowest degree of non-contradiction, thinking that acting on its basis is prohibited. As such, it is important to clarify the difference between a lack of knowledge of contradiction and knowledge of non-contradiction. The first is surmised evidence, though upholding it is confirmed by certain evidence. The second involves a quest for certain evidence to which one limits oneself. It is well known that seeking certainty in *all* matters is considered an excessiveness that leads inevitably to non-enforcement of rules and such non-enforcement inevitably leads to negligence of the rules of the Sharīʿa. Ibn al-Qayyim comments on the statement, 'No policy may be accepted unless it is in accordance with the Sharīʿa.' He says,

> The right policy is an act through which people are closer to righteousness and further from evil, even though such an act has neither been ordered by the Prophet nor established by revelation. If the statement 'in accordance with the Sharīʿa' means 'does not disagree with what the Sharīʿa states,' then it is correct. If the intended meaning is 'the only acceptable policy is what the Sharīʿa has stated', then it is wrong and places the Prophet's companions in error.[20]

A further explanation of this is outlined below:

1. The non-existence of knowledge is not equivalent to knowledge of non-existence. Ibn Taymiyya affirms this, saying,

> The non-existence of knowledge is not equal to knowledge of non-existence, particularly in the statements of Muslim scholars whose numbers are known only to God, the Lord of all the worlds. Hence, Imām Aḥmad and other scholars say, 'Whoever claims consensus is lying. This is the opinion of al-Marīsī (d. 218 AH)[21] and al-Aṣamm (d. 201 AH).[22] One should only say, 'I know of no dispute over this.' Scholars who mentioned consensus, such as al-Shāfiʿī, Abū Thawr and others explained that what they meant by this was that they were not aware of any dispute and that this was the sort of consensus they claimed.[23]

   Imām Aḥmad's statement shows that he is very keen that consensus is not taken to mean knowledge of no dissent, but that it is sufficient not to know of any dissent.[24] In this sense, when a large number of *mujtahid* scholars have exercised their *ijtihād* in a particular question or event, not knowing of any dissent with their verdict from a reliable scholar means the conditions of consensus are met. The present and past practices of the Muslim community confirm that unanimous consensus takes place and is acted upon in this way.
2. Knowledge of non-existence is not possible without knowledge of what exists. Ibn Taymiyya emphasizes the fact that non-existence has no material form. It cannot be known until what exists has been known. He refers to some scholars of scholastic theology (*ʿilm al-kalām*) who say that it is not possible to know of what does not exist unless it is made into something, because they claim that knowledge must relate to something existent. But he asserts that knowledge of non-existence is acquired through the knowledge of what exists. He explains that when we know that 'there is no deity other than God', we visualize an existing deity, and we know that what we have visualized does not apply to anyone other than God. From this, he explains, we realize that knowledge of what exists and its

qualities are the basis and that knowledge of absolute and conditional non-existence branches out of it. Moreover, he asserts that knowledge that something does not exist is of no use to the person who knows it except that it perfects his knowledge of what exists. The perfect knowledge of what exists, he continues, does not in itself impart to the knower any quality of perfection but his knowledge of the non-existence of flaws, in what exists, for example, gives him knowledge of its perfection.[25]

3. Knowledge of non-contradiction occurs when a person knows what the Sharīʿa includes. Such knowledge requires a thorough induction (*istiqrā'*), which leads to certain evidence. This means that limiting oneself to knowledge of non-contradiction leads to limiting oneself to evidence based on certainty. This, in turn, leads to the rejection of evidence based on surmise, which is a cancellation of an appropriate and recognized type of evidence and all the rulings based on it. Doing so leads to negligence of such rulings. Therefore, the Sharīʿa did not rely exclusively on certainty when considering acts of worship, people's transactions or other actions. That would have led to the discarding of a large number of *maṣlaḥas* for fear of committing a small number of *mafsadas*. Thus, whatever leads to the cancellation of a Sharīʿa-approved *maṣlaḥa* or the occurrence of a preventable *mafsada* should be discarded.[26]

The difference between 'absence of knowledge of contrary evidence' and 'ignorance of contrary evidence' is as follows.

For absence of knowledge of contrary evidence to be considered, two things are required: knowledge that the intended action is beneficial and knowledge that the intended action is within the genus of the actions approved by the Legislator. These two qualities suggest that the intended action is most probably legitimate. Only at this point of high probability does the action become a recognized *maṣlaḥa*. We then look as best we can for evidence that might prevent the actions. When no such evidence is found, the action is fully considered a *maṣlaḥa*.

Ignorance of contrary evidence is of different degrees:

1. Ignorance that the action is beneficial, which comes under ignorance of the reason for considering the action.
2. Ignorance that the action is within the genus of the actions approved by the Legislator, which comes under ignorance of the reason for considering or discarding the action. As the *maṣlaḥa*'s inclusion within the genus of the actions approved by the Legislator is the cause making it necessary, ignorance of such inclusion is in fact ignorance of the reason for its consideration. Likewise, as non-inclusion of the *maṣlaḥa* within the genus of the actions approved by the Legislator is considered evidence against its necessity, such ignorance of its exclusion is in fact ignorance of contrary evidence.
3. Ignorance that the intended action is prohibited by the Sharīʿa.

The absence of knowledge of the benefit of the action precludes its consideration as a *maṣlaḥa* until its benefit becomes apparent. Similarly, the absence of knowledge included within the genus of the actions approved by the Legislator precludes its consideration as a *maṣlaḥa* until this inclusion is known. Not exerting one's best efforts to look for legal contrary evidence does not imply the absence of knowledge of contrary evidence. In fact, here the action is not recognized by the Sharīʿa due to a lack of specificity and no ruling is given until this has been ascertained. On the other hand, if it is known that the action is unbeneficial, or not included in the genus of the actions approved by the Legislator, or that there is contrary legal evidence, then the action is not considered a *maṣlaḥa*. The difference between the two, therefore, is in accordance with the degree of ignorance of contrary evidence. Such ignorance of contrary evidence presupposes ignorance of all three degrees. Conversely, the absence of knowledge of the contrary evidence presupposes ignorance of the third degree only. This, in precise terms, is ignorance of the cause of prohibition, not of the case itself. On the basis of what has been stated above, the absence of knowledge of the contrary evidence implies absence of knowledge of any evidence contrary to preponderant surmise, while ignorance of the contrary evidence implies unawareness of the preponderant surmise and what precludes it.

This distinction has various applications in decision making. Rational decision theory relies, *inter alia*, on a premise that is similar in effect to the requirement of knowledge that there is no contrary evidence. By contrast, wise decision theory relies on a premise that is similar in effect to the requirement of the absence of knowledge of contrary evidence. The two are not dissimilar.

When we compare the indications of rational decision theory and the requirement of knowledge of the absence of contrary evidence, we understand the relation between the degrees of non-contradiction of the Sharīʿa-based *maṣlaḥas* and the theories of decision making as follows:

1. Both suppose that the decision maker is able to make a thorough and complete induction to gain all the information that is relevant to the decision, without exception.
2. Both suppose that the decision maker is able to completely understand all that is relevant to the decision, from all aspects, in so far as he does not overlook anything.
3. Both suppose that the costs of induction and complete and full understanding are within people's resources and that such costs have no limits, which means that whatever they are, they remain within people's resources.

Examining real life and Islamic legal evidence, we realize that such suppositions are unrealistic. The Qur'an states, 'And you [people] have only been given a little knowledge' (Q. 17:85).

However, what is required under the Sharīʿa is only the absence of knowledge of contrary evidence, in accordance with its own conditions. This is in line with wise decision theory. Both suppose the following:

1. That the decision maker is only able to make an incomplete induction. One cannot make a complete and thorough induction because of the inability to gain full and thorough information about any decision. Therefore, one needs to gain only what is sufficient to enable the decision to take

place. This is also what seems to be indicated within Islamic textual evidence, as the Qur'an states, 'God does not burden any soul with more than it can bear' (Q. 2:286). In addition, the Prophet is quoted by Abū Hurayra as saying, 'When I forbid you from something, keep away from it and when I order you to do something, do of it what you can.'[27]

2. The decision maker does not have a perfect mental ability to deal with all that is relevant to the decision, particularly if it is a complex one. Any person's mental and intellectual ability is limited to a small number of questions within a limited perspective.[28] This seems also to be what is indicated by the Qur'anic statement, 'God does not put two hearts within a man's breast' (Q. 33:4).
3. The decision maker's resources are limited in time and place as well as in physical and financial ability. One cannot therefore meet the mental and financial costs of the requirement of thorough knowledge, except to a low level that makes securing the involved *maṣlaḥa* beneficial. In other words, the cost of securing the *maṣlaḥa* must not be equal to, or higher than, its benefit.[29]

Based on the above, it could be concluded that rational decision theory is not in line with the suppositions of taking decisions on the basis of *maṣlaḥa*, whereas wise decision theory is in general agreement with such suppositions.

It is clear, therefore, that it is important to observe what the theory requires of the person in practice, keeping it at a moderate level that causes no excessive hardship to people. This is based on the Qur'anic verse, 'God wants ease for you, not hardship' (Q. 2:185).

4.2. Regulator No. 2: The *maṣlaḥa* must not exclude a better *maṣlaḥa*

Operating the concept of exclusion requires the ability to distinguish the larger from the smaller, and the greater from the lesser. When both cannot be gained, obtaining the smaller excludes the larger and vice versa. This means that some of what may be gained is lost.

Al-ʿIzz ibn ʿAbd al-Salām says in this regard,

> Rulers, governors and their deputies should act according to what is best for their people to prevent harm and corruption and to ensure benefit and soundness. None of them should limit himself to what is good when he is able to do what is better, unless this will cause much hardship. They do not choose their actions according to what they prefer for themselves.[30]

Distinction between the larger and the smaller is meant to achieve the greater and abandon the lesser. Therefore the non-exclusion aims to ensure the more plentiful. An example is the fact that it is impermissible to leave money belonging to an orphan without investing it, as it would thereby be exhausted by living costs and zakat. The regulator that 'the *maṣlaḥa* must not exclude a better *maṣlaḥa*' performs the function of preventing the reduction of benefits and seeking to increase them. This means that the securing of benefits should be in such a way that leads to increasing them. Al-Taftāzānī (d. 793 AH)[31] says, 'The increase of benefit is the option to be sought.'[32]

This means that *maṣlaḥa* is the option that is originally more beneficial and more preferable. This also means that *maṣlaḥa* is intertwined with the increase of benefits and the prevention of their decrease. *Maṣlaḥa*, as it always seeks what is best, is one of the qualities of 'good' believers as indicated in the Qur'an, 'Those who listen to what is said and follow what is best. These are the ones God has guided; these are the people of understanding' (39:18).

Ibn Taymiyya says,

> What is obligatory in belief is to follow the better of any two options. It is not permissible for anyone to believe in a principle while believing that a contrary principle is better. Where he has a choice between two actions, one of which is better than the other, then that remains the better option, though it is permissible for him to do the lesser option when the better is not possible. He should however believe that the other option is superior and should like it more, and this is in one sense, following what is better.[33]

What is obligatory in action is to believe that the better but impossible option is better than the lesser but possible one, although it is permissible to do the lesser one. Moreover, the function of 'seeking as much as possible' is to achieve all that is possible, leaving only what is impossible which is not required, as in Q. 2:286, 'God does not burden any soul with more than it can bear', and the Prophetic statement, 'When I order something, do of it what you can.'[34]

Hence, there is no obligation requiring what is beyond one's ability. The ultimate objective is to achieve the best that can possibly be achieved. It is thus an acceptable substitute for the total. Al-Sarakhsī[35] says, 'The majority is an acceptable substitute for the total.'[36] What we make of this rule is that when the ruling applies to multiple things and where a majority of these multiple things is obtainable, the ruling applies to this majority. The applicability of the ruling is not affected by the unavailability or non-existence of the smaller number.[37]

The proper original state is that the possible majority takes the place of the impossible total. In other words, the impossible total is substituted and the possible majority is its substitute. When the total is beyond one's ability, it becomes impossible to achieve and this leads to its being substituted, whilst the majority that replaces the total becomes the substitute. The original case is that the lesser or the least preferable is accepted only when the larger number and more preferable is impossible. Likewise, the larger and more preferable number is accepted only when the total and most preferable is impossible. The highest in this example is the one to be sought. When it is impossible, it is substituted, with the lower, which is possible, being the substitute. Therefore, the rulings and conditions of the substitute and the substituted apply to them.

The process of transfer from the substituted to the substitute has certain regulators and rules specified by jurists. Among these is one stated by Ibn al-Qayyim,[38] 'To settle for offshoots and substitutes is acceptable only when the originals are not possible.'[39] Al-Sarakhsī mentions two rules: 'To perform the substitute when one is able to perform the original is not sufficient'[40] and 'The original rule is that the condition of impossibility, when it does not apply, precludes opting for the substitute.'[41] Therefore, the securing of a substitute benefit is not considered a *maṣlaḥa* except when the original benefit is not possible to secure. When the impossibility condition is not met, the substitute benefit is not called a *maṣlaḥa*. As the substituted is the original *maṣlaḥa*, the substitute is only counted as a *maṣlaḥa* when the original is not possible. The substitute is different from the substituted, they are not equal in kind or quality. The substitute is given the ruling of the substituted when the latter is not possible. Jurists have stated a number of relevant juristic rules, as follows:

1. The substitute replaces the substituted in the ruling applicable to it, not in its qualities.[42] This is when the substituted remains best, but is unobtainable.
2. Variation in the substitute is clear evidence of inequality.[43] This is the principle that if it is different from the thing substituted, it is not as good.
3. Variation in the benefit is clear evidence of different substance.[44] In other words, if the benefit is different, the substitute cannot be the same as the thing substituted.

Based on the above, if we have three benefits for the same purpose: a higher, a middle and a lower, all of which are possible to achieve, but cannot be combined, then only the achievement of the higher one is a *maṣlaḥa*. The achievement of either the middle or the lower is not a *maṣlaḥa* unless the one above it is unachievable. Yet it (the higher unachievable benefit) remains a benefit. This is because the achievement of the *maṣlaḥa* is the original purpose, while the achievement of something else, when the original *maṣlaḥa* is unachievable, is a substitute. The original is not identical to the substitute. The two are different in quantity, quality, kind and ruling. They only have the same ruling when the original is unachievable. Had it not been so, the original and the substitute would be one and the same thing. Al-Sarakhsī says, 'The original is not accomplished (or compensated) by substitution'. In other words,

> Complementing the original by the substitute is different from doing it fully when it can be done. When only some of the original is

> available, it cannot be completed, complemented or compensated by the substitute because that would mean combining the original and its substitute, which is not allowed.[45]

Were it possible for both original and substitute to be combined, their combination would become a new original, with neither of them a substitute for the other. In this case they would be of the same kind and quality and have the same ruling. The conclusion is that the *maṣlaḥa* is different from the inferior substitute benefit, which comes below it when the *maṣlaḥa* is possible to achieve. They have the same relationship as the general to the specific. The benefit here is more general than the *maṣlaḥa*, which means that every *maṣlaḥa* is a benefit. Likewise, the *maṣlaḥa* is more specific than the benefit, which means that not every benefit is a *maṣlaḥa*. The *maṣlaḥa* is a specific type of benefit: the highest possible benefit only. Any other benefit that is not the highest remains a benefit, but cannot be called a *maṣlaḥa* because the *maṣlaḥa* must be identical to the most beneficial. Differences in the sum of benefit where identity with the highest is presumed are taken into account from the Sharīʿa point of view. Al-Sarakhsī says,

> The effect of differences in the quantity where equality is required is greater than the effect of differences in quality. Do not you see that in usurious transactions the difference in quantity makes the contract unlawful, while the difference in quality does not? Yet the difference in quality makes it unlawful to complement the best by [more of] what is of lesser quality.[46]

Securing any benefit is not necessarily a *maṣlaḥa*, but rather securing the highest benefit alone is the *maṣlaḥa*. This principle operates only when the choice is between two or more benefits that cannot be combined but where one of them is possible to achieve. Therefore, one of them must be higher than the other and is given precedence. Securing it in this way is a *maṣlaḥa*. Where the choice relates to one benefit only, which may be procured or left out, the *maṣlaḥa* is always to procure it, no matter how big or small it is. Thus, comparing a benefit that is a *maṣlaḥa* to be secured and a lesser benefit is useful only when we are balancing between two or more benefits. In a case relating to one benefit only, such a comparison is of no use. The balancing here is actually between the *maṣlaḥa* of securing the benefit and the *mafsada* of abandoning it. The first comparison is between benefits to which the regulator that 'a *maṣlaḥa* should not exclude a better *maṣlaḥa*' is applicable. The second comparison is between a *maṣlaḥa* and a *mafsada*, to which applies a different regulator requiring 'the prevention of *mafsadas* and the securing of *maṣlaḥas*'. Likewise, it is not allowed, Islamically, to discard benefits or to bring about harm, and *mafsadas* cannot be prevented except through replacing them with *maṣlaḥas*.

Al-Suyūṭī says, 'Excluding what is "existing" is prohibited, but one may exclude what does not exist.'[47] What is understood from this is that when comparing two or more existing benefits, it is prohibited to exclude the higher one (Figure 6). Therefore, when there is only one benefit, it too should be secured. There is no question here of choosing the higher because there are not two or more benefits to compare, or to exclude one as unattainable. In such cases, seeking a higher benefit is to try to secure what does not exist and this cannot be an option or an alternative. Hence, it is discarded. This is unlike abandoning the securing of benefits, which is a *mafsada*. To bring about *mafsadas* is prohibited by the Sharīʿa. It is not possible to avoid the bringing about of *mafsadas*, except through securing their opposite *maṣlaḥas*.

To sum up:

1. When there is a single benefit, it should be secured whenever possible and this is a *maṣlaḥa*.
2. When there is conflict between two or more benefits, the *maṣlaḥa* is in securing the highest one.
3. Higher benefits are not left out in favour of lower ones, except when the higher is not possible.

The point is that what constitutes a *maṣlaḥa* for the Muslim community must not be abandoned, except where it is impossible to achieve.[48]

Figure 6: A *maṣlaḥa* should not exclude a better one

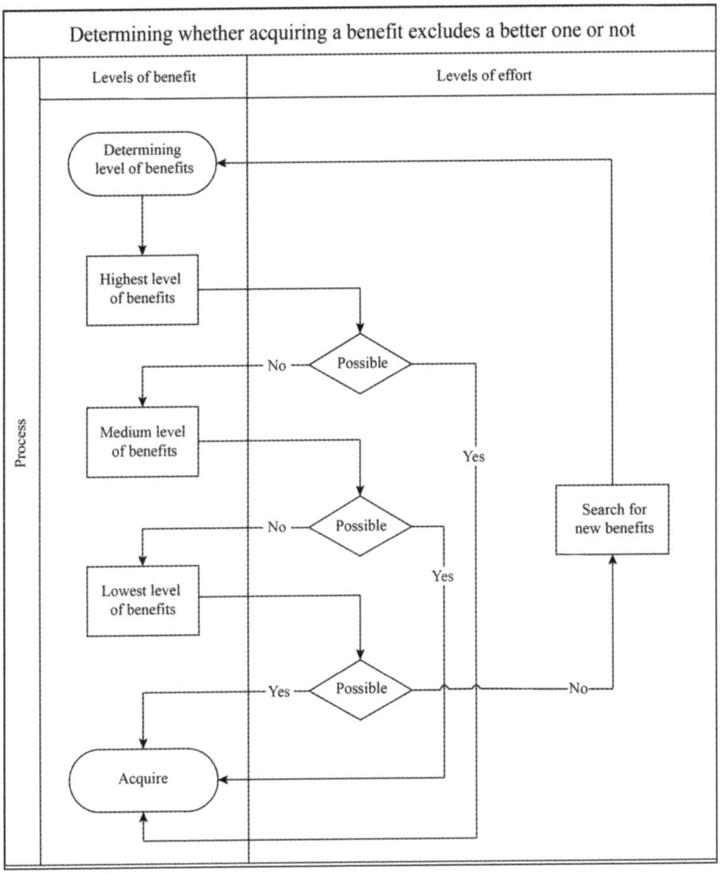

4.3. Regulator No. 3: Securing a *maṣlaḥa* must not lead to an equal or larger *mafsada*

The function of this regulator is to test the *ma'āl*, or the outcome of an action and whether it brings about a *maṣlaḥa* or not. The *ma'āl* is defined as 'the outcome that results from an action, whether good or evil, and whether it is intended by the person concerned or not'. The meaning of the *ma'āl* of an action is that 'the action is given the verdict of its outcome, whether the person concerned has intended that outcome to take place or not. If the action produces a required outcome, then it is required. If it leads only to an evil outcome, it is forbidden.'[49]

Looking into the outcome of actions is important and necessary. Al-Shāṭibī asserts that it is important from the Islamic point of view to consider the outcome of actions, whether they are in agreement with the Sharīʿa or against it. This is so because a *mujtahid* scholar does not give a ruling on an action of a person, stating whether it should be done or abandoned, until he has looked into the ultimate outcome of that action. The action may be legitimate because of a *maṣlaḥa* that it should secure or a *mafsada* that it should prevent. However, it may have a contrary outcome. On the other hand, an action may be illegitimate because it leads to a *mafsada* or to the prevention of a *maṣlaḥa*, but could nevertheless have a contrary outcome. If an absolute verdict is given allowing the first action, the fulfilment of the *maṣlaḥa* it brings may lead to a *mafsada* equivalent to or greater than its *maṣlaḥa*. This prevents issuing an absolute verdict of legality. The same applies in reverse to the second action. If it is given an absolute verdict of prohibition, the prevention of its *mafsada* may lead to an equal or greater *mafsada*. Hence, it is not right to give an absolute verdict of prohibition. It is indicated that *mujtahid* scholars find this area difficult to traverse, yet 'very rewarding work, of lauded outcome and in consistency with the objectives of the Sharīʿa'.[50]

Considering the outcome in this way does not rely on a person's intention or purpose; it relies instead on the result and the fruit of the action. In this life an action is commended or criticized, allowed or prohibited according to its result. This is because this life should be based on people's *maṣlaḥas* and on justice and fairness. Therefore, the prohibition of an action that leads to a *mafsada* that is equal to or greater than the *maṣlaḥa* it seeks to achieve does not look at the intention but at the outcome. Indeed, according to the aforementioned approach, looking at the outcome is the basis of looking at the means so as to allow or disallow it. Thus an action is given a verdict that is seen to be consistent with its outcome, whether intended by the doer of the action or not.

We may therefore say that the relation between the rule of *sadd al-dharāʾiʿ* (blocking the means) and the outcome of actions is that of causality. If the means leads to a *mafsada* or harm, it is blocked; and if it leads to a *maṣlaḥa* or something good, it is allowed. Hence, the means is the cause and the outcome is the resultant effect. Both the consideration of the outcome and the blocking of means are applications of the principle of securing *maṣlaḥa* and preventing *mafsada*. It is clearly apparent that, according to this approach, the consideration of the outcome, one form of which is the blocking of means, aims only to secure *maṣlaḥas* that are usually sought by a *mujtahid* scholar due to the fact that such *maṣlaḥas* have been upheld in the divine legislation and rules. After all, the ultimate objective of the Sharīʿa is to 'ensure all good things in this life and to prevent corruption and harm wherever and whenever they may exist'.[51]

5. Estimating the Outcome

Securing a particular benefit cannot be judged as good or bad until we have looked at the outcome of securing it. It may be legitimate because of a certain *maṣlaḥa* that it aims to achieve, or a certain *mafsada* that it aims to prevent. Yet it may produce an outcome that is at variance with what has been intended. Likewise, it may be illegitimate because of a certain *mafsada* it may produce or a *maṣlaḥa* it may prevent, yet it may in actuality produce a better outcome. Needless to say, the means themselves need to be legally acceptable and hence what is being discussed here is not a legitimatization of illegal means on the basis of their outcomes.

Thus, the verdict on securing a certain benefit cannot be determined until we have estimated the outcome of securing it. Securing it cannot be described as good or evil until its outcome becomes known. The outcome will not be known until the total sum of all likely results, shown in Figure 7, is known.

Figure 7: Representing outcome possibilities

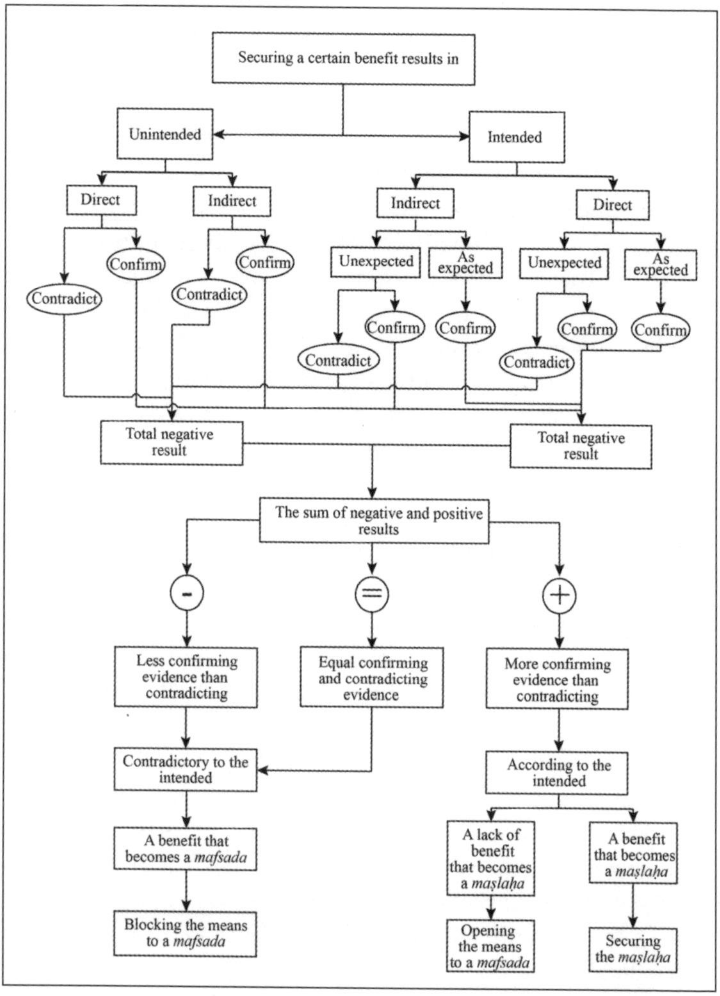

Looking at the model above, it should be noted that the results are divided into intended and unintended results and each type is subdivided into direct and indirect results. Whatever comes under the intended results ends up either as expected, which always confirm what is intended, or as results contrary to expectation. These latter results sometimes confirm what is intended and at other times contradict it. Whatever comes under the category of unintended results either confirms the intention or contradicts it. Before securing benefits, there is a need to look into all the above-mentioned possibilities and estimate those possibilities that are contrary to the intended so that they are subtracted from what is intended. The two may be equal which means that the result is zero, or in other words, securing the benefit leads to a *mafsada* that is equal to the benefit. In this case, it should be prevented by blocking the means to it. This is in line with the rule that gives the prevention of harm precedence over securing the benefit.[52] If the benefit is greater than the *mafsada*, this gives us a positive result, which means that securing the benefit represents a preponderant *maṣlaḥa.* If the *mafsada* is greater than the benefit, this gives us a negative result, which means that achieving the benefit leads to greater harm. The verdict in this case is that the means must be blocked.

This does not mean that the estimation of the intended and unintended results always occur at the same time. Most probably the estimation of the intended results takes place during or before beginning to secure the benefits. The estimation of the unintended results on the other hand, occurs after or during the achievement of the benefits. Hence, it is related to the ruling on the continuity of securing the benefit.

When we look at all the factors mentioned under the present subheading, namely the expected and unexpected outcomes, securing the *maṣlaḥas*, blocking and unblocking the means, we find that they all have a clear pattern that may not be discerned at first sight. This pattern indicates that the dynamism of action and reality brings about a change in the outcome as time passes, to the extent that a certain *maṣlaḥa* may change, either by bringing it directly, or by opening the means to a *maṣlaḥa* or blocking the means to a *mafsada*. Each one of these may be considered as a policy that aims to secure *maṣlaḥas*. Henry Mintzberg[53] discusses the concept of deliberate strategies, unfulfilled strategies and emerging strategies in the context of administration. A summary of his view is that policies which may be applied in a way that achieves their purpose, in a manner that they are considered fulfilled strategies, should be called deliberate or 'intended' strategies. On the other hand, policies that could not be achieved should be called unfulfilled or 'unintended' strategies. Many have written about these two types within the field of administration. The third type, which refers to strategies that have been fulfilled at variance with their primary purposes, but according to a second or third purpose, are the emerging strategies. They are called 'emerging' because they come into the scope of the work without any effort or intention on the part of the administration. He concludes that there is hardly any purely intended policy or purely emerging policy. In most cases, policies are complex, formed by a mixture of intended and emerging policies. This is noted when seeking *maṣlaḥas*, which is considered a policy of securing benefits. The process of securing benefits does not often bring about a result that is similar or identical to what is intended at the beginning. It is often the case that the result is somewhat different, yet remains a preponderant *maṣlaḥa*. Identifying the real result from the expected one is normally impossible. Hence, the result is complex. The conclusion is that the *maṣlaḥa* is, as known, preponderant and that a pure *maṣlaḥa* is almost impossible. The implementation of the concept of complex policies is as follows:

1. The scope of *maṣlaḥa* and *mafsada* is changeable. Sometimes the outcome of a certain *maṣlaḥa* becomes a *mafsada* so the means to it is blocked. The reverse is also true with a *mafsada* leading to an outcome that is a *maṣlaḥa*, so the means to it is open. In practice, this means that the final outcome of whether it will be a *maṣlaḥa* or a *mafsada* is not apparent at the beginning. Matters are judged on the basis of their final results. This means that we should not give any final judgement except after looking at the concept and its practical application. As Mintzberg puts it, 'the strategy and its implementation' as something may emerge during an implementation that differs from the initial objective. Where a *maṣlaḥa* turns out to be a *mafsada*, the *mafsada* emerges from the environment into which the *maṣlaḥa* has been brought. The same applies to the *mafsada* that changes into a *maṣlaḥa*: the *maṣlaḥa*

emerges from the environment into which it is brought or from which the *mafsada* is prevented. The separation between the *maṣlaḥa* and its procurement does not exist in reality. Therefore, the main problem with the outcome is indeed in the imaginary separation between the *maṣlaḥa* and its procurement. This inevitably leads to a flaw in estimating the outcome.

2. The policy of intended *maṣlaḥa* relies, in its conception, on separation between the concept and the outcome of its implementation. This means that the concept is limited to the intended results only while the outcome relies on what emerges from procuring the *maṣlaḥa*, whether it is intended or not.[54]
3. The policy of procuring *maṣlaḥas* is an intended policy which means that it can be studied in advance, while the policy of the outcome is an emerging one, which means that it is not limited to intended matters only. It belongs to consequences that cannot be studied at the outset. They are identified for certain once the results are clear and by observation that comes only after the *maṣlaḥa* has been procured. No condition of planning need be attached to such certain identification.
4. The opening and blocking of means are merely tools to be used when the learnt outcome is different to the studied objective. If the difference leans towards a preponderant *maṣlaḥa*, the tool of opening the means is used so that nothing of the *maṣlaḥa* is lost. If the difference leans towards a preponderant *mafsada*, the tool of blocking the means is used, so that nothing of the *mafsada* occurs.
5. Opening and blocking the means change from a tool into a policy to be implemented when necessary. They remain tools as long as the outcome stays within the intended objective. However, they become a practical policy when the outcome departs from the intended objective,[55] requiring a corrective policy. It is then that a suitable policy of means is adopted, whether by opening or blocking means, at the proper place and under suitable conditions as needs dictate. It is clear then that 'blocking the means', or *sadd al-*

> *dharāʾiʿ*, is a type of *maṣlaḥa* and giving it a special name is meant only to distinguish it from other types. All scholars who approve action in accordance with *maṣlaḥa* make it a condition that it should be preponderant and not lead to an equal or greater *mafsada*. The summary of this condition is that it cannot be acted upon if it is not preponderant or if it leads to a greater *mafsada*.[56]

6. Features of *Maṣlaḥa* Regulators

Each one of the regulators of *maṣlaḥa* has a partial function related to an aspect of the soundness of the *maṣlaḥa*. These are like features of the main functions. Some of these regulators relate to the essentials of the *maṣlaḥa*, others to its conditions and still others to what prevents it. The details are as follows.

6.1. Features of Regulator No. 1: The *maṣlaḥa* must not contradict the Sharīʿa

The features of this regulator include its examination of the essentials of the *maṣlaḥa*. It determines whether the *maṣlaḥa* exists, whether it is real or imaginary. It functions before the process of weighing, looking into past relevant Sharīʿa evidence. Its function is to prevent the *mafsada* from violating the Sharīʿa while its method is to establish the basis of the *maṣlaḥa*.

6.2. Features of Regulator No. 2: The *maṣlaḥa* must not exclude a better *maṣlaḥa*

This regulator examines the conditions of the *maṣlaḥa* to identify the higher and the lower benefits, distinguishing between the *maṣlaḥa* and general benefit. It functions during the process of weighing up evidences (*tarjīḥ*) and looks at the present status. Its function is to secure the *maṣlaḥa* of the highest benefit. Its method is to compare varying benefits.

6.3. Features of Regulator No. 3: Securing a *maṣlaḥa* must not lead to an equal or larger *mafsada*

This regulator examines what may block the *maṣlaḥa*. Through it we distinguish whether its procurement leads to a *mafsada* greater than it. It functions after the process of weighing up evidences and looks at the expected or future conditions. Its function is to block the means to *mafsada* and open the means leading to *maṣlaḥa*. Its method is to estimate the outcome of securing the *maṣlaḥa*.

The enforcement of these regulators provides us with the tools necessary to estimate the benefits of the *maṣlaḥas*. Thus, regulators are tools and using them is a test to determine that the subject of regulation is in line with the objective. As the aspects of regulation differ, so do the tests. Table 6 clarifies these tests:

Table 6: Tests set by the regulators

Regulators/ Tests	**No.1: The *maṣlaḥa* must not contradict the Sharīʿa**	**No.2: The *maṣlaḥa* must not exclude a better *maṣlaḥa***	**No.3: Securing a *maṣlaḥa* must not lead to an equal or larger *mafsada***
Type of test	Fulfilling the essentials	Fulfilling the conditions	Absence of blockers
Field of test	Existence or not; real or imaginary	Higher or lower; *maṣlaḥa* or benefit	Estimated or not; secured or abandoned
Time of test	Before weighing: looking at previous rulings and evidence	During weighing: looking at the present *maṣlaḥa* and examining real life	After weighing: looking at expected and future conditions
Function of test	Prevention of the *mafsada* from violating the Sharīʿa	Securing the *maṣlaḥa* of the highest benefit	Opening or blocking the means
Basis of test	Consideration of the evidence	Consideration of the *maṣlaḥas*	Consideration of the outcome

Chapter Four

MAṢLAḤA PREFERABILITY

One of the most difficult standards, yet most valuable and important to acquire, is that which seeks to balance between *maṣlaḥas* and *mafsadas*. It is said that 'a wise person is not the one who can distinguish good from evil, but the one who can distinguish the better of two good things and the lesser of two evils'. To ignore balancing, or to err in balancing at the time of application, causes great disorder. It may lead to giving preference to types of *maṣlaḥa* that are not recognized by the Sharīʿa, or to ignoring other types that must be fulfilled. In consequence, certain duties and recommended practices may be omitted, and certain prohibited or reprehensible matters may be committed.[1]

This chapter explains the considerations and bases of different kinds of balancing and preferability, giving examples of the balance between the options available for each.

1. Definition of Preferability, or *Tafāḍul*

1.1. The linguistic meaning

Speaking about the various meanings of the derivatives of the Arabic root *'faḍl*, Ibn Manẓūr says,

> *Faḍl* and *faḍīlah*, [which are words for] goodness, are the opposites of *naqṣ* and *naqīṣa* meaning vice. *Al-faḍīla* means a high degree of *faḍl*, or distinction. *Fiḍāl* and *tafāḍul* mean having different degrees of *faḍl*. The verb *faḍḍala* means to give a higher rank. *Tafāḍul* among people means that some of them are better than others. To say, *faḍḍaltahu*

> *ʿalā ghayrihi*, means 'You have assigned to him a higher grade than the one assigned to others, or judged him to be so.'[2]

It is also said that *faḍḍalahu ʿalā ghayrihi* means 'to distinguish that person, which is to acknowledge that he has distinction or a quality that distinguishes him from others'.[3]

Al-Afḍal is the one or the thing that is highest in rank or best in quality. Ibn Ḥazm (d. 456 AH)[4] says, 'Were it possible for *al-afḍal* to be of a lower degree, its distinction would be gone and become meaningless. No one would seek to have it.'[5] Al-ʿIzz b. ʿAbd al-Salām says, '*Tafḍīl*, which is assigning preference, means nothing but assigning attributes and ranks.'

The process of preferability depends on five elements: the assigner of preferability, known as *al-mufaḍḍil*; the higher and the lower in preferability, *al-fāḍil* and *al-mafḍūl* respectively; the cause of distinction; and the nature of distinction. *Al-mufaḍḍil* is the determiner of distinction. You see, then, that the essence of preferability relies on the cause and nature of distinction. It is the pivot around which the whole process turns. According to linguists, it is 'all qualities of goodness, or the nobility of lineage. Leadership of any community is based on either one of these two factors.'[6]

1.2. Preferability according to Muslim classical scholars

Some Muslim classical scholars expressed certain views concerning the types of distinction, or *faḍl*, and how it should be subdivided. According to Ibn Ḥazm, it has only two types: one type is granted by the Divine Legislator, which depends on no action by the person concerned. The other type is earned through action as a reward from the Divine Legislator. The first type is shared by all creatures: animals whether endowed with the faculty of speech or not, inanimate objects and so on. To give some examples: at the time of their creation, angels had distinction over all creatures; prophets had distinction over all humans and jinn; the month of Ramadan has distinction over all other Islamic months; Friday, the day of ʿArafa (ninth day of the lunar month of Dhū al-Ḥijja) and the first ten days of the month of Dhū al-Ḥijja have distinction over all other days in

Islam. This is concerned with the distinction granted by the Divine Legislator. The distinction earned as reward for action applies only to a creature endowed with speech, which limits it only to angels, humans and jinn. It is this type that has been subject to controversy and is the subject matter of this chapter. Ibn Ḥazm divides the nature of distinction into seven different subdivisions: one, which he calls 'essence', applies to the action itself; another, which is 'quantity', applies to features or aspects of the action. The other subdivisions apply to quality, time, place and contribution.[7]

Al-Rāghib al-Aṣfahānī[8] defines distinction, or *faḍl*, as what is beyond that which is necessary. He divides distinction into two classes: commended distinction, such as knowledge and forbearance, and censured distinction, such as anger as opposed to proper manners. He adds that the commended distinction is used far more than the censured one. When it is used to identify the better or further thing or action, it may be subdivided into three subcategories. The first is applicable to class, such as the distinction of animals over plants. The second is applicable to species, such as the distinction of man over all other animals.[9] An example of this subcategory is the one outlined in the Qur'an, 'We have honoured the children of Adam and carried them by land and sea. We have provided good sustenance for them and preferred them above many of those We have created' (Q. 17:70). The third subcategory is that applicable to self, as in the case of one person having distinction over another. Al-Rāghib then states that the first two subcategories cannot be acquired by one who is deficient either by becoming more deficient or by acquiring distinction. A horse or a donkey, for example, cannot acquire an aspect of distinction applicable to man. The third subcategory, which applies to self, may be circumstantial, which means that it can be earned. This is clear in the Qur'anic verse, 'God has preferred some of you above others in provision. Those who have been given more are unwilling to pass their provision on to the slaves they possess so that they become their equals. How can they refuse to acknowledge God's blessings?' (Q. 16:71), and also, 'We preferred some of the prophets above others…' (Q. 17:55).[10]

Abū al-ʿAbbās al-Qarāfī (d. 684 AH) speaks of another categorization of preferability between actions, stating that equivalent actions may be distinguished on the basis of preferability: 1) between the status of the doers; 2) between the actions themselves; and 3) between the circumstances of those who benefit from these actions when they benefit other people. By 'equivalent actions' al-Qarāfī means that they are equal in all other aspects.[11]

2. Where Preferability Lies

Maṣlaḥa is the opposite of *mafsada*, and in life things are composites of the two. There is no situation that is not composed of a mixture of *maṣlaḥas* and *mafsadas*. When making a choice, a person only needs to know such mixtures according to their time, place and status on the one hand and according to the presence of *maṣlaḥas* and *mafsadas* on the other. Such a person can then make decisions, choosing the action that avoids the *mafsadas* and attains the *maṣlaḥas*, so as to reach the purpose for which the action is undertaken. This fulfils the liability to take due care before acting. It is also the sum and substance of the 'Situational Management Theory', which suggests that there is no ideal, uniform method of action to be followed at all times. The choice of the appropriate method is influenced by circumstances and the factors posed by each situation.[12]

Hegel's Dialectics[13] look at the intellectual relation between matters, suggesting that it is normally made up of 'Idea', which is, as far as this study is concerned, *maṣlaḥa*, and its opposite (*mafsada*), and what is composed of them, which is where the preferability lies. This applies to different aspects of the subject matter of this study, such as:

1. The decision maker, that is the liable human being. Human beings are rational, which represents 'Idea'. They also have a soul that incites them to evil, which represents its opposite. Thus, man needs to balance between his sound mind and heart, which motivate him to goodness, and his evil-inciting soul. He cannot do that unless he brings his actions in line with the requirements of the Divine

Legislator: doing what He commands and refraining from what He forbids.

2. Making the decision, which is the intellectual side of the matter. Making the decision is not the action itself or its implementation. It rather represents a methodical way of thinking based on certain regulators and on the consideration of various measures and environmental factors relevant to the decision. When this is done on sound basis, the result is sound and healthy. The opposite leads to decline. When we look at the total sum of the decisions people make at the level of societies, states and nations, we realize that people build their nations and develop to the extent that some of them dominate the whole world. They then start to decline after a long or short period. The following Prophetic *ḥadīth*, 'Indeed, God sends someone to restore the status of this faith at the outset of every one hundred years',[14] seems to suggest that humanity moves in accordance with a precise law. According to this law, once a nation has attained the leadership of the world, the opposite elements begin to work within it leading to its decline, unless it rekindles its source of strength. Every nation has its own factors of decline. Therefore, no matter how long we continue to act on the basis of *maṣlaḥas*, they will come to an end unless we regularly maintain these *maṣlaḥas* to prevent their corruption through *mafsadas*. Such maintenance is achieved by performing a continuing process of preferability. The more we neglect this, the more the *maṣlaḥa* decreases until a stage is reached when a reformer is needed to restore the proper situation.
3. The decision taken, which will need to be in accordance with reasoning that follows the rules of the Sharīʿa.

To sum up, the situation, which is a composite of variables including *maṣlaḥas*, is where preferability applies. The role of the administrator is to monitor the different elements of that situation to set them in a proper way to ensure the realization of the *maṣlaḥas* that ensure the administrative objective and avoid the opposite *mafsadas*. This concept leads to important matters without which preference cannot be appropriately assigned. These are:

1. A situation that is chosen as a *maṣlaḥa* (for being less harmful) does not render this lesser *mafsada* a *maṣlaḥa*. The reverse is also true: the presence of a preponderant *mafsada* (chosen as a necessity) does not render the lesser (abandoned for necessity) *maṣlaḥa* a *mafsada*. This is what Ibn Taymiyya meant when he said, 'Good things are good, and evil ones are evil.'[15] Simple as this sentence is, it is a comprehensive maxim. When good and bad things, *maṣlaḥas* and *mafsadas*, are in plenty, most people will either incline towards the good, negating the evil with it, or go to the bad, removing the good thereby. Hence, the evil things do not remain evil in the first case, and the good things do not remain good in the second.[16]
2. Preferability may change: a preferred thing may become less preferable due to the introduction of a preponderant *maṣlaḥa*.[17]
3. Preferability is relative: it differs from one place to another, from one time to another, from one status to another and from one person to another.

Therefore, when something is in itself a *maṣlaḥa*, it does not necessarily follow that doing it is also a *maṣlaḥa* and preventing it is a *mafsada*. The reverse is also true: if something is a *mafsada*, it does not necessarily follow that doing it is a *mafsada* and preventing it is a *maṣlaḥa*. The ruling on achieving something and the ruling on the essence of that thing are not necessarily the same as one of them does not automatically entail the other.

3. Rules and Relativity of Preferability Dynamism[18]

We mean by 'dynamism' the progress of the preferability process, which relates to the extent of change in the process of preferability. The rules of preferability dynamism mean the rules that regulate and govern the process of determining distinction and preferability.

3.1. Rules of preferability dynamism

By nature, preferability refers to the continuous change in the presence of *maṣlaḥa* and *mafsada* in different actions according to each specific situation. It appears as though there is a continuous process of change between *maṣlaḥa* and *mafsada*, and the degree or amount of each one of them in a particular action and how they relate to each other. A decision maker needs only to monitor this process of change to determine where the *maṣlaḥa* lies so as to act within the particular situation.

Based on the above, we will look at some of the rules of preferability dynamism. These are based on two premises:

> Premise 1: Taking change and relativity into consideration. Change means looking at the preferability as it is in actual fact, while relativity means looking at it from the perspective of the onlooker.
> Premise 2: Change and relativity overlap. Each expresses the other from a different angle, with either of them capable of making an impact on the other.

The general rules that apply to preferability dynamism are:

> Rule 1: Pursuing what is in itself better is superior to pursuing a lesser option. The first step in decision making regarding a matter that is required by the divine law is to pursue the option that helps to better fulfil one's responsibilities. So, pursuing the better option is the first practical step the decision maker takes. It is universally known that duties and prohibitions vary in ranks: some duties are of a higher degree than others and some objects of prohibition are more evil than others. Therefore, a wise person will more diligently pursue the best possible outcomes.[19]
> Rule 2: Pursuing something may be encouraged at times, but not so at other times. This depends on whether or not *maṣlaḥa* will be achieved by doing it and on the variation in the actions performed to achieve the goal and the nature of this goal in and of itself. This is because one action

may be recommended at one time, but not so at another, in accordance with what the *maṣlaḥa* dictates based on Islamic textual evidence.[20]

Rule 3: What is better may vary according to the variation in the nature of acts of worship, their timings, places and other considerations. Thus what is better may vary on these bases and also according to a person's capability and his different actions. Thus, the variation of distinction is due to the variation of its considerations, which may increase or decrease according to the need to identify which aspect of a particular matter is preponderant.[21]

Rule 4: The presence of more than one good option, with no possibility of combination or exclusion, leads to opposing goals. This has the following possibilities:

i. Comparing between two good things that cannot be combined: the better one is given priority by ignoring the lesser or the least beneficial one.
ii. Comparing between two evil things that cannot both be avoided: the worse one is prevented by tolerating the lesser one.
iii. Comparing between a good thing and a bad one, where the two cannot be separated. In such a case, doing the good thing means the bad one also takes place, while abandoning the bad one means that the good thing is also left out. In this case a decision should be made on the basis of balancing the benefit of the good thing and the harm resulting from the evil thing.

Based on the foregoing, an evil thing is tolerated in two situations: 1) to prevent a greater harm, if such harm cannot be prevented without tolerating the evil thing; and 2) to secure what is more beneficial than abandoning it, when such a benefit cannot be secured without tolerating it. Likewise, a good thing is abandoned in two situations: 1) if doing it leads to abandoning what is better; and 2) if it leads to a bad thing whose harm is greater than the benefit it provides.[22]

Rule 5: The original rule in balancing things is to emphasize the already existent right and to perform the right that is sought. Emphasizing the existent right is accomplished through rejecting falsehood. This means that emphasizing this right is the foundation while declining falsehood is based upon it. Doing the right that is sought is achieved by refraining from what is forbidden, which means that it is the foundation, while refraining from prohibitions is based upon it. Thus, emphasizing the existent right and doing the right that is sought are foundational matters in the Sharīʿa while declining prohibitions and falsehood are subsidiary ones. This is premised on the fact that commandments in the Sharīʿa are the roots and prohibitions are their branches.[23] Furthermore, it is not essential that these two types of right are identical. The two may vary. Preferability and the various ranks of *maṣlaḥas* and *mafsadas* change according to the variance between the existent right in a specific situation and the right that is sought, which is intended to be achieved through it.

Rule 6: In balancing the preferability between the genus of what is commanded and the genus of what is prohibited, commandments are given precedence over prohibitions, as complying with commandments is of a higher distinction than abandoning what is prohibited, and the reward which the Divine Legislator grants to humankind for doing what He has commanded is greater than the reward granted for abandoning what He has forbidden. Likewise, the punishment for breaking commandments is greater than that for doing what is forbidden.[24]

Rule 7: When balancing between *mafsadas*, the outcome of prohibition should be considered in line with that of permission. The volume of the *mafsada* that necessitates its prohibition must not be considered in isolation of the need that requires the same action to be permitted, or even declared to be recommended or obligatory in certain circumstances.[25]

Rule 8: Distinction is according to what the Sharīʿa determines, and its effect should be considered in accordance with the degree and effectiveness of distinction between the balanced options. So, if we suppose that Sharīʿa evidence makes a particular option preferable, no blame is attached to a person who does what is permissible rather than what is preferable, nor should the permissible be discouraged because of the preferable. Thus, this rule indicates that distinction should not be increased beyond what the Sharīʿa has determined, because a preference may be only marginal or ineffective.[26]

Rule 9: The original rule in *maṣlaḥa* preferability is diversity and shifting of preference, not sticking to one preference alone. Hence, according to this rule, it is not appropriate to give a preference to one kind and stick to it, even though the person considers it better and believes that persisting with it is better. It is not necessarily true that persisting with what is better is always better. It is argued that diversity ensures following the example of the Prophet in a cohesive manner where a consideration of time, context and circumstances is taking place. And this in addition will benefit the individual by the diverse special qualities of every kind, as it was the habit of the Prophet himself who used to shift from one option to another rather than persisting with one option. It is suggested that this serves several purposes, which are:

i. Following the Prophet's Sunna;
ii. Promoting unity and cohesion of hearts within the Muslim Ummah, as the comprehension of this rule will help them to be united while accepting diversity;
iii. Preventing recommended practices from being thought of as similar to obligations;
iv. Making the best of each one of the different available options;
v. Emphasizing the relevance and importance of textual evidence in the introduction and selection of rulings;
vi. Shifting from one available option to another regarding a given issue will ensure that none of the available legitimate options will become neglected or even forgotten.

In summary, this rule asserts that securing the benefit of *maṣlaḥas* requires shifting between available legitimate options, rather than sticking to one only.

> Rule 10: What is better and has greater distinction does not necessarily lead to dispensing with what is lesser. A person may need the lesser option and be unable to limit his actions to what is better only. The rule operates within the arena of acts of worship and habits. This rule argues that everything that the Prophet has pointed out serves a wise and beneficial purpose. Therefore, what are classified by Islamic legal theorists as recommended and voluntary acts should not be ignored with attention only paid to what are classified as obligatory acts. This is due to the fact that recommended acts will be better in their time and place than other acts, even those of the obligatory category.[27] An example of this principle is the initiation of the greeting '*al-salām ʿalaykum*', which is of greater virtue than returning it, even though this response is an obligation.
>
> Had it been the case that a better or more distinguished action brings about the total benefits of all lesser actions, such lesser ones would not have been legislated in the first place. Thus, the fulfilment of the better action or achieving its benefit does not necessarily mean the fulfilment or achievement of the lesser one. Nor does the fulfilment of the lesser action necessarily lead to the exclusion of the better one. This means that the more distinguished option may be undertaken without the lesser one, and it may also be undertaken incorporating lesser ones. The fact that all of this is possible does not make the two options mutually interlinked.[28]

Decision making is a process based on balancing different alternatives according to their distinction. The best is given overall precedence and a better option takes precedence over a lesser one. This process relies mainly on understanding the meaning, grades and bases of distinction. Therefore, according to the aforementioned understanding, all that is said about preferability deals in essence with the method of drawing a balance between the different options on the basis of their respective merits. It is thus directly related to the Sharīʿa-approved decision, which is the one based on the claim to secure the highest possible distinction, both in this life and in the life to come, and doing so is the fulfilment of one's responsibility before God.

3.2. Value judgement

The difference between the preferability of factual and value judgements lies in factual judgement being based on differences in the subject matter of what is being judged, while value judgement is based on differences related to either the person who is required to make, or the person who is subject to, such judgement. Both together constitute the situation that reflects the appropriate action in the balancing process. The relativity (value judgement) in this process may be outlined as follows:

1. A person may be better in observing his religious duties by performing the lesser option. In this case, the lesser option is preferable for him. A more meritorious option for one person may not be equally preferable for another, due to differences of situations, physical conditions and personal capabilities.[29]
2. Some people may be adversely affected by knowing the better option, Ibn Taymiyya argues. He explains that such a person is always seeking what is better, but cannot live up to it and becomes unhappy with the lesser option being maintained. Ibn Taymiyya asserts that it is not in the interest of such a person to learn what is better than his method if such knowledge leads him to abandoning his method without undertaking the better one. At the same time, it is not right for him to believe that his own method is better than other options, when it is not. It is in his interest, his *maṣlaḥa*, that he should maintain his method hoping to fulfil his obligations.

   Thus, every person is asked to act according to their own ability. One should not be moved from a lesser state of obedience, even though it may incorporate imperfection or inferior status, unless such a move places one in a better state of obedience. This, as Ibn Taymiyya argues, should not be explained to a person if such an explanation would lead him to completely turn away from his own method, realizing that it is not the best option as he had expected. He would thus abandon his method, which is a good one and should not be abandoned without opting for something else. To apply this to administration, an administrator may begin to implement a certain plan, but half way through its implementation, he becomes aware of a better plan. He, therefore, discards his original plan and pays full attention to the better one. Again before it is fully implemented, he finds a third and even better plan. Once more, he discards what he has started and begins anew. The end result is wastage of resources and efforts. He has neither completed any plan to begin reaping its benefits, nor achieved the best that he had aspired to do.

3. An action judged to be fine and acceptable when performed by one individual may be judged as inappropriate if performed by another.[30] The reason is that people vary in relation to what is required of them and to the prioritization of their duties. Likewise, they vary in gain and its prioritization. Therefore, it is wrong to apply what is good for some people to all of them. Much error in this area is the result of such generalization. A person describes the actions of a group of people and makes it generally applicable to all other people, considering anyone who does not follow it a 'misguided' person. This group's line of action may indeed be wrong, and also may be right while there is another line of action that is also right. Often, the one who has chosen a different approach declares the other right way as totally erroneous, rejecting its rightful elements. Thus, some Muslims reject what others do, even though it is right, simply because it is unlike their own custom and tradition.

It is argued here that the same applies to judging *maṣlaḥas*, as applying several methods of judgement, without being restricted to one only, spares the subject of the law the unhealthy situation of generalizing special habits and restricting what is right.[31] This is due to the contrast between the good and evil that can exist in each person. At the macro level, as a community is composed of a group of people, good and evil are present in the same community, pulling against each other. The same applies to societies, states and nations, each of which is the composition of several of its predecessors.[32] To relate this to administration, we may give the example of a company that applies a system of working hours based on a split shift and another whose working hours run in one continuous working period. Members of each company may adamantly advocate their own system, claiming it to be the only right system. This is just an aspect of rigidity that leads to applying a specific group's tradition to a different unrelated situation, thus spoiling its benefit by making it of general application. This is particularly true when it is applied to people who find a system hard or totally inconvenient but are judged as offenders when they break it. The fact is that each system may be suitable to the company applying it, but not to the other. Aspects such as the location of the working place, its closeness to the locality where its employees live, convenient roads and ease of access are all directly relevant to the suitable system of working hours applied by each company. Different conditions make different systems more suitable.

4. An example of relative preferability may be seen in the case of a person who is unable to perform a preferable good action without accompanying it with something bad. The normal case is that a bad thing earns punishment, but in this case it is lesser than the good thing to be done. There are two different situations that may apply here:

   i. Where this is inevitable: in this case the lesser bad thing is no longer considered bad. This is because when an obligatory or a recommended action cannot be accomplished without a particular thing, that thing becomes obligatory or recommended. Moreover, if the *mafsada* accompanying doing that thing is lesser than the *maṣlaḥa* it achieves, then its prohibition is waived.
   ii. When it is possible, yet difficult, to do good things without having to do a bad one: this is the case of a person who finds it hard to overcome the difficulty, or against his natural temperament. In such a case, he finds himself unwilling to fulfil these good things, whether obligations or recommended actions, without allowing himself to do

certain things that are prohibited or reprehensible, but whose harm is lesser than the benefit of the good things.

According to Ibn Taymiyya, in both cases, if the hardship involved is acceptable as an excuse, giving up the good things is not counted as sinful, but if the hardship cannot be accepted as an excuse, then giving up the good things is sinful. Where there is neither an excuse, nor a difficulty, then giving up the duties is nothing less than following one's own desire.[33] The difficulty of disobeying one's own desire is discounted: it cannot be accepted as an excuse, nor can it constitute a hardship.[34]

5. People's different viewpoints lead to variance in the direction of balancing *maṣlaḥas* and assigning preferability. To give an example: someone may look at a community by focusing on the 'mistakes' they have committed. Therefore, he criticizes and rejects them. Another person looks at the same community, focusing on the good deeds they have done, and he praises and likes them. The first one may go as far as considering the good deeds of this community as bad ones, while the other may consider their bad deeds as good ones. The reason is that both persons do not apply a proper criterion for balance and judgement. One person makes the good his criterion of judgement, balancing only *maṣlaḥas*, thus judging the community as completely good. The other makes evil the basis of judgement, balancing only the *mafsadas*, and thus judging the community as totally bad. The proper procedure is to take into account both good and evil aspects of the society (or, following Hegel, 'Idea' and its opposite), which reflects a composite of *maṣlaḥas* and *mafsadas*.[35] More will be said about this when speaking about the situation and its role in decision making. It is only when the situation is properly taken into consideration that the process of preferability will be correct. To give an example in relation to administration, we may cite different views in relation to a particular action. Mobile phone companies may consider that equipping cars with facilities to install and easily use mobile phones may

increase demand for such phones, judging this as good and appropriate. On the other hand, traffic police may consider that this leads to an increase in road accidents, judging it as inappropriate.

6. This brings us to the point that some evil is better done than left undone, even though inclination to evil is a flaw of character. All creatures have their flaws, but not all of them are required to attain perfection. Indeed, this is not within their ability. When good and evil deeds are mixed together, things may be ambiguous, as one thing may become tied up with another. Indeed, people differ in their outlook and in their ability to deal with things when they become entangled, or when confusion arises. In this regard, people may be classified as follows:

   i. Those who look at good things, giving them preference, even though this may exclude serious evil things;
   ii. Those who look at evil things, giving them preference, even though this may exclude extremely good things;
   iii. Those who pursue a middle course, looking at both sides together. They may find themselves in one of two positions that do not help them have full understanding of the situation. These two positions are:

      a. They cannot determine the full measure of the *maṣlaḥa* and *mafsada*, which leads to a flawed process of preferability;
      b. They may be able to determine such measure, but cannot find help to do what is good and abandon what is evil, because desires are in conflict with wise judgements.[36]

Therefore, it is necessary to distinguish between choosing one of the legitimate options as a result of balancing preferences by the person choosing it, and choosing a specific option because it is necessary. It may be that what gives preference to a specific option is its being easy for the person making the choice, or some similar factor. Therefore, balancing the options should not be undertaken by the person who will be affected by this process. Furthermore, what is given preference because of necessity is judged on the basis of that necessity. Judgement of a particular option should not be based on its being easy for a particular person. To give an example, some people may find it easy to perform many of the recommended acts of worship. They, therefore, wish that these were made obligatory for all people. This is, however, contrary to the Divine Legislator's purpose with regard to recommended acts of worship. Therefore, no preference between two things should be made unless it is based on textual evidence. No person should let their own view determine the distinction without such evidence. In fact the acceptability of a deed as an action of worship requires that.[37]

7. If we measure people's errors and delusion in balancing between different options, we find that the majority of their errors are due to their non-acceptance of many true aspects of preferability, not due to accepting false considerations. Moreover, it is noticeable that when something relates to worldly *maṣlaḥas*, very accurate measures are employed, but no such accuracy in measuring, or enthusiasm for it, is used in evaluating the *maṣlaḥas* related to the Hereafter.
8. Asceticism and godliness should be weighed against the *maṣlaḥa* contradicting them or the *mafsada* accompanying them. They should not be observed in a *mafsada* that involves a greater *maṣlaḥa*. True godliness, as Ibn Taymiyya asserts, is attained through knowledge of the better of two good options and the greater of two evil ones, and the Sharīʿa is based on attaining and perfecting *maṣlaḥas* and preventing or reducing *mafsadas*. According to him, a person who does not balance between doing or leaving out a particular action and what his choice of bringing about a legitimate *maṣlaḥa* or precluding a *mafsada* involves will most probably neglect some duties or do some forbidden things, thinking his omission or commission to be an act of godliness. Godliness cannot

be subject to personal desire, or what is easy or hard for the self. In truth, piety and asceticism are achieved on the basis of proper balancing between options undertaken on the basis of Islamic rules in the first place and then on the relative personal circumstances of the person seeking to attain either state.[38] Ibn Taymiyya indicates that some people tend to think that despite being hard for the self, suppressing its desires is always better.[39] He asserts, however, it is not true that harder is better, nor is it right to say that what is easy is less good. The best actions are those that ensure 'better obedience' to the Divine Legislator and bring more benefit to the doer. This may happen to be the easier or harder of any two options. When the Divine Legislator commands something that is hard, He does so because it brings the subject of law benefit, not to afflict them.[40]

9. It is argued that the best action is that which best 'earns the Divine Legislator's pleasure' among other available and possible alternatives. In most cases, the best is not available in complete form. Therefore, it is suggested that the subject of the law should choose the better one of two good things and prevent the worst of two evils. The best at all times and in all situations lies in 'belief in God and doing good deeds'.[41] The best of all actions is that which is 'more obedient to God and more useful to man'. Whatever brings better benefit to the doer makes him 'more obedient to God' in doing it. Hence it is the better option.[42] We may put this in a mathematical equation as follows:

$$\text{The best} = \text{More obedient to God} \cap^{43} \text{more useful to man}$$

Hence, what is proposed here is that a Muslim, when giving advice to others, should ensure that such advice is tailored for what is best for each of their personal situations. In fact, 'the absolute best', according to Ibn Taymiyya, is that which is similar to what the Prophet was like, in public and private.[44]

On the basis of the foregoing, the process of balancing should be based on certain rules that may be summarized as follows:

1. Equality of rank does not necessarily mean equality of merit.[45]
2. Fair balancing requires that everything is given its right.
3. All qualities of a living person are subject to increase and decrease of merits.[46]
4. A prerequisite of fair balancing is knowledge of the two options and the reasons for preference.[47]
5. Multiplicity of options does not necessarily require distinction of one over others.[48]

Therefore, when *maṣlaḥas* and *mafsadas*, benefits and harms, good deeds and evil ones are present and contradicting, a tool is needed to distinguish the better from the lesser. This is based on four main principles:

1. Knowledge of the different ranks of right and wrong, good things and bad ones, the better of two good things and the worse of two evils.
2. Knowledge of what is obligatory and what is not, as well as what is recommended and what is not.
3. Knowledge of the conditions of ability and inability that make something obligatory or recommended, and that being obligatory or recommended is conditional upon knowledge and ability.
4. Knowledge of the nature of the addressees and their types. According to Ibn Taymiyya, this is important, because it will cater for the needs of different people. This will entail ordering people to observe what is best for them 'in obedience to the Divine Legislator' and forbid what is beneficial for them to be forbidden from. They also should not be ordered to observe something good that leads to something worse than what they are forbidden from.[49]

It is important to know that merits are relative and vary in relation to time, place, the person concerned and their status. The interrelation of these factors means that the situation or position in which a decision needs to be taken is also relative. Moreover, rules have their exceptions. Hence, preference and distinction are related to the situation that requires taking a decision. This is the essence of relativity or value judgement in balancing preferences and leads to flexibility and removing hardship from people. As people's needs are varied, and their desires are even more so, forcing one type of *maṣlaḥa* on them may constitute hardship for them. So, taking the decision according to every particular situation is in fact an implementation of the concept of relativity or value judgement in the process of balancing preferences. This is necessary for understanding the suitable aspect of *maṣlaḥa* in a particular situation and acting upon it.

In this regard, Muhammad Muṣṭafā Shalabī asserts that the purpose of the Sharīʿa is to separate people from their 'improper' desires. Had their *maṣlaḥas* been based on their desires, they would have been mutually contradictory, or they would have undermined the purpose they are meant to serve. The Qur'an states, 'Had the truth been in accord with their desires, the heavens and the earth, together with all that lives in them, would surely have been in utter corruption' (Q. 23:71), and also says, 'If you were to pay heed to the greater part of those on earth, they would lead you away from God's path. They follow nothing but conjecture and they do nothing but falsify' (Q. 6:116). Moreover, benefits and harms in this life are relative, not fixed. Something may be beneficial to one person and harmful to another at the same time. One person may find something to be beneficial in one situation but harmful in another, or beneficial at certain times but not at others. Moreover, the same thing may have different purposes for different people. If one person achieves his purpose, he benefits, while another may suffer because his purpose could not be achieved as a result. It is rare that all purposes are the same in any matter.[50] The more relative a certain matter is, the more the need arises to understand the variations in situation, the elements of the decision to be taken, its operation and how it differs according to situation, time, place, person and status. So, no person is required to do what is not necessary for that person. This is all part of the tools and means of making things easy, which is a religious requirement.

Chapter Five

TYPES OF *MAṢLAḤA* PREFERABILITY

According to Islamic understanding, the Divine Legislator, God, enjoins justice and good conduct. Justice means equal treatment of any two that are of the same status. Likewise, textual references indicate that the Divine Legislator has forbidden injustice altogether and made it totally forbidden to all His creatures. In a *ḥadīth qudsī* (a tradition in which the words of God are related), the Prophet quotes God as saying, 'I have taken it upon Myself to wrong no one and made injustice forbidden among you. Therefore, do not be unjust to one another.'[1]

Hence, according to the aforementioned understanding, under this generality of demanding equality between equal matters comes equality in religious matters. If the Divine Legislator has made two actions or two actors equal, then preferring one of them over the other is seen to be gross injustice. Likewise, if the Divine Legislator has accorded preferability to one of them, then treating them equally is also gross injustice.

Decision makers in Islamic issues often dispute over determining preferability of certain options when none of them have any distinctive merit; rather, they are of equal value. And sometimes what gives one alternative a speciality is counterbalanced by another equal speciality of the other. Hence, it does not seem to be accurate to assign distinction to either. Yet we find differences on which one of the two is preferable, despite the fact that seeking to determine preferability in such cases is problematic as this is based on the assumption of distinction between the cases in questions in which this does not seem to have been proven. The proper action in this regard should be to identify whether these two are equal, or whether either of them has distinction over the other. If the latter, it may be asked if the distinction is total, or in certain aspects.[2]

If the decision maker is not fully aware of the details of this area where differences vary according to the variations of situations in many actions, that lack of awareness will inevitably lead to much confusion.

Additionally, according to Islamic understanding, there is a need for the process of assigning preferability to be accompanied by 'divine' guidance. Without this, human beings will be deluded by their power, relying on it, feeling no need for guidance by the Divine Legislator. Hence, what is emphasized is that comparison and balancing will not lead by their own to the right decision, rather this divine component is a major factor for achieving an accurate outcome. Thus, we find in the Prophetic supplication:

> God! Originator of the heavens and the earth! You have knowledge of all that is imperceptible and all that is present. It is You who will judge between Your servants concerning all that over which they differ. Guide me by Your grace to the right over which people differ. You certainly guide whomever You will to a straight path.[3]

The *duʿāʾ istikhāra* (guidance-seeking supplication) is based on this very point. It begins, 'My Lord, I am seeking Your guidance to the best choice based on Your knowledge...'[4] This divine guidance on determining preferability was very important in early Islam to the extent that the Prophet is reported to have taught his companions this supplication in the same way that he taught them a chapter from the Qur'an.

Therefore, Islamically, although one should take all precautions to ensure that one makes the right decision, it is necessary at first to place one's trust in divine guidance and appeal for guidance to what is right. Then, this will be followed by taking the necessary steps and measures, including the determination of *maṣlaḥa* preferability.

What is meant by *maṣlaḥa* preferability is to determine which of two or more options is preferable, which means it is given a higher distinction when balancing them. As stated earlier, the process of determining preferability is based on four main pillars:

1. The determiner of preferability, the Divine Legislator;
2. The preferred option, which is the one that brings the greatest benefit;
3. The lesser option(s), including all other options;
4. The distinction aspects, which explain giving preferability to the selected option. These have different elements:

    i. Reason for preferability: identifying the option bringing greatest benefit;
    ii. Consideration for preferability: the various beneficial considerations;
    iii. The regulator of preferability: selection of that specific choice which constitutes a *maṣlaḥa.*

On the basis of the foregoing, when the greater and lesser options cannot be taken together, a process of evaluation of different opposing *maṣlaḥas* is resorted to. Such a process is basically indubitable. The stronger is given precedence over the weaker, the greater over the lesser and so on. The Qur'an states, 'They ask you about intoxicants and games of chance. Say, "In both there is great evil although they have some benefits for people, but their evil is far greater than their benefit…"' (Q. 2:219).

In addition, in the process of determining preferability public interest is given priority over personal interest, as in the case of pulling down a building, even though it may be an endowment, in order to widen a mosque or a public road. So, greater harm may be prevented by allowing a lesser harm; the less stringent prohibition may be observed in order to prevent the more stringent one and the the lesser of two evils may be overlooked in order to prevent the greater one.

We find such considerations discussed by some classical authors. For instance, al-Maqqrī (d. 758 AH) says,

> Adopting the more beneficial option is, by consensus, incumbent. A lesser *mafsada* is overlooked in order to secure a greater *maṣlaḥa* when

> it is impossible to combine action on both. This is different from the case over which the Mālikī scholars and others differ in their views, when a small measure of what is prohibited is mixed with a great measure of what is permissible. This latter case is different because both elements can be treated individually by separation, division and similar measures that ensure refraining from what is prohibited and doing what is permissible.[5]

Preventing *mafsadas* takes precedence over securing *maṣlaḥas*, as stated by al-Zaqqāq (d. 912 AH) in the last rule included in his book *al-Manhaj*. Al-Maqqrī says, 'The care which the Sharīʿa takes to prevent *mafsadas* is as important as the care which it takes to secure *maṣlaḥas*. When securing [the *maṣlaḥa*] is not demonstrably greater, the prevention [of the *mafsada*] is given priority.'[6]

Al-Shāṭibī writes at length on this topic:

> When the benefit is not free of an accompanying harm, or in the reverse situation, how can there be permission and prohibition of the same thing? For example, how can it be said about wine that the original status is its permissibility because it gives pleasure and encouragement and alleviates worries, as also the original status is prohibition because it overshadows one's mind, turns the drunk away from the remembrance of God and from prayer, when the two situations are inseparable? How can it be said about a medicinal mixture that its original status is prohibition because of its horrible smell, bitter taste and side effects, and equally, it is permissible because of its curative benefit, when the two cannot be separated? To say so means that in all such cases, the original status is both permissibility and impermissibility, which is impossible.

He adds,

> It may be said that where there are opposing factors, it is the greater that determines the ruling, and anything against it is simply overlooked. In answer to this point we say that this confirms what has already been said. It is evidence that benefit is not always absolutely permissible, and that harm is not always absolutely prohibited. Verdict on permissibility or otherwise is based on what is stated above. This

> is necessary for this life and the life to come, even though there may be along the way a certain harm to be expected or a certain benefit to be denied.[7]

Al-Shāṭibī also states,

> Where removing harm altogether is possible, removing the general harm is prioritized, and therefore causing general harm should be prevented as the public *maṣlaḥas* are given priority over the private ones. Proscription of the pre-emption of traders, the prevention of a city dweller from selling to a nomad, the necessity of providing a guarantee by manufacturers though they are originally treated as trustworthy, and the extension of the Prophet's mosque against the wish of the landowners – all are examples providing proofs for that. This means that the public *maṣlaḥa* is given priority over the private one, yet in a way that does not drastically affect the private *maṣlaḥa*.[8]

Al-Shāṭibī goes on to say,

> Conflict may occur in two things where neither comes under the other's heading, nor do they come under a single general rule. An example is that of an adult who cannot find water for his ritual ablution (*wuḍū'*) nor can he perform the dry ablution (*tayammum*). The choice here is between abandoning prayer, which is incumbent by the Qur'anic order of performing prayer, because of the inability to fulfil the requirement of making ablution for the prayers, or the reverse of that. Prayer is included under the general rule of necessities (*ḍarūriyyāt*), while ablution and purification are included under the general rule of complements (*taḥsīniyyāt)*, according to some scholars. Another example is that of a person who is unable to determine the proper direction to take in prayer. He faces a conflict between the command of performing prayer and the command of taking the direction of the *Ka'ba* during prayer. The basic rule is that, in the balancing process, the particular takes the status of the general to which it belongs. If the general is given greater or lesser value, the same applies to its particular items. So, the particular is always considered within its general. When the general is granted preferability, the same is given to its particular.

> It has been already stated that the particular rule is subordinate to the general one to which it belongs. Yet, the general rule cannot exist except through particulars, which constitute its elements. Therefore, if the particular rule is left undone, the general rule may be consequently left undone, because the latter is composed of the former. If other particulars, which do not belong to the same general rule, are assigned greater value, these would then, inevitably, be given preference over the other general rule. It has already been stated that the obligatory 'necessary' general rule takes precedence over others. Hence, its particulars must also be given precedence. This extends also to the general rules that include these particulars, so there is no need to speak about them separately.[9]

Ibn al-Qayyim asserts the importance of this process of determining preferability when he states, 'The Sharīʿa is based on the principle that the greater of two *mafsadas* is prevented by tolerating the lesser one, and on securing the greater of two *maṣlaḥas* by abandoning the lesser one. Indeed, the *maṣlaḥas* of life and religion are based on these two basic principles.'[10]

From these comprehensive texts, it is evident that when there is conflict between expected *maṣlaḥas* and *mafsadas*, judgement based on balancing between the two is necessary. No one questions an action when *maṣlaḥa* is preponderant in it. It is the balance between different *maṣlaḥas*, or between *maṣlaḥas* and *mafsadas*, or between different types of *mafsadas* that causes great difficulty. We often find two opposing parties, each of whom claims to express the right which serves public interest. Numerous have been the cases where two groups go to war claiming that they are only fighting to bring about *maṣlaḥa* and to oppose *mafsada*. In Islamic history, those who assassinated ʿUthmān and ʿAlī, the third and fourth caliphs respectively, made such claims.

The crux of the matter is the proper evaluation of the situation so as to ensure that *maṣlaḥas* are realized and *mafsadas* are prevented. Difference in the weight assigned to different options does not entail a difference in the basis on which they are weighed. Moreover, the method of determination of *maṣlaḥa* and whether it is judged rationally or on the basis of religious texts presents another facet of the problem. Is it sufficient that a particular option does not contradict the Sharīʿa to classify it as a *maṣlaḥa*? Or does the jurist have to have supporting textual evidence indicating that this is the case?

In actuality, the discussion in this regard is related to customary matters rather than worship-orientated issues. According to al-Shāṭibī, as far as customary matters are concerned, the rules of the Sharīʿa aim at securing the *maṣlaḥas* and preventing the *mafsadas*. Al-Shāṭibī says,

> Should it be asked whether these two aspects apply to all rules of customary acts and acts of worship, the answer is that what appears to people of understanding is that in customary actions results should be intended and sought as the material *maṣlaḥas* are clearly evident in them. Acts of worship are different because they are not established for rationally intended results. Therefore, results are not considered in acts of worship because the meanings and causes of action in this kind are traced to the genus of *maṣlaḥas* and *mafsadas* that are intended by these acts. These are apparent in customary matters, but not so in acts of worship. Hence, taking the results into account and working towards their achievement is important in customary matters, particularly in matters that require *ijtihād*. A *mujtahid* scholar can only expand his area of discretion by taking results and reasons into account and paying them due consideration. Without this, *mujtahid* scholars would not have been able to arrive at rulings based on *maṣlaḥas* except through a clear religious text or scholarly consensus, and thus the whole exercise of analogy (*qiyās*) would be invalid, which is not right. Hence, taking into account the purposes for which rulings have been stated is necessary, and these purposes constitute the resultant effects of rulings.[11]

Based on the above, it is clear that determining *maṣlaḥa* preferability may be divided into two main classes: determining preferability by type and by degree. The details are considered in the following section.

1. Determining Preferability by Type

It would be assumed that even before the revelation of the Sharīʿa, it was clearly apparent that securing pure *maṣlaḥas* and preventing pure *mafsadas* is something good and commended. The same applies to giving preference to securing the best benefits and preventing the worst harms, according to their respective degrees of importance. Again, preventing greater harm by sacrificing a lesser benefit is also good.

Generally speaking, determining preferability means that which has more merit is given precedence over the less meritorious. This process of determining preferability by default confirms that competing factors are not equal and hence the basic rule is that there can be no process of preferability among equal things. Therefore, the subject of discussion cannot be complete unless it considers the possibility of things being equal, how to determine preferability in these things, and how to determine preferability by degree. This involves ten types:

1. Choosing between a *maṣlaḥa* and a *mafsada*;
2. Choosing a *maṣlaḥa* that is equal to a *mafsada*;
3. Choosing between a *maṣlaḥa* and another *maṣlaḥa* that is equal to a *mafsada*;
4. Choosing between a *maṣlaḥa* that is equal to a *mafsada* and another *mafsada*;
5. Choosing between a *maṣlaḥa* and an unspecified option;
6. Choosing between a *maṣlaḥa* and an unknown option;
7. Choosing between a *maṣlaḥa* that is equal to a *mafsada* and an unspecified option;
8. Choosing between a *maṣlaḥa* that is equal to a *mafsada* and an unknown option;
9. Choosing between a *mafsada* and an unspecified option;
10. Choosing between a *mafsada* and an unknown option.

1.1. Choosing between a *maṣlaḥa* and a *mafsada*

The basic rule in *maṣlaḥas* is to secure them and in *mafsadas* is to prevent them. Therefore, a *maṣlaḥa* is always given preference over a *mafsada*. Here is an example in relation to administration.

Suppose that someone bought an old book, read it and then offered it for sale. He got two offers: one giving him a 50 per cent profit and the other a 50 per cent loss. Which offer would he accept? The answer is clear. He would sell it to the person offering him the 50 per cent profit. However, the important question is how and why has he taken this decision?

The two options available to him are: one that gives him an additional benefit of 50 per cent, while the other incurs harm amounting to a 50 per cent loss. The difference between +50% and -50% = 100%. This means that the first option is 100 per cent more beneficial. These are the only two options that this person has, and they are equal in all their other aspects. Therefore, the first option provides higher benefit, which means it is the *maṣlaḥa* option. If someone is working as an agent for the owner of the book, this agent would not properly fulfil his liability unless he accepts the first option.

1.2. Choosing a *maṣlaḥa* that is equal to a *mafsada*

When the *maṣlaḥa* and *mafsada* of a particular action appear to the decision maker to be equal, what is he to do? Which option does he choose? Take the example of a doctor working in the Accident and Emergency Department in a hospital. During his shift he receives a case in which an elderly unconscious patient is brought in, having suffered a clot on the brain. He makes the necessary diagnosis and decides to give him a medicine known as RTPA, which causes the blood clot to be broken into small portions. He considers that unless the patient is given this medication, he would be paralysed. According to him, the success rate of this treatment is 70 per cent against 30 per cent failure. Another A&E doctor who is a friend of the patient also comes visiting. He expresses a different opinion saying that the rate of success of the proposed treatment is only 30 per cent while the failure rate is 70 per cent.

As the two doctors differ, they decide to consult a third A&E doctor. If this doctor were to take the total average of both views, he will need to decide on the basis of a 50 per cent chance of successful treatment in which the proposed medicine will dissolve the clot and an equal chance of failure in which the treatment will cause brain haemorrhage. It is a difficult choice with no clear preponderant benefit or harm to base the decision upon. This doctor cannot make the decision himself because he is away from the A&E Department. It is the doctors that are present who will have to arrive at a decision. Should the doctor in charge operate the juristic rule that says, 'Preventing *mafsadas* takes priority over bringing *maṣlaḥas*', he will decide not to give the treatment in order to prevent exposing the patient to brain haemorrhage. This will be preferred to the possibility of dissolving the clot in his brain, which leads to his recovery.

This rule is supported by examples from human nature. Take the example of a man holding an apple. On seeing an obviously hungry child he calls out to him and throws him the apple. The child will try to catch the apple before it falls to the ground, knowing that it will relieve his hunger. If the man throws both an apple and a stone at the hungry child, the child will instinctively try first to avoid the stone. He will then look where the apple has fallen and pick it up to eat. Needless to say, the child's action is instinctive and he is unaware of the juristic rule, which nonetheless is clearly supported by this illustration of human nature. The important question, however, is: does such a case of equal benefit and harm exist in reality? Or is it merely theoretical? And what is the difference? We will elaborate on this below.

That the benefit resulting from a certain case is equal to the harm that it may cause is possible theoretically, but this does not mean that it actually occurred. The theoretical possibility of two equal benefits and harms is due to certain reasons and conditions, such as:

1. The difference between the benefit and the harm is so little that it is ineffectual in a given situation. For example, one may want to buy a plot of land that could bring a profit of £1 million when sold, or could bring a loss of the same amount. If the profit was one pound more, or the loss one pound less, would that affect the decision? Obviously not. Even though there is a difference in effect, it is too marginal to affect the judgement.
2. The absence of some information that is necessary to give a clear picture of the difference between the available options.
3. Time may be too short to allow the real difference to be seen clearly. In the case of the A&E doctor above, had he been

present, he may have had to rely on his own diagnosis of the case. He should have given a judgement based on his own discretion without taking the opinion of any one of the other doctors, if time did not allow.

4. The exclusion of other factors of preferability is a reason why the difference between the available options remains unclear. Again, in the doctor's case above, he did not give greater weight to the view of the treating doctor, although he is the specialist and the one in charge, while the other doctor is merely a visiting friend.

Whether the choice to be made is between *maṣlaḥas* or *mafsadas*, the fact that a difference may be too ineffectual to change the *maṣlaḥa* into a *mafsada* or the *mafsada* into a *maṣlaḥa* does not mean that it cannot be used to determine the option of choice. If we do not exclude such a little difference, we can use it to opt for a preferable option. Such a difference may be seen as marginal because we are unable to appreciate its real effect, not because it is actually marginal. With the great technological advancements that humankind has achieved, it is now possible to evaluate many new aspects of things and assign initial values to even small differences. This enables us to add other considerations that will clarify such differences. Thus, whenever the choices available to us appear equal, we can add a new factor, hoping to make one option clearly preferable.

The same may be said if we were to have additional information about each option to help in making a decision. If we do not ignore the difference on the basis that it is too marginal, nor exclude any consideration, and if we make every possible effort to have all information that may be of help in determining preferability, then it becomes almost impossible for the options to be equal. After all, it is not possible for a *maṣlaḥa* and a *mafsada*, benefit and harm, to be equally present in one situation. This is precluded religiously and logically. From the religious point of view, there is no possibility that the same thing is commanded and prohibited at the same time so that if one leaves it, one abstains from a commandment and if one does it, one commits a prohibition. Such a situation leads to confusion and contradiction in legislation.

It simply cannot be imagined that divine law could include it. Logically, this is impossible because it cannot be imagined that the same thing is equally beneficial and harmful at the same time, place and situation.

So, what brings equal *maṣlaḥa* and *mafsada* is non-existent, even though it is included in the classification we are outlining. Every action is either good, because it is of preponderant benefit, or bad due to its preponderant harm. The idea that something is better done because of its benefit and better undone because of its harm, and both benefit and harm are equal, is a strange notion. There is absolutely no evidence that such a thing ever exists. Instead, evidence suggests the reverse. Whenever *maṣlaḥa* and *mafsada*, benefit and harm, pleasure and pain exist side by side, one of them must inevitably outweigh the other forcing the choice to be in its favour. The two causes of *maṣlaḥa* and *mafsada* are always in opposition, and each brings its own effect. Hence, each will prevent the effect of the other. Their contradiction means that each of them negates the other. They cannot bring both their effects together, because this involves putting two contradictory things together. If one of them is negated, it produces no effect; and if it is ineffectual, it cannot negate the effect of the other. It cannot be imagined that each will be effective and ineffective at the same time. Such a situation cannot exist. This proof is similar to that of mutual exclusion.[12] Thus, one of them must be stronger than the other, producing its effect on the other, which drives the decision in its favour.[13]

Furthermore, when *maṣlaḥa* and *mafsada* are equal and theoretically exist together as postulated in one of the cases above, they cannot together be either essential or incidental. Rather, one of them would be essential and the other incidental. Hence, we need to determine which one is essential and make the choice accordingly. If benefit is essential, then the harm is incidental. This makes the benefit aspect weightier on the basis that the essential is given greater weight than the incidental. This is due to the fact that the essential benefit is permanent while the incidental harm is temporary and will be eventually removed. The reverse is also true. If the harmful aspect is essential and the benefit is incidental, the harmful aspect becomes weightier, because it is permanent, while the incidental benefit will eventually be removed.

This idea of giving more weight to what is essential is endorsed by the Sharīʿa. Juristic rules provide numerous examples and this is further demonstrated in practice. The following rule provides an example: 'If the incidental is removed while the ruling of the essential is still operative, the incidental is treated as having never existed.'[14]

This is exactly what we proposed: when an incidental *mafsada* has gone, leaving the essential *maṣlaḥa* in place, the *mafsada* is deemed not to have existed. Consider the case of an essential *maṣlaḥa* that is accompanied by an equal incidental *mafsada* that is expected to be removed, compared to an incidental *maṣlaḥa* accompanied by an equal but essential *mafsada* that is expected to remain. The former is given precedence, because the *mafsada* is expected to be removed, as compared with the one expected to remain. Likewise the former *maṣlaḥa* is essential and the latter one incidental, so the *maṣlaḥa* with the greatest benefit is the one to be given preference.

1.3. Choosing between a *maṣlaḥa* and another *maṣlaḥa* that is equal to a *mafsada*

Suppose that you want to visit two of your relatives, both of whom you have not seen for some time, but you know that one of them is in his house at present and he normally receives visitors at this time of day. With the other, you have only a 50 per cent chance of finding him at home at this time. Whom do you start with? Needless to say, you will visit the one whom you are sure to find at home. You will make your choice on the basis of having two options:

1. You definitely know that you will make good use of your time;
2. The possibility of making good use of your time is only 50 per cent.

The first option offers a highly probable benefit. In the second option the benefit of visiting a relative is offset by the harm of wasting your time if the relative happens to be out. It thus offers an outweighed benefit, because the two possibilities are equal. Since the prevention of harm is given precedence over ensuring benefit, the type of weighing preference here is between a preponderant benefit and presumed harm. In other words, it is between a *maṣlaḥa* and *mafsada*. The *maṣlaḥa* is always given precedence over the *mafsada*.

1.4. Choosing between a *maṣlaḥa* that is equal to a *mafsada* and another *mafsada*

It is known that when a *maṣlaḥa* is equal in its effect to a *mafsada*, it is theoretically considered a *mafsada* and given its ruling on the basis of the rule that says that the 'prevention of *mafsadas* is given precedence over securing *maṣlaḥas*'. Therefore, if we were to balance between such a *maṣlaḥa* and a *mafsada*, we choose the least of them, as when we are faced with several *mafsadas* we choose the lowest of them.

To give an example: suppose that someone is looking for a teaching job, but the only job he is offered is in a remote area where the loss of being with his family is counterbalanced by the benefit of having a job. He looks at the benefit and the harm as equal. Should he accept the offer? The answer is that he should accept the offer, because it involves two options:

1. Accepting the job in the remote area where the benefit of employment is counterbalanced by the harm of being away from one's family;
2. Refusing the job offer, which means that the harm of unemployment is counterbalanced by the benefit of staying at home with one's family.

Applying the rule that 'preventing *mafsadas* is given precedence over securing *maṣlaḥas*',[15] the harm indicated in the first option is considered a theoretical *mafsada*. Therefore, it is given precedence over the second option because incurring a theoretical *mafsada* is better than incurring a real *mafsada*.

1.5. Choosing between a *maṣlaḥa* and an unspecified option

The basic rule is that what is unclear should be left undecided. This means that only one choice is left, which in this situation is the *maṣlaḥa*. However, this is only true if the unclear option cannot be clarified. This is the case when the limits of non-clarity are known to occur between a minimum that is within the *mafsada* and a maximum that is within the *maṣlaḥa*. Thus it is not possible to know if the unclear option is a *maṣlaḥa* or a *mafsada* and make an informed choice.

To explain by example, let us suppose that someone has a sum of money, which he wants to invest. He has two options: either to submit a bid in a tender to buy the equipment a certain company has been using on a project that has been completed, or to buy shares of a famous company. The first option may bring him a profit between 30 per cent and 70 per cent, which means that the rate of profit is unspecified. The second option indicates that he will most probably realize a profit of 50 per cent, according to market and economic expectations. Which option should he choose?

The starting point is that an unclear option is left out until it has been clarified, in accordance with the juristic maxim that says, 'The unspecified matter remains undecided until it is made clear'. Therefore, the second option is given priority, provided that it remains impossible to find out the details. Should the details become known, we will then consider how beneficial it is. Should its benefit be greater than the second option, that is more than 50 per cent, we choose the first option. Should the two options give the same benefit, we look at other aspects of preferability. If the benefit that the first option will bring is less than 50 per cent, then the second option is given priority, on the basis of the rule that gives preference to the greater benefit. It should be noted that the difference between the unspecified and the *maṣlaḥa* is a difference of kind, not of degree.

It should be noted that there are several methods to eliminate the lack of specification. One of these is to make what is certain our basis. If the benefit range in our example above is between 30 and 70 per cent, then we take the lower figure, which is 30 per cent, in accordance with the juristic rule that says, 'In figures, the basis is the lowest.' When we cannot be certain of the ultimate figure, we take the lowest one, because the greater one includes it. Thus, the lowest is the one that is certain.[16]

Another method is to calculate the degree of benefit through other considerations that may lead to the unspecified option offering greater or lesser benefit. What is important is to realize that the lack of clarity decreases and the degree of clarity increases when we use more than one consideration to assess and measure the degree of the benefit.

1.6. Choosing between a *maṣlaḥa* and an unknown option

What seems to be the emphasized position within Islamic classical scholarship is that not every unknown is pardoned. Only ignorance that is normally difficult to avoid is pardoned. Al-Qarāfī says, 'The criterion that determines what is pardoned of what is unknown is that it is normally difficult to avoid. What is not so difficult or hard is not pardoned.'[17]

To give an example: suppose that a man goes to a doctor and tells him that he is going on a work trip to a desert area. He fears to catch cold or to suffer allergy. He wants to take some medicines as a precaution. The doctor prescribes two medicines and tells the man to choose one. One of the two medicines is available, but the other, which is the better and more effective, is not. He buys the first one from a pharmacy, as he cannot find the second. Later a friend of his tells him that he has one packet of the second medicine and he could spare him a few tablets. He takes these and puts them in an unmarked package for preserving medicines.

One day during his trip, he needs the medicine, but he discovers that he has to choose either the one he knew, since it was still in its original packet, but which has some side effects and could cause him a stomach ache, or take the other medicine in the unmarked package. He is uncertain whether the tablets in it are the ones he has taken from his friend or some other medicine in a similar package that has been with him just before starting his journey. Which one he should take?

The basic answer is that he should take the medicine he is certain of, in preference to the one about which he is unsure. This, however, applies only if he cannot remove the status of 'unknown' from the second medicine. He may be able to do so by, for example, remembering the size or colour of the tablets, or by reading what is written on them. If he can make the medicine 'known' then he compares it to the other. If he is sure that it gives the same effective treatment without producing side effects, he should give it preference over the other.

As we can see in this example, the unknown option is in fact known in itself but its benefit or harm is unknown. Thus, it is not completely unknown.

1.7. Choosing between a *maṣlaḥa* that is equal to a *mafsada* and an unspecified option

A *maṣlaḥa* that is equal to a *mafsada* is theoretically considered a *mafsada*. Therefore, the choice of preferability sought here is in fact between a *mafsada* and something unspecified. What is unspecified is partially known. Had it been totally unknown, it would have been called 'unknown'. The basic rule is that the unspecified should be left undecided until it becomes specified. Normally, we know the lowest and highest points of the unspecified. What we do not know is its exact position between these two points. Therefore, explanation is sought for the unspecified option and it is then judged according to its status. If it appears to be a preponderant or pure *maṣlaḥa*, it is given preference over the *maṣlaḥa* that is equal to a *mafsada*. On the other hand, if it appears to be a preponderant or pure *mafsada*, the *maṣlaḥa* that is equal to *mafsada* is given preference over it. If it turns out to be another *maṣlaḥa* that is equal to a *mafsada*, this comes under determining preferability according to degree, which we will deal with in what follows. If the unspecified matter cannot be clarified, the *maṣlaḥa* that is equal to a *mafsada* is given preference over the unspecified option, following the rule that states that, 'The unspecified is left undecided until it becomes clear.'

1.8. Choosing between a *maṣlaḥa* that is equal to a *mafsada* and an unknown option

The unknown is different from the unspecified only in the degree of ignorance of its nature. Therefore, they are treated in the same way. What is required is that the best efforts are exerted to know what is unknown, and to ascribe it to its specific original status. If it appears to be a preponderant or pure *maṣlaḥa*, it is given preference. On the other hand, if it appears to be a preponderant or pure *mafsada*, it is discarded. If it is a *maṣlaḥa* that is equal to a *mafsada*, such a case will be discussed when speaking about determining preferability according to degree. If it cannot be made known, it is discarded.

1.9. Choosing between a *mafsada* and an unspecified option

In this case, there is a need to learn or clarify the details of the unspecified option and look into the measure of its *maṣlaḥa*. If it is preponderant or equal, it is given preference over the *mafsada* option. If it is a *mafsada*, this will be discussed in more detail when talking about determining preferability according to degree between various *mafsadas*. If we cannot learn or clarify the details of the unspecified, we choose the *mafsada* option as a necessity.

1.10. Choosing between a *mafsada* and an unknown option

This is the same as the previous case. We need to learn about the unknown and treat it according to its nature. If it appears to be a pure, preponderant or equal *maṣlaḥa*, it is given preference over the *mafsada* option. If it is a *mafsada*, this will be discussed in more detail when explaining determining preferability according to degree. If we cannot learn the unknown, we leave it undecided and choose the *mafsada* option as a necessity.

2. Determining Preferability by Degree

Determining preferability according to degree is based on the assumption that available options are not equal in degree. Therefore, the discussion will start by speaking about the possibility of equality of degree and what it entails.

When options are of equal type, we cannot distinguish between two similar things except through a difference of degree.

Distinction can only be in a case of difference. If they are identical in one aspect and different in another, we differentiate between them on the basis of the aspect in which they differ. This is what is meant by determining preferability according to degree. It aims to identify an aspect by which preferability is determined, when both options are of the same type. In every type there is a low, a high and a middle degree. Sometimes, the high is better than the low, while the reverse occurs at other times, and the middle may be better than both in some cases. The aspect of preference differs according to the type and considerations of the degree. Yet the two options may be equal in this, which leaves the person in a difficult position. Should one refrain from judgement, or should one make an arbitrary choice due to the lack of a determiner?

Scholars have discussed this in considering the methods by which they choose one of two equally valid opinions. Some scholars advocate the abstention from giving a ruling. Others give the right of choice to the mufti or the judge, or to the person seeking a ruling directly, once the different views are explained by the mufti. A final group seeks a compromise position. These positions will be explored in what follows.[18]

1. Scholars who prefer not to give a ruling based on surmise: Saḥnūn[19] says, 'There is no harm if the judge orders reconciliation, refraining from making a ruling based on surmise.'[20] Al-Shāṭibī says, 'If I find two valid opinions within my school of thought, I do not give a fatwa based on a surmised choice of either of them, although I am a follower of senior scholars […] If I cannot determine which of the two is more widely accepted and do not find any preference expressed by any senior scholar, I refrain from issuing a ruling.'[21] Ibn ʿĀṣim[22] (d. 299 AH) states that the verdict should be left unimplemented, and the judge should call for reconciliation when the case is unclear and the right cannot be distinguished. This applies whether the lack of clarity is due to the nature of the evidence provided by the two conflicting parties or to the text used to reach the verdict being so unclear that it falls short of indicating preponderance.[23]

2. Scholars who say that the issue may not be left undecided: They say that the judge or the mufti must issue a ruling on the basis of one of the two views. This is because, they argue, issuing a verdict after having exerted effort does not mean that the person who issues it is following his desire. It is rather permissible. Such is the view of the Mālikī scholars. The view of the Ḥanafī scholars is summed up by Ibn ʿĀbidīn[24] (d. 1252 AH) in his assertion that Ḥanafī scholars maintain that when preference cannot be determined because of the equality of the options, the judge should exert all effort and then choose the option he is more comfortable with. Once he has upheld one of the two equal options, he cannot take up the other unless he receives an additional item of evidence greater than him being 'more comfortable' with the chosen option.[25]
3. Scholars who adopt a compromise position: In one sense al-ʿIzz b. ʿAbd al-Salām is one of the scholars who opine that in a case of equality and contradictory evidence, no verdict should be given. He says, 'Should the two options be equal in all aspects, abstention from giving a verdict should be adopted; because, in such a case, the normal basis of verdicts, which is (preponderant) surmise, is non-existent.' However, he maintains that it is impossible for two certainties or two surmises to be mutually contradictory: 'It cannot be imagined that two certainties or two surmises should contradict each other, because this leads to a combination of confirmation and negation of the same thing at the same time. Yet, mutual contradiction may occur between the evidence supporting each.'[26]

The same applies to administration. An administrator does not look at evidence, but rather realities. This means that he considers what is known and what is believed to be true. No contradiction is possible in this area according to the case which al-ʿIzz b. ʿAbd al-Salām explains. Hence, preferability is determined on the basis of type, which is perfectly possible for the administrator.

Al-ʿIzz b. ʿAbd al-Salām also says concerning situations where *maṣlaḥas* and *mafsadas* are equal, 'If it is impossible

> to secure all or prevent all, then a choice should be made if they are of equal degrees. If they differ in degree, choice of a preferable option is sought where it is known, and abstention from judgement is observed when it is unknown.'[27] Ibn ʿAbd al-Salām's statement on equality of degrees as a condition for making choice is a subtle distinction. He therewith takes into consideration that, when there is equality of degrees, a small difference does not preclude choosing an option.
>
> For example, if available options are equal, he may try to determine preferability according to considerations other than those in which the options are equal. If they remain equal, or if such preference is impossible to determine, he may give preference to one option on the basis of its acceptability to those who will implement it or those who benefit by it. He may endorse whatever they accept, preferring it to all other equal options. Their acceptance of it makes its benefit more stable. Should this lead again to equality, he may draw lots, giving preference to whichever the draw indicates. If the drawing of lots serves no purpose other than excluding one's own desire, it is sufficiently useful. Moreover, it is better than abstention from judgement that may lead to an interruption of *maṣlaḥas*. It is also better than losing one's reward from the Divine Legislator by following personal desire. For Ibn ʿAbd al-Salām, the drawing of lots is permitted by legislation in order to help choose one of two equals, prevent grudges and accept what 'destiny has decreed and God has judged'.[28]

All this comes under the prevention of *mafsadas*, because it prevents the *mafsada* of leaving *maṣlaḥas* undone or unfulfilled as a result of the inability of evaluating a small difference between them, which does not affect the fact that they are beneficial. It also prevents the *mafsada* of one becoming used to inaction or bringing one's personal desires into play. Establishing preference between *maṣlaḥas* according to their degrees, *mafsadas* according to their degrees, and all that takes their rulings – all of this has been established in order to ensure that one follows the Divine Legislator's law and does not follow personal desire.

2.1. Choosing between *maṣlaḥas*

The basic rule in determining preferability of *maṣlaḥas* is to give preference to the greater over the lesser, following the rule of choosing the greater *maṣlaḥa*.[29] To give an example: suppose that a person wants to sell his car. He takes it to several car dealers and receives three offers: £60,000, £50,000 and £65,000. To which one would he sell? Needless to say, he will sell it to the one offering £65,000, because it is the most beneficial. This does not mean that the other two offers are not benefits, rather that the important thing is to ensure the greatest benefit, which constitutes the *maṣlaḥa*.

2.2. Choosing between *maṣlaḥas* that are equal to *mafsadas*

To start with, a *maṣlaḥa* that is equal to a *mafsada* is considered a theoretical *mafsada* on the basis of the juristic rule that says, 'Preventing *mafsadas* takes precedence over securing *maṣlaḥas*'.[30] Therefore, choosing between options where the *maṣlaḥa* of each one is equal to the *mafsada* it produces is essentially a process of choosing between theoretical *mafsadas*. This is not resorted to except in situations where the equality cannot be overcome by giving preference to one of the two options. This is perhaps the most difficult type because every option is composed of a *maṣlaḥa* that is equal to a *mafsada*. To explain the aspect of *maṣlaḥa* in it, we may give the following example.

Suppose that a medical doctor, who is a member of the Médecins Sans Frontières (Doctors Without Borders) organization, works in an area of high mountains and rainforests in South America. He is requested to take a shipment of medicines to a remote village. Unless the medicines arrive in the village within two days, mortality among the villagers will increase. Thus his action is a *maṣlaḥa*. However, each of the two possible ways of travel carry a danger and so are equal to a *mafsada*: either he takes a small plane with a single engine to fly struggling against strong winds and high mountain tops, or he travels by a motor vehicle through rough and narrow mountain passes overlooking steep slopes. In both cases the risk of accident is estimated at 50 per cent. Which option should he take?

The answer is that when two options are equal from all aspects, we make a preference on the basis of 'the essential' versus 'the incidental'. When we consider the first option, the essential state is that a plane reaches its destination with nothing to prevent it. Its route is easy and passable. Bad weather is incidental, because the normal case of weather is that it is free of hurricanes and tempests, which normally last for a short period. In the other option, the essential characteristics are that the road is rough and narrow, winding around high mountains and overlooking steep slopes. All this is essential and will not change. Hence, the essential in the first option is that it involves no risk, while the second option is essentially risky, compared with easy routes. Thus, the contradiction is between an essential and a seemingly incidental factor. The essential is safety and the apparent factor is the possibility of a fatal accident, leading to failure of the mission. Therefore, the essential is given precedence because the incidental factor is not premised on a solid basis.

The first option is thus considered a *maṣlaḥa*, pursuant to its essence, which involves no danger, while the second option is considered a *mafsada*, pursuant to its essence which involves danger. This is what is meant by determining preferability pursuant to the essential and the incidental. It has already been established before that it is impossible for two opposites to be present in one thing and one aspect. Therefore, determining preferability between equal options pursuant to their essence is always possible.

2.3. Choosing between *mafsadas*

The basic rule in determining preferability between *mafsadas* is giving precedence to the lesser one, which is to prevent the greater by choosing the lesser. An example is a businessperson who buys shares of a petrochemical company. Later, war breaks out leading to disruption of security and economic stagnation. Hence, costs of shipment and insurance go up, while sales go down, and the company's profits are thus wiped out. When the company's budget is announced, it indicates immediate losses as well as further losses expected in the following year. The businessperson has two options: either he sells his shares now at a loss of 10 per cent, or waits and sells later at an expected loss of 30 per cent. There is, however, a small chance that the company's shares will recover and go back to their original value in the near future. Which option should he take?

The right choice for the businessperson in such a case is to cut down his losses. He has to choose between a loss of 10 per cent and a loss of 30 per cent. The lesser harm is given preference over the greater harm to save the difference between the two harms. To prevent the greater harm is a *maṣlaḥa* according to the juristic rule that says, 'Harm should be removed.'[31] Another relevant juristic rule is, 'When two *mafsadas* preclude each other, the greater is avoided by allowing the lesser one.'[32] Moreover, this gives precedence to the potential harm over the certain one. Likewise, the more probable *maṣlaḥa* is given preference over the rare *mafsada*.[33] It is possible that two factors are considered in determining preferability. Yet, whichever of them is upheld should be followed; and if one of them is removed, its import is not removed unless the other consideration is also removed.

2.4. Choosing between two unspecified options

The basic rule is that choosing between two unspecified options is not undertaken until the lack of specificity is removed by explaining the details. To refrain from seeking explanation and details only because one believes something to be unspecified is not acceptable to the Sharīʿa. Ibn Taymiyya says something to this effect when he speaks of preferability and determining preference: 'One should have enough details for explaining such a lack of specificity. Otherwise, many people may consider this to be unspecific, leaving it out when it comes to details, either due to ignorance, or injustice or to pursue one's desire.'[34] Seeking details of the unspecified is not abandoned in the case of securing *maṣlaḥas* or preventing *mafsadas*, except in the case of a valid excuse.

When an unspecified option is explained, it may take several forms, each one of which represents one type of determining preferability, as follows:

1. A *maṣlaḥa* versus a *maṣlaḥa*;
2. A *maṣlaḥa* versus a *mafsada*;
3. A *maṣlaḥa* equal to a *mafsada* versus a *maṣlaḥa* equal to a *mafsada*;
4. A *maṣlaḥa* equal to a *mafsada* versus a *maṣlaḥa*;
5. A *maṣlaḥa* equal to a *mafsada* versus a *mafsada*;
6. A *maṣlaḥa* equal to a *mafsada* versus an unknown option;
7. A *maṣlaḥa* versus an unknown option;
8. A *mafsada* versus an unknown option;
9. An unknown option versus an unknown option.

When the type of preference is made clear, its ruling is operated as detailed above. As for determining the preferability of an unknown option against another, it is discussed under the next heading.

2.5. Choosing between two unknown options

The basic rule is that choosing between two unknown options cannot be done until they become known. Only then can the way to determine preferability be clear enough to be assigned. The same possibilities of options mentioned when discussing choosing between two unspecified options apply here.

One of the issues that requires careful consideration is when the choice is to be made between an unknown option and a pure *mafsada*. To give an example, suppose that we have two options concerning a certain situation: 1) an unknown option in which we do not know the measure of benefit or harm; and 2) a pure *mafsada* that brings only harm. In such a situation, the unknown option is given preference, because a pure *mafsada* rarely happens, compared to the unknown option, which is most probably different from the pure *mafsada*. When we compare the two options we conclude that the first option is at worst a probable pure *mafsada*, while the other is in any case a certain pure *mafsada*.

Discussing the preferability of the likely *maṣlaḥa* over the rare *mafsada*, al-Maqqrī asserts that surmise is given the status of knowledge when the evidence suggests the non-existence of knowledge. He cites in this regard the Qur'anic verse, 'Do not pursue that of which you have no knowledge. Indeed, ears, eyes and heart shall all be called to account' (Q. 17:36) and 'Yet of this they have no knowledge. They follow nothing but surmise, but surmise can never take the place of truth' (Q. 53:28). Thus, he concludes that surmise is negated unless it is proven by certain knowledge, in which case it should be acted upon. This could be the case when it is proven that reaching certainty is unattainable or improbable and there is a necessity or need for the surmise. Al-Maqqrī provides a rule that regulates all of this: 'Do not give preference unless you have authority and evidence. Beware of what is unbeneficial as much as you can, because it may cause harm. Consider ignorance of anything to not harm you unless you are required to know it.'[35]

The removal of ignorance could be improbable or impossible and high probability suggests that it is rare the unknown option will result in pure harm, which is totally rejected. Therefore, the unknown option is given preference over that of pure harm. This comes under the heading of giving preference to surmised pure harm over ascertained pure harm.

Chapter Six

CRITERIA OF *MAṢLAḤA* PREFERABILITY

When a decision is to be taken, weighing up the available options takes several forms. For example, when someone buys a mobile phone or a book, he pays more than the total value of the raw material used in making the mobile phone or the book, such as the metal parts, or the paper. How can the increased value be justified? The answer is that the increase is for the value added by the manufacturing process. This is equal to the price of the commodity or service being bought or consumed minus the value of the raw material used in it. Needless to say, goods and services vary. Likewise, their values at the time of sale or consumption vary according to taste or the need for these goods and services. Were it not for different tastes, goods would not be sold, and were it not for different needs, no person would serve another. These differences also lead to using different measures and standards to estimate values of products or the values added to them.

The aspects of variation of values are the criteria of preferability. Although they measure the same thing, which is the preferability, each criterion is different from the other. Each one is independent and uses a different measurement unit for estimating the relevance of a certain option to what is intended of it. For example, the ruler measures length in centimetres, which is a unit related to metres. When lengths are measured in inches, this unit is related to yards. Both are units measuring length, but they use different standards.

Likewise, each of the *maṣlaḥa* criteria is a unit of measurement, but it measures only one aspect of it, which is immeasurable by any other criterion. The process of determining preferability is applied only in cases of full contradiction where it is not possible to combine useful options or prevent harmful ones. Each criterion is applied independently from other criteria only when the options are equal in all other respects.

The purpose of using these criteria for determining *maṣlaḥa* preferability is to evaluate the benefit of every option using different aspects, with each criterion measuring one type of benefit. Determining the most beneficial option for a person requires evaluating the benefits using all possible aspects, so as not to bring about something that is a *maṣlaḥa* from one angle but leads to a *mafsada* from another. Such a resulting *mafsada* would then not have been taken into consideration, due to no criterion for its evaluation being used, or because evaluating the *maṣlaḥas* relied on one aspect. Generally speaking, the function of the criteria of preferability, according to the rules of Islamic legal theory, is to prevent and remove what could preclude taking the decision on the basis of the *maṣlaḥa*. This is because, in some cases, it is not possible to understand the cause that serves to justify a ruling as a decision of *maṣlaḥa*.[1] The criteria being discussed in this chapter are meant to show such a sufficient measure of benefit so that the decision of *maṣlaḥa* is taken based on it.

1. The Criterion of Rank

This criterion is of three types:

1. Rank according to objective;
2. Rank according to importance;
3. Rank according to basis.

1.1. Rank according to objective

Objective is used here to refer to the main Islamic objectives, which are the five comprehensive essentials (*al-kulliyāt al-khams*), namely, the preservation of religion, self, mind, offspring and property. However, they are here divided in a way that is different from the scheme that many scholars have adopted, which typically places them in five ranks, giving top rank to religion, then self, then mind, then offspring, then property, or an alternative order. In our discussion here, however, they are placed in two classes: a main objective, namely the preservation of religion, and four subordinate objectives, namely the preservation of self, mind, offspring and property.[2] The reason is to stress that the preservation of religion takes priority at all times, and it never fails in any action. If it fails in any option, that option is nullified.

Speaking about sacrificing oneself to preserve religion, or about declining the implementation of some religious aspects in order to preserve oneself, or saying that the first is in accordance with the essence and the second is an exception, is not absolute. In fact all are according to the essence, which is the preservation of religion. An example of the first is that a person exposes himself to be killed during his defence of his faith. An example of the second is the permission of the verbal denial of the faith when one is so forced that it could lead to one's death. Such a verbal denial of faith is permitted on the condition that the person who utters it is firm in his conviction of the truth of faith. His verbal denial is not considered a sacrifice of one's religion, because it is the religion that orders the preservation of self in this way, and there is no sacrifice of one's religion in obeying the Divine Legislator's orders. Also, the preservation of Muslims' lives is, in itself, preservation and strengthening of faith through the preservation of those who follow and implement it. Likewise, the preservation of mind is ranked ahead of the preservation of self, offspring and property if the preservation of mind is more conducive to the preservation of religion. The preservation of offspring is given priority over the preservation of self, mind and property if this helps more to preserve the faith. Such priority is also given to the preservation of property if that leads to the preservation of religion. Religion is always the lead objective, while the other four follow. They serve it and branch out of it, and a branch is never given priority over the stem. One branch may be given priority over another on the basis of its rank in preserving the religion.

Hence, the available options are the preservation of self, mind, offspring and property. A person may give priority to any of these when they cannot be combined together, according to an order of priority that takes into account what serves the preservation of religion most. It should be noted that the preservation of religion is not included as an option, because it is seen to be incumbent on all Muslims, in all situations and at all times and places. The Qur'an states, 'Say: my prayers, my worship, my living and my dying are for God alone, the Lord of all worlds' (Q. 6:162). This means in mathematical language a conditional probability, which is that the probability of giving priority to any of these four objectives is conditional on the preservation of religion. This is mathematically represented by the equation:

The probability (secondary objectives | main objective)

This is because the preservation of religion is the main objective while the secondary objectives are the preservation of self, mind, offspring and property. Thus, preservation of religion is given top priority in all matters, and everything else may be prioritized or not according to the position given to it by the religion.

It may be said that when there is a contradiction between the preservation of mind and the preservation of offspring, property or self, the higher is given priority over the lower. Such a case is further said to be a contradiction between two of these four with no direct impact on the preservation of religion.

However, there seems not to be a contradiction due to the fact that, although the preservation of religion always takes priority, and the priority of self-preservation over the preservation of property, for example, may be self-evident according to human reasoning, it is also required of the subject of the law by religion. It, therefore, comes under the preservation of religion. In fact, there is no imaginable situation of determining preferability without having a religious ruling that the subject of the law must follow. The preservation of religion is achieved through knowing such rulings and implementing them. This is another indication that the preservation of religion always takes precedence, whether directly or indirectly.

To give an example: suppose that a certain institution wants to invest either in the education sector or the health sector, by building a school or a hospital. Which of the two is more conducive to the preservation of religion? An analysis of this case leads to the following:

1. The hospital is related to the preservation of self, while the school contributes to the preservation of mind. The preservation of religion needs both, but the better for this purpose is determined according to the need for either. The one needed more is given priority.
2. The first step to be taken is to consider whether it is possible to have both. If so, then this is the option that serves the religion best by helping to preserve both self and mind. The investment may, for example, take the form of building a teaching hospital that serves also as a college focusing on a certain medical specialization.
3. If the two cannot be combined, the level of sufficiency in each sector is considered. It is more conducive to the preservation of religion to invest in the sector where the level of sufficiency is lower.
4. In the case of an equal level of sufficiency in both sectors, we consider the specializations where sufficiency is below the required level. Investment is then channelled to that specialization according to its degree of shortage.

To sum up, the preservation of religion may be achieved through various means, including the preservation of self, mind, offspring and property. The element that preserves the religion best is known through these. To preserve the whole takes precedence over preserving its parts. When it is impossible to combine preservation and development of all of these, priority is given to whatever preserves the highest number of parts over what preserves a lower number. Should this prove to be unattainable, the part that is most keenly needed is given priority. This process is continued: whenever two options are equal we add another criterion to help give priority to one of them. The 'particular' and the 'comprehensive' will be highlighted when discussing the overlap of ranks of importance.

1.2. Rank according to importance

Importance has two criteria: realistic and psychological. The realistic criterion includes what is necessary, needed or complementary. These are degrees that differ in importance according to circumstances. The psychological criterion is most apparent when the degrees of importance are close to each other in reality, or even equal. In this case, preferability is given to whatever the decision maker feels to be important. Experience in the field of administration proves that when all considerations are equal, the decision maker bases his choice on what appears more important.[3]

Here is an example of ranking things according to importance. The municipal council of a borough in a town allocates a budget that is sufficient to build a new road for a district that has no proper road to access it, or to widen an old road to a different district, or to plant trees along the main road in the town centre. Which of these options should be given precedence based on importance? There are three choices:

> Option 1: A district with only a dust road that will remain so unless it is asphalted. In other words, this district will not have a paved road unless this project is carried out. Thus, the *maṣlaḥa* will not be gained unless this project of asphalting the road is carried out. Where a purpose cannot be achieved without something, that thing is deemed necessary for that purpose. Therefore, the importance of this project for this district is categorized as 'necessary'.
>
> Option 2: A district with an asphalt road that needs to be broadened. If the broadening project is not approved, the residents of this district will have to face some difficulty. Such difficulty cannot be removed without the broadening of this road. Whatever leads to an easing of a problem is needed for it. Therefore, the importance of this project for this district is of the 'needed' category.
>
> Option 3: The main road in the town needs to be planted with trees to adorn the entrance and exits of the town. Such tree planting will make the road more pleasant for users, giving

them aesthetic pleasure. Whatever gives pleasant feelings is related to complements. Therefore, the importance of this project for this town is of the 'complementary' category.

Thereupon, the head of the municipal council has three options and he needs to choose only one. When he compares the options according to their importance, he notes the following differences:

1. The first option: the benefit for the residents cannot be achieved without it.
2. The second option: gives the residents easier and better benefit, but the benefit is complete without it.
3. In the third option: the benefit is complete without it, and users incur no hardship without it. The pleasant appearance of the road is complementary to its width and ease, both of which are complementary to the fact that the road exists.

Therefore, what is necessary is given precedence over what is needed, just as the needed is given priority over what serves as a complement. In other words, the first option, which is the asphalting of the road, is given priority over the other two. The order of importance of the three options is as follows:

1. The option whose benefit cannot be achieved without it, which is called the necessary option.
2. The option whose benefit is not facilitated without it, which is called the needed option.
3. The option whose benefit is not improved without it, which is called the complementary option.

The necessary option is given precedence over the needed and the needed over the complementary. The lower option complements the higher one and the higher is the basis for the lower. Thus, the first option, which is asphalting the road, is given precedence over other options.

In undertaking the process of preference, the relation between the necessity, the need and the complement is taken into account. The question is looked at from a partial perspective, taking every rank or point of importance separately. They are then viewed from a holistic perspective that considers the complementarity and overlap of the three purposes. This holistic perspective is highlighted by al-Shāṭibī: 'When it is confirmed that the complement serves the need and this, in turn, serves the necessity, it is the necessity, then, that is required.'

Here are five points that need to be outlined:

1. The necessity is a basis to other needed and complementary purposes.
2. If the necessity is flawed, this entails that the other two are flawed absolutely.
3. Should the other two be absolutely flawed, it does not necessarily mean that the necessity is absolutely flawed.
4. If either the complement or the need is absolutely flawed, the necessity may also be flawed in some form.
5. The need and the complement should be kept safe for the sake of the necessity.[4]

To explain, we begin with the first. As stated previously, religious *maṣlaḥas* are based on preserving the five types mentioned earlier. If this world's existence is based on these five, to the extent that their loss constitutes a total loss of this world, in as far as it relates to people and the tasks assigned to them by the Divine Legislator, then matters of the life to come cannot also be maintained unless these five are achieved.

If the religion does not exist, then the reward that is aspired for will not exist; if the ones charged with a task, humanity, do not exist, then there will be no one to believe in religion; if the mind does not exist, there can be no believing in religion; if offspring does not exist, life will not continue; and if property does not exist, people will not be able to live. Property here means all that humans can possess and defend to their ability if acquired through a legitimate channel. Food, drink and clothing are included here, as are all other possessions. If nothing of this exists, life could not continue.[5]

1.3. Rank according to basis

The rule here is 'Wherever an obligation cannot be fulfilled without a particular matter, that matter is also obligatory.' The operation of this rule defines the difference between the basic option and the subordinate one. Although the basic option is complemented by the subordinate one, it may be fulfilled without it, although then it will lack its benefit. Therefore, the process of determining preferability on the basis of the basic and subordinate options is different from other processes of determining preferability, because as a matter of *maṣlaḥa*, the basic option must include whatever is subordinate to it. The available choice in this case is in fact a combination of the basic option and whatever is subordinate to it. The preferability process, therefore, is between this group and another group that includes a different basic option and its subordinate ones.

For illustration, let us take the university as an example. The basic objective in a university is education. Students, lecturers, subjects, research and other areas are all supporters of this objective. They are there to serve the basic process. Hence, they cannot be given priority over it. Students and lecturers must stop anything that distracts them from learning and teaching. In the subjects taught at the university and in the research, focus must be determined according to degree of importance. Suppose the rector of a university has several options relating to next year's budget, some of which are directly related to the basic process while others concern the subordinate issues. How is he to choose between them? Some people may suggest that the options related to the basic process must be given automatic priority. Whatever is related to subordinate issues comes only after the needs of the basic process have been satisfied. This is not absolutely correct. Every basic option cannot be complete unless it incorporates its supporting subordinate options. The following example clarifies this.

Suppose that the rector of the university determines that a certain department needs a 5 per cent increase in the teaching staff to cover the needs of the increased number of students. He decides to go ahead with this increase, and determines the number of staff members to be appointed, their salaries, accommodation, visas and so on. All these decisions are considered as basic processes. There are, however, numerous other decisions that need to be taken, including the provision of offices for the new staff members, freeing them from strenuous administrative tasks, the distribution of work among them in a way that makes the best use of their respective academic skills, organizing the processes of consultation based on their academic rank, and conducting consultation, teaching, research and supervision in a way suitable to their respective academic standing. All of this requires tens of complementary administrative decisions at the levels of the board of the university, rector, dean of faculty, head of department and other personnel. These are complementary subordinate decisions. Unless these complementary decisions are taken in the appropriate manner and at the right time, the basic option loses its effectiveness and its benefit is considerably reduced. Therefore, when the process of preferability is conducted between two basic options, each of these is considered together with the subordinate options it requires. Thus, the preferability is not determined between basic options or subordinate options alone. The process is conducted as follows:

1. Each basic option is grouped together with all the subordinate options it involves.
2. Each basic option with the subordinate options related to it is considered as a single group.
3. The merits of each single group are looked into to determine which group is most beneficial.
4. The most beneficial group is adopted and necessary decisions are taken on its basis.

Thus, we may move from choosing the highest beneficial basic option and its complementary option to the next most beneficial ones.

2. The Criterion of Stability

When benefits are stable, they are more beneficial. If they are unstable, they are less beneficial. Therefore, determining preferability between benefits according to the considerations of stability is in effect a balance between the degrees of usefulness of each. It is thus not a weighing of benefits, but a weighing of the factors that help to make use of them. It has seven types:

1. Stability according to constancy;
2. Stability according to customs;
3. Stability according to understanding;
4. Stability according to comprehensiveness;
5. Stability according to life expectancy;
6. Stability according to handling;
7. Stability according to alternative availability.

The following is a detailed discussion of each of these types.

2.1. Stability according to constancy

When we look at benefits and harms, we find that they are often relative. Each one necessarily needs time, place, situation and person. It changes when any of these change. As it is natural that they change when their related elements change, it is undeniable that rulings based on *maṣlaḥa* and tradition change with time.[6] Here are some examples.

1. Benefits that change according to time: heating is beneficial in winter and unnecessary in summer.
2. Benefits that change according to place: small, fast cars are beneficial on asphalt roads, but unusable on rough country roads.
3. Benefits that change according to situation: taking a bath is beneficial when the water temperature is moderate, but is harmful when the water is too hot or ice cold.
4. Benefits that change according to person: a medicine is beneficial to a sick person but can be harmful to a healthy one.

In fact, all benefits and harms may change, except good deeds and sinful deeds whose respective benefits or harms are constant. What is constant takes precedence over what is changeable. Therefore, compliance with the Divine Legislator's orders and refraining from sins are given preference over all other things. This is a kind of precedence for constant benefits over changeable ones. It is out of the Divine Legislator's grace that this does not exclude changeable benefits as compliance with the Divine Legislator's orders and refraining from sins combines both constant and changeable benefits. By contrast, concentrating on changeable benefits, paying no heed to compliance with the Divine Legislator's orders and refraining from sins, deprives humans of the constant benefits, as well as many changeable benefits that cannot be obtained except by doing good deeds of obedience and refraining from sinful deeds. The best choice to ensure the maximum benefit is to combine the constant benefits, giving them priority, with the changeable ones in such a way that the latter do not exclude the former or cause a flaw in them.

Thus, whenever a benefit is constant, doing it is a *maṣlaḥa*; and whenever it is changeable, doing it is a *mafsada* compared with the constant one. Whenever the benefit is temporary and of short duration, its usefulness is less, compared with the constant benefit.

2.2. Stability according to customs

On the basis of the juristic rule that says, 'Customs are to be considered in issuing rulings',[7] the stability of society and the inadmissibility of what constitutes hardship for people are given high importance. This is governed by the fact that all actions should conform to customs that ensure the fulfilment of a *maṣlaḥa* endorsed by the Sharīʿa.

The reason for which a certain action is done is the *maṣlaḥa* that it involves and its stability as a practice that people accept.[8] This statement confirms the necessity of considering what the community accepts, unless it is in conflict with the Sharīʿa. That is because this ensures clear *maṣlaḥa*, including encouraging people to do what they like and are familiar with. This brings them the benefit of the stability of many *maṣlaḥas*, ensuring their availability. It also gives them assurance, for benefits that encourage people to do what they like incur people's assurance and pleasure and become closely available to everyone. In other words, this will make the social environment more conducive to making the best of these benefits.

Suppose that a rich businessman in the private sector wants to invest in tourism. He conducts several economic studies to identify the tourist projects that appeal to families in a particular city. These studies tell him that they prefer a tourist resort that will keep the family entertained for at least a full week. It should also be next to appropriate accommodation and shopping facilities. Preferences indicated a particular area because of its fine weather in summer. He builds a hotel, an amusement village and a shopping mall. After the opening, the tourist facilities become full of visitors. Yet some time later, demand falls and losses start to accumulate. He brings in consultants to identify the causes and recommend suitable measures. The results are as follows.

1. The amusement area was not arranged or divided in accordance with the social family structure in the country of investment. The special amusement taste of every social group was not taken into consideration, neither in quality, nor quantity or type. This has led to problems for the consumer, because of location and quality overlaps. Moreover, entertainment facilities have not been designed to suit the traditions of dress code in that city.
2. In the light of the above, it has been concluded that most visitors did not make more than three visits to the amusement village, because of the impression they had from previous visits.
3. The whole project was designed to attract high-income and upper-middle-class people. These normally have a wider choice for tourism. It would have been wiser to design the project for people in the middle and lower-middle classes, and to reduce the type of investment. Most people in these classes are happy with a clean and spacious area with unsophisticated and inexpensive amusement facilities, and good catering facilities. This has cost the amusement project a loss of 70 per cent of potential consumers, because of high prices.

4. Regarding the shopping mall and on the basis of item 3, it has been noted that most goods in the shopping mall are either too expensive for consumers or are not usually bought by them. They are unsuitable for the life pattern of the prospective consumers, which resulted in the inactivity of the shopping mall.

To sum up, social unsuitability leads to hardship that causes a lack of visitors, which in turn causes loss. Perhaps the businessman might have seen a similar facility in another country, which he admired and decided to copy. He studied only part of the purely economic feasibility without looking at the social feasibility. He did not take into consideration the local population's traditions and what amusement they prefer. Economic feasibility is not considered a real feasibility unless it takes into account the special characteristics of the market, the nature of the consumers and what they can afford in the short and long terms. Otherwise, it is merely a financial study with no practical importance.

The benefits the businessman wanted the project to have were unstable because they were contrary to the traditions of the consumers. It is the project that observes and respects people's traditions and social practices that will often be successful. Therefore, an option that conforms to tradition is given preference over one that does not so conform. This is because its superiority is in the degree of its benefit stability. This is the case when the two options are equal on all other aspects of preferability.

2.3. Stability according to understanding

There are several degrees of understanding the benefit of the option to be taken. There are also levels associated with these degrees. Because the process of understanding is relevant to a person's ability and method of understanding, scholars of Islamic legal theory (*uṣūl al-fiqh*) have taken care to clearly define its levels and regulate its rulings. This aspect is of great importance with regard to every decision to be taken, irrespective of all other considerations. It, in fact, affects the understanding of all such considerations. Therefore, an indication to the scholarly views and the definition of levels of understanding will be provided before giving examples.

The contemporary legal theorist and jurist Yaʿqūb al-Bāḥusayn states that understanding has different degrees; and there are different levels for each degree of understanding. He adds that understanding

> may either be firm or not firm. What is not firm may be more probable, less probable or of equal probability. Also, a firm understanding may either be consistent with reality or not. A firm understanding that is consistent with reality is certainty (*yaqīn*) or knowledge (*ʿīlm*), while a firm understanding that is inconsistent with reality is ignorance (*jahl*). An understanding that is not firm, but more probable is called surmise (*ẓann*), and that which is less probable is illusion (*wahm*), and that of equal probability is suspicion (*shakk*).[9]

Certain benefit is the subject of firm understanding and consistent with reality. Thus it is known with certainty. Surmised benefit results from a more probable understanding that is not firm. Suspected benefit comes from an understanding that is not firm with no more likelihood of being right than being wrong. Illusory benefit is the product of an understanding that is not firm with little probability of correctness. Ignorance of benefit is the firm understanding of a benefit that is inconsistent with reality. These degrees of understanding benefits are illustrated in Figure 8.

It is clear in this model that although surmise is not equal to certainty in nature and reality, it has the same ruling. Likewise, suspicion and illusion are not equal to ignorance in nature and reality, but both have the same ruling as ignorance. Action on the basis of certainty or surmise is permissible and may be obligatory at times, while action on the basis of ignorance, suspicion or illusion is not permissible, and may be forbidden. What follows is a detailed explanation of these degrees.

Figure 8: Degrees of understanding benefits

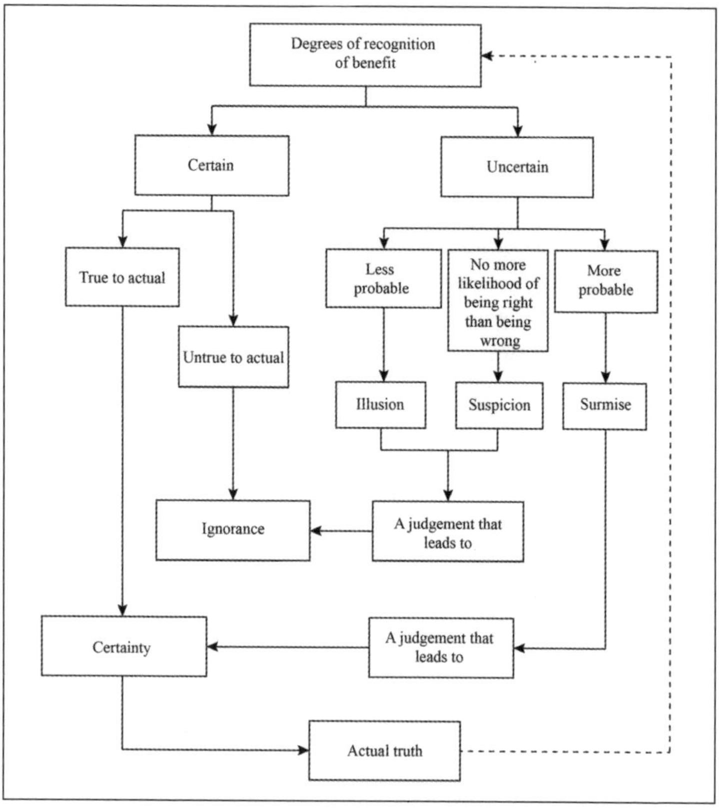

2.3.1. Certainty

Certainty is 'a belief that something is of a particular form, believing that it cannot be of another form, and the belief is correspondent with the reality of that thing, and not liable to be removed.'[10] This definition has been adopted by a large number of scholars of logic and Islamic legal theory. Therefore, it is necessary to explain what this definition excludes and what may be said in elaboration of it.

When scholars say 'a belief that something', they exclude suspicion, because suspicion means equal probability and thus it is different from belief. The phrase 'believing that it cannot be of another form' excludes surmise, because surmise allows the possibility of a less probable opposite side. 'The belief is correspondent with the reality of that thing' provides a restriction that excludes ignorance, which is based on a firm belief that is inconsistent with reality, while 'not liable to be removed' provides a restriction that excludes belief by someone who is a 'follower' of a specific scholar or school of thought who even if they are right about something may have their belief about a matter removed by their bias. A follower who is in the wrong is excluded by the earlier restrictive phrase 'correspondent with the reality of that thing'.[11]

Jurists allow a broader area for what could be considered 'certain' than scholars of Islamic legal theory and scholars of logic, adding to it what is surmised. This is due to the fact that juristic rulings are based on face value. In numerous cases, the Sharīʿa ruling considers something to be a certainty, while reasoning allows the possibility that reality takes a different form. Something is judged to be true on the basis of appropriate Sharīʿa-approved evidence, such as the testimony of witnesses. According to the Sharīʿa, it is as certain as something one sees with one's own eye. However, it remains a testimony of individuals, who could, rationally speaking, be subject to forgetfulness and deliberate lie. Al-Nawawī (d. 676 AH) indicates this fact when he states that it should be known that scholars may use terms like knowledge and certainty when they actually mean apparent surmise, not absolute certainty and true knowledge.[12]

2.3.2. Ignorance

According to scholastic theologians, ignorance is of two types: a) simple ignorance, which means a lack of knowledge of something that is normally known; b) complex ignorance, which means a firm belief that is contrary to reality.[13] Some scholars maintain that ignorance is of three types:

1. The lack of knowledge, which is the essence of ignorance. Some scholars view ignorance as a state that leads to actions that do not conform to order, while knowledge is a state leading to actions that conform to order.

2. Believing something to be contrary to what it actually is.[14]
3. Doing something in a way contrary to how it should be done.

Simple ignorance can be quickly overcome by learning and having information, whereas complex ignorance can be overcome only with difficulty. Some scholars have even opined that it is untreatable.[15]

2.3.3. Surmise

Ibn Fāris[16] (d. 395 AH) considers surmise to indicate two different meanings: certainty and doubt.[17] Some say that the certainty referred to here cannot be a tangible certainty; rather it is a certainty arrived at through reflection. A tangible certainty cannot be anything other than knowledge. The Arabic term *ẓann*, which originally means surmise, has been used in both senses in the Qur'an and the *ḥadīth*. For example, it occurs in the sense of certainty in the following verse, 'I certainly knew (*ẓanantu*) that one day I would have to face my account' (Q. 69:20), and in the sense of doubt in, 'No! You doubted (*ẓanantum*) that the Messenger and the believers would ever return to their families and this thought seemed pleasing to your hearts. You thought an evil thought and you were a people doomed to perish' (Q. 48:12). In his *Al-Kulliyāt*, Abū al-Baqāʾ al-Kafawī (d. 1638 AH) quotes al-Zarkashī as outlining two regulating rules for the meaning of '*ẓann*' or surmise in the Qur'an. The first is that wherever *ẓann* is commended and coupled with a promised reward, it denotes certainty; and whenever it is condemned and coupled with a threat of punishment, it denotes doubt. The second rule is that where the term *ẓann* and its derivatives are followed by the Arabic particle '*an*' then it indicates doubt, and whenever it is followed by the form '*anna*' it denotes certainty.[18]

In the traditions of the Prophet, he is quoted as saying, 'Beware of surmise (*zann*), for it is the worst of false tales.'[19] *Ẓann* here refers to doubt. In most cases the word denotes one of these two meanings, especially doubt and suspicion. It is also used in the sense of accusation. Another derivative is *maẓanna*, which refers to the expected time or place of something.[20]

The technical meaning of *ẓann* is 'Believing that something is more probable while accepting the opposite possibility.' It is also said that it means 'the side of the doubt which is given a stronger probability'.[21]

Another definition is 'Accepting two alternatives, one of which is weightier than the other.'[22] Others say that it refers to the weightier option by giving more weight to the right side. In this sense, it is the opposite of illusion, which gives weight to the wrong side.[23] It is said that 'If one side is weightier, then the less weighty side is called "illusion", while the weightier is called "surmise", if it allows the possibility of the existence of a less weighty option.'[24]

Scholars speak about the use of *ẓann* in the sense of 'certainty', as well as in the sense of 'illusion'. In *Al-Kuliyyāt*, al-Kafawī[25] speaks about the explanation of indications saying, 'The word *ẓann*, or surmise, may be used alongside "certainty" to denote a firm opinion that is consistent with reality and not attributed to its cause, as well as to denote a firm opinion that is inconsistent. It is not used to denote what is not firm.'[26]

Jurists associate surmise with doubt because they use it to denote oscillation between the existence and non-existence of something, whether the two possibilities are equal or one is deemed more likely. However, according to al-Taftāzānī (d. 792 AH), the famous view is that 'surmise denotes the more likely alternative, but it might also be used in the sense of illusion'. To say that 'surmise', that is *ẓann*, is used to denote both suspicion and certainty means that it is a word with two opposite senses. However, it appears that the usage of the word to denote either certainty or illusion[27] is not frequent. It may be only a figurative usage with clear distinctive hints.[28]

When indications of surmise are achieved, it is considered an avenue leading to the following rulings.

1. A report narrated by a single or small number of transmitters (*khabar al-wāḥid*) must be acted upon if the transmitter is reliable.
2. The testimony of two witnesses, and the report of two evaluators, must be accepted if they are trustworthy.
3. Acting on the basis of analogy, even though the cause of the base ruling is surmised.

4. In case of suspicion, the ruling of a former situation is presumed to continue.[29]

2.3.4. Suspicion

Linguistically speaking, suspicion is the opposite of certainty.[30] In technical terminology, it is used by jurists in a sense that is rather different from that of scholars of theology and Islamic legal theory. According to the latter, it means 'Allowing the possibility of two alternatives, neither of which have a merit over the other.'[31] Al-Jurjānī defines it as 'Oscillating between two opposites when in doubt, without giving either a weightier value.'[32]

It is noted that all of these definitions agree on the ambiguity of the subject matter, due to the existence of two options, neither of which is preponderant over the other. Some of these definitions are considered to elucidate the object of suspicion, rather than suspicion itself, which is a human attribute. Whoever defines it as 'something of equal possibilities' is not giving a definition to the characteristics of a person who is in a state of suspicion, but rather the suspected matter, the object of suspicion. Anyone defining it as 'oscillating between two opposites, or allowing two possibilities, or equality of two opposites, or standing in between two possibilities without leaning towards either', looks at a person's attitude in the matter. This is closer to explaining the meaning of suspicion, because it is a human characteristic, not the object of suspicion.[33]

The question of equality between two or more alternative options in the state of suspicion has near scholarly agreement. However, Imām al-Ḥaramayn (d. 478 AH) includes within suspicion cases where the alternative options are not equal, yet neither of them has attained a sufficient degree of probability that enables a rational person to make a decision.[34]

Jurists consider suspicion to mean oscillation between the existence and non-existence of something, whether the two alternatives are equal or one of them more probable.[35] This is stated by al-Nawawī and others. Ibn al-Qayyim says, 'Whenever jurists use the term suspicion, they mean oscillation between the existence of something or its non-existence, whether the two cases are equal or one is more probable.'[36]

Jurists maintain that suspicion as a terminology relates to the mental conceptualization of terms as individual entities, rather than to the affirmation and establishment of rulings. Therefore, suspicion involves no ruling, as it is, for the jurists, contrary to knowledge and its opposite, which do involve rulings.[37] Hence, no religious ruling is issued on the basis of suspicion. Should there be an already existing ruling, its continuity is presumed at variance with suspicion. Al-Zarkashī mentions several cases in which a ruling can be based on suspicion, though this is only when it is impossible to arrive at certainty.[38]

2.3.5. Illusion

Illusion is something that occurs to the mind. Linguistically speaking, to *tawahhama* (which is the verb) something means to 'imagine and visualize that thing, whether it exists or not'.[39] In technical terminology, it is said that illusion is the less probable alternative,[40] which is compared with surmise when the two alternatives are of equal standing (according to those who understood surmise to accommodate such possibility).[41] It is also mentioned that, like suspicion, it belongs to the category of conceptualization and not of affirmation,[42] so the basic principle is that no rulings may be based on illusion.

2.3.6. Continuity of degrees of understanding

The degrees of understanding are like interlinked rings of a chain: the lowest, which is ignorance, is thus linked to the highest, which is certainty. Certainty (*yaqīn*) represents a degree of full understanding, which is 100 per cent. It is followed by surmise (*ẓann*), which is a lesser degree of understanding ranging from 51 to 99 per cent, and the higher degree is given precedence over the lower. Next comes suspicion (*shakk)*, which is again an incomplete degree of understanding at the rate of 50 per cent. This is followed by illusion (*wahm)*, which is an incomplete degree of understanding ranging from 1 to 49 per cent. The lowest is ignorance (*jahl*), which is zero degrees of understanding (Figure 9).

Figure 9: Continuum of degrees of understanding

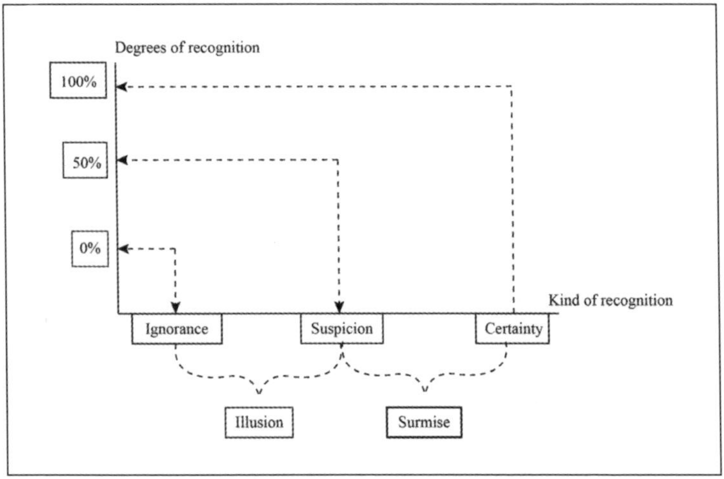

Certainty and ignorance are constant and unchangeable, while surmise, suspicion and illusion are all changeable. In some cases when a high degree of surmise is required, suspicion may be at a higher point than 50 per cent. This means that the area of surmise is decreased while the area of illusion is increased. This is represented by Figure 10.

Figure 10: Suspicion of benefit above 50 per cent

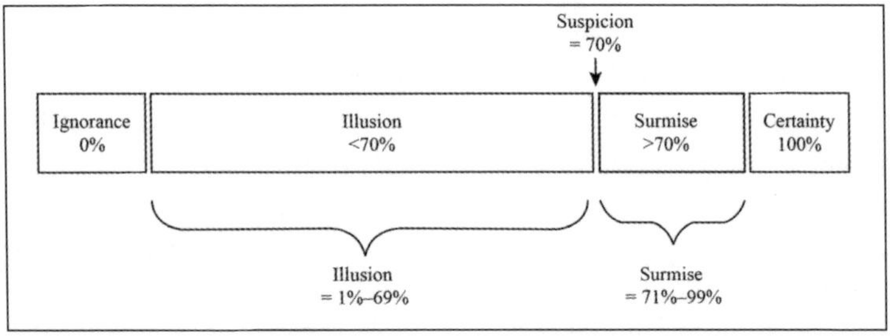

In the above example where the area of surmise is decreased, it is apparent that illusion becomes more probable. The basic rule is that more probable illusion prevents action. However, although illusion cannot attain the near certainty of the more probable surmise, action may be taken on its basis as a precaution against harm. A case in mind is a false report suggesting that a bomb has been planted in a hotel lobby. The report comes from an unknown source. There seems to be no reason to believe this report or take any action, other than to take precautionary measures in order to prevent harm. The cautious approach means that the report is not dismissed. Hence, the concerned authorities evacuate the hotel and undertake a thorough search. Only when they are absolutely certain of complete safety do the authorities allow people to return. This is a clear case of dismissing the more probable illusion regarding this report and taking action on the basis of the less probable surmise so that harm is prevented. Such an action may also be taken as a precaution to secure *maṣlaḥas*. The smaller rate of surmise, which is 28 per cent in this case, is given precedence over the greater rate of illusion, which is 69 per cent, out of precaution, to save people's lives should there really be a bomb in the hotel.

The reverse may be the case in matters that require only little illusion for action to be taken. This means that suspicion comes at a point lower than 50 per cent, and therefore there is a larger area for surmise and a smaller one for illusion. This is shown in Figure 11.

Figure 11: Suspicion of benefit below 50 per cent

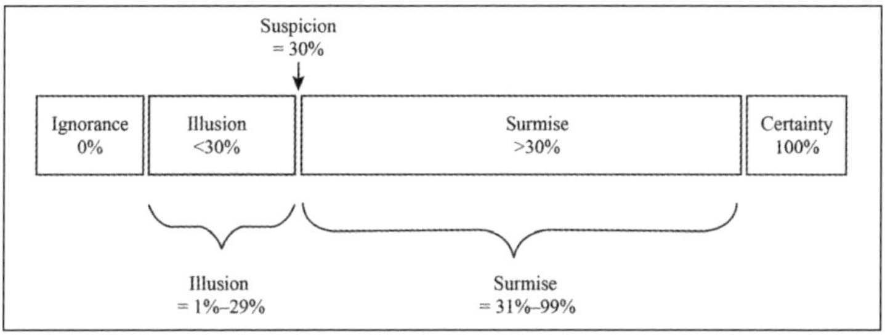

An example is that of a pilot who, just before take-off, notices that his meters indicate marked variance in the level of fuel the plane has been given. He conducts a thorough test but cannot find anything wrong. He concludes that should he take off, he will most likely reach his destination safely. Nevertheless he does not do so. Regulations will not allow him to do so, even though the plane is on the runway, ready to fly. He must return and allow the technical staff to carry out a thorough check of the fuel, its reservoir, passages, meters and engines to determine the cause of the variation. Only then a decision will be taken on whether or not the plane should be allowed to fly. Although the surmise suggests that the flight is safe by 68 per cent, which means it, religiously speaking, has the same verdict as certainty, and that the illusion is only 29 per cent, which means it takes the verdict of the non-existent, the plane is not allowed to fly. The reason is that necessary precautions must be taken to prevent any possible harm, which is, in this case, the danger of a fault occurring during the flight. This is also to ensure the *maṣlaḥa*, which is, in this case, the preservation of the lives of the passengers and the crew.

Therefore, the two rules of taking necessary precautions to abandon what is controversially thought to bring harm or to secure what is controversially thought to bring benefit, which have been stated by Al-ʿIzz b. ʿAbd al-Salām, affect the point at which the degree of suspicion is placed in between surmise and illusion. The decision is taken on the basis of its position so as to relate it to the objective of deciding which alternative is more likely.

When precaution applies to what is controversially harmful, it raises the degree of suspicion towards benefit to the level normally occupied by surmise, indicating a greater probability of harm and the need to prevent the action. In this case, suspicion as to its benefit becomes an illusion and cannot be acted upon, as was explained by the example of the grounded plane. By contrast, when precaution applies to what is controversially beneficial, it lowers the degree of suspicion towards benefit to the level normally occupied by illusion, making it more probable that the action will be beneficial and should be acted upon. In this case, suspicion as to its benefit becomes more probable surmise and must be acted upon, as was seen in the example of the report of a bomb in a hotel.

On the basis of the above, the point for which evidence is sought is whether a given measure of surmise is acceptable from the Sharīʿa point of view, so as to admit the soundness of what it indicates. If not, the converse inquiry is whether it is unacceptable, so as to be discarded along with what it indicates.[43] That such questions are asked about evidence means that the degree of preponderant surmise differs according to the nature of what is surmised and the general tradition concerning it. From another view, it is necessary to take such difference into account, so as to determine the degree of surmise that is sufficient to confirm a ruling.

Generally speaking, certainty may be acted upon with regard to the present or the past only. As for the future, Islamic textual sources indicate that everything relating to it is known only to the Divine Legislator. The Qur'an states, 'Never say about anything, "I shall do this tomorrow," without adding, "if God so wills." Should you forget, then mention your Lord and say, "I pray that my Lord will guide me even closer than this to what is right"' (Q. 18:23-24). The expected *maṣlaḥas* and benefits, as well as capabilities, goals and purposes are equal in this regard. Complete certainty regarding decisions meant for the future is impossible from both the religious and rational points of view. Hence, every decision involves a certain degree of risk.

2.4. Stability according to comprehensiveness

Al-ʿIzz b. ʿAbd al-Salām says, 'One action may combine several *maṣlaḥas*.'[44] He gives an example of a ruler being told of the general *mafsadas* that are clearly apparent among Muslims. He issues a single order for them to be removed. Such an order results in countless benefits. This becomes one of the reasons for preferring some benefits over others. An example follows from the field of administration.

Take the case of the managing director of a large company that employs 1,000 people. The company decides to give a special reward for the ones who have demonstrated excellence in their work. The managing director is appointed as head of the committee to determine the type of reward and its quantity. After consultation, two alternatives are suggested: either a monetary reward equivalent to one month's salary, or certain administrative privileges during working hours in addition to a letter of thanks. The managing director is requested to make a choice between the two. Which one should he adopt?

The choice is between two forms of reward, each of which serves the purpose for which the reward is given, but one is monetary and the other incorporeal. The incorporeal reward gives the employees some privileges in choosing their working hours plus an expression of gratitude. This option will only significantly benefit the recipient employees within their work, whereas the monetary reward benefits the workers in addition to their families and dependants. In other words, the monetary reward achieves the purpose for which it is given and has a wide benefit, whereas the other option benefits almost exclusively the recipient workers. Hence, it might be concluded that the monetary option provides more comprehensive benefit than the other option, and therefore it is to be preferred.

This means that in relating the choice of the incorporeal reward to the monetary one, we find that it has a more particular scope, while the latter has a more comprehensive scope. The comprehensive option is always given preference over the particular. Therefore, we say that whenever an option ensures several benefits, whether intended by the original purpose or not, without losing any part of the benefit intended by the original purpose, that option is better in the process of determining preferability. Whenever a benefit is broadened in scope, it is considered more comprehensive, while a benefit that is limited in scope is less comprehensive.

2.5. Stability according to life expectancy

Every benefit has a life expectancy, which has three stages: 1) growth; 2) maturity; and 3) decline (Figure 12).

Benefits are arranged in preference according to these stages as follows. A benefit in the growth stage is given preference over the one in the maturity stage, and the latter is given preference over the one in the stage of decline.

Suppose, for example, that a certain person obtains a licence to operate a car hire company. He wants to buy a fleet of cars to start this business. He has three options:

1. Buying new cars;
2. Buying used cars in the middle of their life expectancy,

for instance, three years old out of six, which is the life expectancy at the best expectations;

3. Buying five-year-old cars.

Figure 12: Life expectancy of benefits

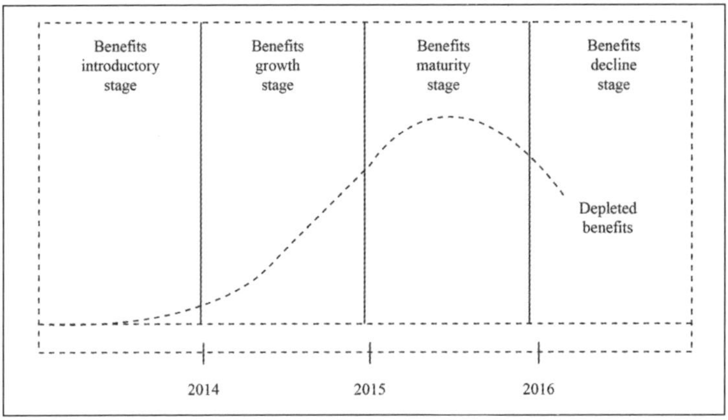

Undoubtedly, when all other considerations, such as the year of manufacture, the number of cars and their value, are equal, the new cars are preferred to the three-year-old ones and both are preferable to the five-year-old cars. This is due to the fact that the first option represents the growth stage on the benefit scale, while the second option represents the maturity stage and the third the decline stage.

2.6. Stability according to handling

Suppose that a professor has completed a certain piece of scientific research that he has been working on, and he wants to publish it in a specialized scientific journal. His first option is to print it and enclose a letter with it before he goes to the post office where he buys a stamp and posts it. His second choice is to send it as an attachment to a covering e-mail message.

It is clear that sending the research paper by e-mail is cheaper and more convenient. The two options are of equal benefit, but the second option of sending it by e-mail is preferable because it is easier to handle and to achieve the desired benefit. The preference here is based on easier handling. The easier option is given preference over the difficult one when both are equal in all other considerations, as it is more in line with the Qur'anic statement 'God desires that you have ease. He does not desire that you be afflicted with hardship' (Q. 2:185). Another supporting evidence in this regard is the *ḥadīth* that states, 'Whenever God's messenger (peace be upon him) had to choose between two options he would always choose the easier option, unless it involved a sin. If it involved a sin, he would be the furthest away from it...'[45] Hence, it seems that the inclination within textual evidence is to advocate basing one's decisions on the easier options that involve no sin.

2.7. Stability according to alternative availability

When the available options ensure a benefit but one of them precludes another alternative benefit and the other does not preclude it, the one allowing the other benefit is to be preferred. Al-ʿIzz b. ʿAbd al-Salām says, 'In such questions, gaining one of the two benefits in line with the alternative of the other is more preferable to gaining one benefit while precluding the alternative of the other.'[46]

An example of this is to give preference to saving the mother's life to that of her embryo. One consideration in this is that the mother has an alternative, as she may be able to give birth to another child in future. If the mother's life is placed at risk in favour of saving her embryo, the embryo, when born, will not have an alternative mother.

3. The Criterion of Volume

The volume of benefit is measured by two criteria: 1) The number of beneficiaries, in which the larger the number, the more widespread its benefit; and 2) How much benefit each one of them derives, in which the more this is, the greater the benefit is overall. Following is a discussion of both aspects.

3.1. Volume according to the spread of benefit

Al-Ghazālī clarifies that the general *maṣlaḥa* is that which benefits the general public, and its benefit is not exclusive to a specific person.[47] It is not peculiar to one in preference to another. Therefore, it varies in its scope: the more people it benefits the more general it is, and the more general is given preference over the less general, according to the juristic rule 'Preference is given against the private benefit in favour of the general benefit.'[48]

An example is the manager of a residential complex that includes 300 families who has an empty plot of land in the middle of the complex. The municipal regulations make clear that it must be utilized as a public facility to serve the residents in the complex. He has two options: either to build a sports arena, including a football pitch and other sports facilities, or to build a centre for family services to ensure children are taken from home to school and back, as well as providing a nursery for children who are under school age. Which is the more preferable option?

The answer obviously favours the second option, because the benefit of the service includes parents and children, in addition to the drivers. The first option provides benefit to the children only. This means that the benefit resulting from the second option is more general than the first. The more general is given precedence over the less general in accordance with the juristic rule that states that the general *maṣlaḥa* is given priority over the private one, when the two are mutually contradictory and cannot be combined.

Hence, the often-expressed notion that the general *maṣlaḥa* is the opposite of the private *maṣlaḥa* is wrong. The opposite of a general *maṣlaḥa* is a general *mafsada*, while the opposite of a private *maṣlaḥa* is a private *mafsada*. A *maṣlaḥa* can only be opposed by a *mafsada*. It is impossible that a general *maṣlaḥa* contradicts a private *maṣlaḥa*. How can this occur when a general *maṣlaḥa* is only qualified as such, because it incorporates a large number of private *maṣlaḥas*? A private *maṣlaḥa* is part of a general *maṣlaḥa*, and the whole cannot be placed in opposition to its parts.

The correct process is for the general *maṣlaḥa* to be given precedence while ensuring the private *maṣlaḥa*. It is imperative that private *maṣlaḥas* are given due consideration wherever possible. They may not be disregarded unless there is a specific textual instruction to disregard them.[49]

To sum up, a general *maṣlaḥa* is of a higher status than a private *maṣlaḥa*, and as such it is given preference. Showing that this is the right view helps rectify some administrative practices that are based on viewing the two as mutually contradictory. Here, what sometimes happens is that whenever an individual applies for a private *maṣlaḥa*, he is told that the general *maṣlaḥa* requires that his application be declined. The person who declines the application takes no measures to make sure whether or not the private *maṣlaḥa* can be achieved without discarding a general one, as, he thinks, the two are completely contradictory. In reality, such a contradiction is very rare. In most cases, combining the two *maṣlaḥas* is feasible at least through one reconciliatory aspect, if not through all aspects. Moreover, if combination is not possible, there will always be a way to compensate the individual by providing him with a *maṣlaḥa* that is similar or close to the one he has applied for, which is not contrary to the general *maṣlaḥa*. This will serve as an alternative to the one he has applied for.

3.2. Volume according to quantity

The value of acts differs according to their respective *maṣlaḥas* and what they entail. If the types of *maṣlaḥas* are of equal nature, then preference is determined according to quantity. A small number of the best *maṣlaḥas* may be given preference over a larger number of good ones. When the types of *maṣlaḥas* or *mafsadas* are equal, the many is given priority over the few.[50]

Here is an example from administration. Suppose that a farmer wants to sell his agricultural produce, and he has two options:

1. He sells them to an agricultural marketing company, making a profit of £100,000, with minimal cost to himself;
2. He takes his produce to the marketplace where he sells them, making a profit of £150,000.

However, when the farmer considers the time he will need to spend going to the marketplace and what he can do during that time if he concentrated on other matters, he finds that the time cost is equivalent to £60,000 in lost opportunities. Thus, the first option appears to be worth £10,000 more. In other words, the first option is more advantageous than the second by £10,000. Therefore, it is given preference. Al-ʿIzz b. ʿAbd al-Salām says, 'Reward varies according to the difference of actions' ranks. When two actions are equal in every respect, a greater reward is granted for the larger amount.'[51] This is indicated in the Qur'an: 'Whoever does an atom's weight of good shall see it then' (Q. 99:7).

4. The Criterion of Time

Ibn Masʿūd, the Prophet's companion, says, 'I have never regretted anything more than regretting a day that has passed, bringing my death closer, without having increased my good deeds.'[52] Ibn al-Qayyim says,

> The best, most sublime and most beneficial thoughts are those that are for God's sake and for reward in the Hereafter. The ones for God's sake are of different types [...] the fifth is thinking about time, its duties and functions and concentrating all one's effort to make good use of it. A knowledgeable person is the product of his time: if he wastes it, he actually wastes all of his *maṣlaḥas*, because every *maṣlaḥa* is the product of time. When time is lost it cannot be regained.[53]

A person who does not allocate adequate time for benefits to be achieved in quantity and quality will inevitably lose some of them. Every benefit has a particular time in which it can be better achieved. There are several considerations regarding time, each of which may be used to distinguish certain benefits from others, giving them higher or lower ranks when preferability is being determined. This is discussed below.

4.1. Time according to duration

What seems to be proposed within Islamic textual evidence is that giving help in doing what is permissible is a means to achieve its *maṣlaḥa*, while the *maṣlaḥa* of the help given comes mostly later in the Hereafter. The Qur'an states, 'Help one another in righteousness and piety' (Q. 5:2). This is, then, a means that is better than the purpose for which it is given and its reward is better and more lasting than the benefit of the person helped. The reason for this is that the reward for the help given, as proposed by this textual evidence, is granted by God on the Day of Judgement. An example follows related to administration.

By 'time duration', we actually mean the duration of the benefit. Suppose that you have a sum of money sufficient to buy a small apartment, which is less than what you have in mind, but sufficient for the present. Alternatively, you can use that money to buy a very luxurious car, or you can use it to take a recreational holiday in foreign countries. Which option will you take? The benefit of trips and journeys, particularly those that are not for scientific or medical purposes, is short lived, ending when one returns home. It is short when compared with the benefit of the other options. The luxury car may bring benefit that lasts for ten years. If you are the type of person who takes good care of cars, then it will give you its benefit for the medium term. The benefit of an apartment is long term, lasting for as long as you live in it. It is clearly apparent that the longer-lasting benefit should be given precedence over the shorter-lasting ones. However, it should be noted that all of these benefits are temporary, not permanent.

Moreover, the concepts of short, medium, and long term are relative, changing according to situation, place, time and person. What is long in someone's view may be considered short or medium by another, or by the same person in a different time, place or situation.

Some may say that all benefits will come to an end, which means that there is no permanent benefit. This is related to our concept of time and its duration. Islamic sources indicate that time does not begin with one's birth and does not end with one's death, and that there will be resurrection, reckoning, reward or punishment and heaven or hell. Hence, according to this understanding, the only permanent benefit is the reward for acts of the subject of the law in which they fulfil their obligation and do their good deeds. Such reward is suggested to benefit man in his present life and in the life to come and hence it is everlasting. Therefore, we find in the Qur'an a censure for those who prefer this life to the Hereafter, 'Yet you prefer this present life, while the life to come is better and longer lasting' (Q. 87:16–17).

Therefore, the permanent benefit is always given preference over the temporary one. Likewise, preference is given to a long-term benefit over a medium-term one, and to the medium-term over the short-term benefit. Thus, the longer benefit is the best when all other considerations are equal. When the choice is between a permanent benefit and a temporary one, the permanent is always given precedence. When it is between different durations of a temporary benefit, precedence is given to the longer lasting. The intention of emphasizing the beneficial works within Islamic textual evidence is to continue to reap their benefits.[54]

4.2. Time according to lapse

The less preferable action may be given time priority when the more preferable has ample time. An example from the acts of worship is that when the time period of an obligatory prayer starts, one should give priority to make the call to prayers (*adhān*), the *iqāma* (second short *adhān* announcing the start of actual prayer) and the regular recommended prayer, before offering the obligatory prayer. Likewise, the less preferable is given priority if it is feared that its time will elapse. An example is that of a person who sneezes during the *adhān* or when reading the Qur'an. He interrupts his action to praise God. Generally speaking, when there are several *maṣlaḥas* and one of them may be lost if delayed and another will not be lost, the one that is feared to be lost is done first.[55]

4.3. Time according to the starting point

The *maṣlaḥa* lies in performing acts of obedience early at their specified times. Nevertheless, delaying the midday prayer (*Ẓuhr*), for instance, when it is very hot in summer and praying is instead later, within the allowed time, is recommended. Although it is contrary to the principle of encouraging early compliance, such a delay means giving preference to a greater benefit over a lesser one. This is due to the fact that walking to the mosque when the temperature is at its highest disturbs tranquillity (*khushūʿ*) which is one of the essential features of prayer. Therefore, what helps maintain tranquillity, which is of a higher degree, is given priority over the early performance of the obligation, which is of a lesser degree.[56]

Here is an administrative example. A doctor is brought a patient suffering from a heart attack. He gives him a Nitroglycerine 0.4 mg tablet under his tongue. After the patient's condition has stabilized, he gives him a Nitroglycerine 10 mg patch. What is the difference between the two medications? And why were they given in this order?

The answer to these questions will explain the purpose for distinguishing benefits in accordance with their time of action. Benefits do not occur at the same speed. Some occur immediately, in one go, while others are slower or more gradual. The difference is in the speed of activity. The speed cannot be known unless we know how long the intended effect will take to materialize. The following details will explain the matter, in light of the previous example.

When the patient is admitted into the Emergency Department and his case is diagnosed, it is clear that he is in need of immediate treatment. Therefore, he is given the Nitroglycerine 0.4 mg pill under his tongue, because its effect is instantaneous. When his condition stabilizes, it is clear that he needs a long-term medicine to maintain this stability until he is fully cured. Therefore, the patch is given, because its effect is gradual and lasts for 12 hours. The important question for the decision maker is to decide which option is more preferable: the one producing the immediate benefit or the one with gradual benefit. The answer is certainly complex. The difference between the two options lies in the timing of and speed of their benefits. This is the difference with which we are concerned at this point, as preferability between the two options is in fact an issue of speed.

Which is the best timing of the benefit: the speedy one that occurs immediately or the slower, gradual one? The answer is that the quick one produces the desired effect. It is what matches the need. If the patient's need is immediate, then the treatment that produces an immediate effect is the one to choose. The reverse is also true. This means that both are needed, and neither replaces the other or is given preference over it in all situations, because both have a suitable speed of effect as long as the speed of the beneficial effect matches the speed required. In this process of preferability, the matching is the determining factor. Matching here means that the speed of the effect matches the urgency of the need. The more the speed of the beneficial effect matches the speed needed for the action, the more proper the option is, and therefore should be given preference over the lesser option.

The aspect of repetition must also be observed. According to their occurrence and speed, benefits are of two types: one with repeated effects and another that produces its effect only once. We have already discussed the process of choosing between two options, one with immediate benefit and one gradual. When the choice is between two types of *maṣlaḥa*, one with a repeated benefit and another with a single but gradual benefit, we need to know the total sum of the gradual benefit and compare it with the total of the repeated benefits within a specific time frame. Then we need to determine the greater benefit so as to decide the preference on its basis, unless the quicker benefit is urgently needed, in which case it is given preference.[57]

4.4. Time according to the start of the benefit

Securing *maṣlaḥas* is meant to obtain benefits. The time of securing the *maṣlaḥa* is not necessarily the same as the time at which it is benefited from. A *maṣlaḥa* may be secured today, but it may bring benefit later on. Thus, *maṣlaḥas* vary in the start time of their benefits. Some *maṣlaḥas* begin their benefit immediately, as is the case of removing harm, and some may begin to give benefit after a period of time that may be long or short.

An example is that a manager of a consultancy and economic studies firm conducts a feasibility study of a project to build a petrochemical plant for three businessmen. The first is a land merchant, the second a stocks and shares dealer and the third an industrialist. The study shows that the project will take two years to complete, at a cost of £100 million, with an expected net profit of £15 million a year. Each one of the three calculates how long it would take for the project to repay its capital. The land merchant works it out as two years, and after that the project will yield pure profit. The stock dealer puts it at three years, while the industrialist estimates it at eight years and eight months. How can the calculation give such widely different figures?

The answer is that they all based their calculations on the date at which they begin to benefit from the project after they recover their capital investment. The land merchant considers that his profit begins once the building phase is complete and production begins. At that moment he evaluates his share in the plant as the invested amount and the accrued profit. The stocks and shares dealer adds another year so that a financial year will have passed and profits will have been declared. His returns begin to accrue at the date when he receives his first dividend payment. The industrialist considers that he has first to recover his initial capital through the annual profits. His net profit begins after that. In other words, what he receives in the early years is repayment of the investment he paid. At the rate of £15 million a year, this will take six years and eight months. He added two years, which are needed for the project to be implemented, making a total of eight years and eight months.

The important question in this example concerns which of the three calculations is most accurate according to this standard. The answer is that the best is the one that fits best with the investor's objectives. People's needs differ, which means that the better and more preferable differs accordingly. What is essential is to apply the right standard in matching the need and the required benefit.

5. The Process of Determining Preferability

We conclude this brief outline of the criteria of preferability with a discussion of the process through which preferability is determined. With so many criteria and options in complex questions, the decision maker may need a methodology to clarify the obscure and look at the different considerations and information that should be taken into account. Such a task may be beyond his mental ability or material resources. So, people normally adopt a process to deal with such matters. As there are so many methods of calculation, we will confine ourselves to two types only, taking them by way of example.

The first is the method of mutual compensation between different considerations. This involves a process of trading off the advantages of one consideration for those of another, so as to choose the most important ones to the question of the decision. The second method relies on balancing out different considerations so as to discard those that contradict each other, leaving the preferable choice clear. The two methods overlap. The details of this will be illustrated with the example of choosing a partner for marriage.

The Prophet, peace be upon him, says, 'A woman is sought in marriage for four considerations: her beauty, her wealth, her family lineage and her piety. Be sure to take the pious, or you will be a loser.'[58] Suppose that a woman receives proposals of marriage from three different people or a man wants to propose to one of three women. How are they to determine whom to choose? In either case there are three options and four considerations that are directly related to the question of the marriage decision. There are also several patterns by which to conduct the process of determining preferability. Only some of these will be briefly mentioned, because a detailed discussion is beyond the scope of this study.

5.1. The ideal choice pattern

In this pattern, the person to make the choice visualizes an ideal option before comparing each of the available options to it. He then takes up the option that comes closest to this ideal and discards the others. With regard to marriage, young people paint a picture of what they want their life partners to be and then seek to find it in reality. This is easy to do, but unrealistic, as a person who follows this pattern sets certain standards that are difficult to fulfil in reality.

5.2. The matching pattern

According to this pattern, the man estimates to what extent each of the women matches the four considerations of beauty, wealth, family lineage and piety. He then follows one of several partial methods to determine the best choice. These partial methods are:

1. Addition: He sets a scale for each consideration and assigns to each girl a mark on that scale, say, one to 100. He then adds up the four marks. The one with the highest total is the one he chooses. However, this is not normally done in practice, because human life cannot be so mechanical.
2. Importance: The young man puts the relevant considerations in their order of importance, as he sees them. He then compares the girls according to the most important of these considerations. He either decides in favour of the girl that scores the highest mark in this consideration and proposes to her, or continues the process of determining preferability, using the second most important consideration, when the two scores of the first most important consideration are equal or close to each other. He may continue to do so until he weighs all considerations.
3. Weights: In this pattern, the young man assigns a weight to each consideration according to its importance. Two considerations may have the same weight or slightly different weights. He gives each girl a mark for each consideration. He then multiplies each mark by the weight assigned to each consideration before adding up the total. The one with the highest total is the most preferable.

5.3. The disagreement pattern

Pursuant to this pattern, a woman, for example, considers to what extent each of the suitors does not match the consideration that is most important to her. She then determines whether to accept his proposal or not. Or, when she receives more than one proposal, she carries out a process of preferability on this basis. She may do this in different ways, such as:

1. The minimum: She puts a minimum requirement for each consideration. Whoever of the suitors does not meet this minimum is left out. The preferability process continues only between those whose qualities are above the minimum of each consideration.
2. The graded minimum: She conducts the preferability process on the basis of the minimum of the most important consideration. If a suitor does not meet this minimum, he is left out regardless of how much he meets the other considerations.
3. The weighted minimum: She adds a weighting of importance to the minimum. She then considers whether a suitor meets the minimum required or not. Then the weighting given to the considerations is taken into account, and the results are set off against each other in relation to the different considerations. The net figure arrived at is the indication of preference.

When using either the matching or the disagreement pattern, one of two approaches may be used:

1. The options approach: The process of preferability is first applied to the options available. It is then undertaken between the equal or nearly equal options on the basis of the different considerations.
2. The considerations approach: The process of preferability is started on the basis of the different considerations. The options that are equal or nearly equal are then made the subject of preferability.

The first approach is used to reduce the options and the second to reduce the considerations when either are too many. Both approaches are meant to reduce the hardship accompanying the process of determining preferability.[59]

It is clear from even this simplified presentation of the process of determining preferability that it is not an easy process. Hence, many people start with reducing the complexity by attempting to reduce the options available and the considerations to be taken into account. While this is acceptable, or even preferable, in individual and not-so-important cases, it could be risky in relatively complex and important cases, unless it is accompanied by methodological regulations. This is because unless the process of determining preferability is conducted on the basis of a clear policy, it may be flawed through bias and lack of objectivity, which can distort reality.

As shown above, the considerations are divided into basic areas, which are rank, stability, time and volume. Each consideration branches out into secondary considerations, which are subdivided into grades. This means that there is a large and complex number of points to be considered. They are not all expected to be considered whenever a decision needs to be taken. However, the more important a question is and the closer to one another its options are, the greater the need to use complex processes with multiple and complex considerations. Hence, the mathematical aspect is introduced. There is also a numerical aspect utilized in computer systems with regard to artificial intelligence, expert systems and decision support systems. Numerous works have been published in this area.[60]

Returning to the question of spousal selection:

1. Islamically, the most important consideration in choosing one's spouse is piety. This is based on the Prophet's advice, 'Be sure to take the pious, or you will be a loser.'[61] As such, certain procedures follow, such as:

    i. The piety consideration is taken out of the process of preferability, because it is of a higher rank than the other three, i.e. beauty, family lineage and wealth.
    ii. Piety is considered the minimum.

2. The other considerations are left to choice. Everyone may choose which of the other considerations should be given priority, in accordance with what they know to be more relevant to their cases and more conducive to ensuring happiness in their family lives.

Choosing between *maṣlaḥas* is first considered on the basis of their rank. When they are of equal rank, then they are considered on the basis of the benefits they produce. Both elements are also valued according to the degree of the *maṣlaḥa*'s acceptability and its consequent stability. All these considerations may vary according to suitable or unsuitable times. Hence, the criteria of *maṣlaḥa* and their distinction, be it according to type or degree, are all subject to the process of preferability. They all operate in the same situation, time and place, as they interact and are interlinked. Therefore, the process of preferability should be first considered in a holistic way, then the details should be looked at and finally the results of the preferability process should be arrived at. If the process is run in this way, the decision maker will be able to determine the most preferable choice.

In this chapter we have discussed determining preferability on the basis of degree, and type, as well as the criteria of preferability. Now, we need to conclude with the following methodological points:

1. The fulfilment of one's liability by choosing an option on the basis of an item in the preferability process, whether on the basis of type, degree or consideration, is understood to be a matter of surmise.
2. The relation between the items of the process of preferability, whether relating to type, degree or consideration, is definitive.
3. When it is found multiple times that a given item in the preferability process leads to the fulfilment of one's responsibility and when this includes type, degree and considerations, this leads to definitive results.

This means that the relation between the items of a continuous whole in this field is definitive, but its presence in the details, the options subject to decision, is a matter of surmise, or probability. However, when assumptions in all the links converge, they complement one another in indicating that one's liability is fulfilled through the details. Thus, they, in their sum, become factually, or at least theoretically, definitive in indicating that the decision taken through them to fulfil one's responsibility ensures the result of a definitive *maṣlaḥa*.[62]

CONCLUSION

This work has introduced a group of concepts that are considered part of the wise thinking and reflection that humanity uses to achieve its *maṣlaḥas*. In Islamic law, these *maṣlaḥas* are governed by rulings, methods and tools that serve as regulations. The study has presented the operating system of the approved *maṣlaḥas* in Islamic law by analysing critically its components and explaining how they operate with one another as a cohesive system.

For *maṣlaḥa* to be governed by Islamic law, it requires regulators with a specific function, which is to allow it to secure its object moderately with neither negligence nor excessiveness. First, there was a need to ensure that *maṣlaḥa* is not contrary to the Sharīʿa, to examine whether or not *maṣlaḥa* exists and is considered by Islamic law. Secondly, it has been clarified that there is a difference between *maṣlaḥa* and benefit, *maṣlaḥa* being the highest possible benefit. Consequently, every *maṣlaḥa* is a benefit, but not the reverse. The regulator of this differentiation is that a *maṣlaḥa* must not exclude a better *maṣlaḥa*. This can be achieved only when the *maṣlaḥa* is considered as the highest possible benefit, without losing any possible better option. The criterion of the highest benefit is constant in the sense that it is always required, possible, comprehensive and inclusive of all that humanity can produce of benefits and ways of securing them. Third, it was established that securing the *maṣlaḥa* must not lead to an equal or greater *mafsada*, and this regulator demonstrated how *maṣlaḥa* may be used in a way that preserves the Sharīʿa's fundamental purposes.

Perhaps the most important contribution of this study is that it shows the role of the religious *maṣlaḥas* in the legitimate adjustment of rulings according to the circumstances of life, which is merely one of the Sharīʿa's tools to adapt people's needs at all times to the requirements of Islamic law.

NOTES

Chapter One: What is *Maṣlaḥa*?

1 Abū al-Faḍl Jamāl al-Dīn Muḥammad b. Makram Ibn Manẓūr, *Lisān al-ʿArab*, ed. ʿAlī Shīrī, 1st edition (Beirut: Dār Iḥyā' al-Turāth al-ʿArabī, 1408 AH/1988), pp. 384–7.

2 Ramaḍān ʿAbd al-Wadūd al-Lakhmī, *Al-Taʿlīl bi al-Maṣlaḥa ʿinda al-Uṣūliyyīn*, 1st edition (Cairo: Dār al-Hudā li al-Ṭibāʿa, 1407 AH/1987), pp. 10–11.

3 Muḥammad b. Muḥammad b. Muḥammad al-Ghazālī, *Al-Mustaṣfā min ʿIlm al-Uṣūl*. ed. Ḥamza Zuhayr Ḥāfiẓ, 1st edition (Medina: Sharikat al-Madīna al-Munawwara li al-Ṭibāʿa wa al-Nashr, n.d.), vol. 2, pp. 481–2.

4 For his profile, see Abū Bakr b. Hidāyat Allāh al-Husaynī, *Ṭabaqāt al-Shāfiʿiyyā*, ed. ʿĀdil Nuwayhiḍ, 2nd edition (Dār al-Āfāq, 1399 AH/1997), p. 222; Al-Ziriklī, *Al-Aʿlām*, vol. 4, p. 313.

5 ʿAbd al-ʿAzīz al-ʿIzz b. ʿAbd al-Salām b. Abū al-Qāsim, *Al-Qawāʾid al-Kubra*, (alias) *Qawāʾid al-Aḥkām fi Iṣlāḥ al-Anām*, ed. Nazīh Ḥammād and ʿUthmān Ḍamīriyya, 1st edition (Damascus: Dār al-Qalam, 1421 AH/2000), vol. 1, p. 18.

6 Ibn Taymiyya, *Majmūʿ al-Fatāwā*, vol. 11, p. 343.

7 Al-Lakhmī, *Al-Taʿlīl bi al-Maṣlaḥa ʿinda al-Uṣūliyyīn*, p. 14.

8 Al-Ḥusaynī, *Ṭabaqāt al-Shāfiʿiyya*, pp. 217–18.

9 Fakhr al-Dīn Muḥammad b. ʿUmar b. al-Ḥusayn al-Rāzī, *Al-Maḥṣūl fī ʿIlm Uṣūl al-Fiqh*, ed. Jābir Fayyāḍ al-ʿAlwāni, 1st edition (Beirut: Dār al-Kutub al-ʿIlmiyya, 1418 AH/1998), vol. 2, p. 39.

10 Q. 5:48.

11 Q. 41:42.

12 Ibn Taymiyya, *Majmūʿ al-Fatāwā*, vol. 2, p. 583.

13 For some of those who reported *ijmā*ʿ (unanimous agreement) in this regard, see section 2.3 of this chapter.

14 Q. 5:3.

15 Ibrāhīm b. Mūsā b. Muḥammad al-Shāṭibī, *Al-Muwāfaqāt*, ed. ʿAbd Allāh Draz (Beirut: Dār al-Maʿrifa, n.d.); also see al-Shāṭibī, *Al-Iʿtiṣām*, 2nd edition (Amman: Al-Dār al-Athariyya, 1428 AH/2007), vol. 2, pp. 55–6.

16 See his profile in Ibn Khallikān, *Wafayāt al-Aʿyān*, vol. 3, p. 256.

17 ʿAlī b. Muḥammad al-Āmidī, *Al-Iḥkām fī Uṣūl al-Aḥkām*, 1st edition (Beirut: al-Maktab al-Islāmī, 1402 AH/1982), vol. 1, p. 54.

18 Muḥammad al-Amīn b. Muḥammad al-Mukhtār al-Shanqīṭī, *Aḍwāʾ al-Bayān* (Beirut: Dār al-Fikr, 1415 AH/1995), vol. 4, p. 214.

19 Ibn Taymiyya, *Majmūʿ al-Fatāwā*, vol. 11, p. 344.

20 Al-ʿIzz b. ʿAbd al-Salām, *Mukhtaṣar al-Fawāʾid fī Aḥkām al-Maqāṣid*, (alias) *al-Qawāʾid al-Ṣughra*, ed. Ṣāliḥ b. ʿAbd al- ʿAzīz al-Manṣūr, 1st edition (Riyadh: Dār al-Furqān, 1417 AH/1997), p. 18.

21 Muḥammad b. Muḥammad b. al-Ḥusayn b. Abū Yaʿlā, *Ṭabaqāt al-Ḥanābila*, ed. ʿAbd al-Raḥmān al- ʿUthaymīn (n.p., 1419 AH/1999), vol. 2, pp. 366–70; Al-Ziriklī, *Al-Aʿlām*, vol. 3, p. 127.

22 Najm al-Dīn al-Ṭūfi, *Kitāb al-Taʿyīn fī Sharḥ al-Arbaʿīn*, ed. Aḥmad Ḥājj ʿUthmān, 1st edition (Beirut: Muʾassasat al-Rayyān, 1419 AH/1998), p. 240.

23 Al-Lakhmī, *Al-Taʿlīl bi al-Maṣlaḥa ʿinda al-Uṣūliyyīn*, pp. 22–5.

24 Muḥammad b. Abū Bakr b. al-Qayyim, *Iʿlām al-Muwaqqiʿīn ʿan Rabb al-ʿĀlamīn*, 1st edition (Beirut: Al-Maktaba al-ʿAṣriyya, 1407 AH/1987), vol. 3, pp. 6–7.

25 For his profile, see Kaḥḥāla, *Muʿjam al-Muʾallifīn*, vol. 1, p. 174.

26 Ibrāhīm b. Mūsā b. Muḥammad al-Shāṭibī, *Al-Muwāfaqāt*, 1st edition (KSA, Al-Khubar: Dār Ibn ʿAffān, 1417 AH/1997), vol. 1, p. 53.

27 Muḥammad al-Ṭāhir b. Muḥammaḍ al-Shādhilī b. ʻAbd al-Qādir b. Muḥammaḍ Ibn ʿĀshūr (1296–1394 AH). He joined Al-Zaytūna Mosque in 1310 and became the Imām and Head Mufti of Mālikīs. He also held the position of *Naqīb al-Ashrāf* in Tunisia, and was one of its most prominent scholars. His works include: *Shifāʾ al-Qalb al-Jarīḥ*, *Sharḥ al-Burda*, *Maqāṣid al-Sharīʿa al-Islāmiyya*, *Uṣūl al-Niẓām al-Ijtimāʿī fī al-Islām* and *al-Taḥrīr wa al-Tanwīr fi Tafsīr al-Qurʾān*. See Al-Ziriklī, *Al-Aʿlām*, vol. 6, pp. 173–4.

28 Muḥammad Ibn ʻĀshūr, *Maqāṣid al-Sharīʻa al-Islāmiyya*, revised by Mohammed Tahar Almisawi, 2nd edition (Amman: Dār Al-Nafāʾis, 1421 AH/2001), p. 48.
29 Q. 16:90.
30 Al-Lakhmī, *Al-Taʿlīl bi al-Maṣlaḥa ʿinda al-Uṣūliyyīn*, p. 28.
31 Q. 16:90.
32 Ibn ʿAbd al-Salām, *Al-Qawāʻid al-Kubrā*, vol. 2, p. 315.
33 Ibn ʿAbd al-Salām, *Mukhtaṣar al-Fawāʾid*, pp. 109–14.
34 Q. 99:7–8.
35 Q. 10:57–8.
36 Al-Ṭūfī, *Kitāb al-Taʿyīn fī Sharḥ al-Arbaʿīn*, pp. 240–1.
37 Q. 2:185.
38 Al-Ṭūfī, *Kitāb al-Taʿyīn fī Sharḥ al-Arbaʿīn*, pp. 236–7.
39 Q. 22:78.
40 Q. 2:220.
41 Q. 7:56.
42 Q. 9:120.
43 Q. 42:40.
44 Narrated by Mālik in *Al-Muwaṭṭaʾ* (as a saying of a Companion of the Prophet) in *Bāb al-Qaḍāʾ*, vol. 2, p. 745. It was also narrated on the authority of ʿUbādah b. al-Ṣāmit as a saying of the Prophet himself. This is in Ibn Mājah's *Sunan*, vol. 2, p. 44 in *Bāb man Banā fi Ḥaqqih ma Yaḍūrru bi Jārih*. Al-Albānī classified this *ḥadīth* as authentic in his *Irwāʾ al-Ghalīl*, vol. 3, p. 413.
45 See also al-Ṭūfī, *Al-Taʿyīn fī Sharḥ al-Arbaʿīn*, pp. 234–80.
46 Narrated by Muslim in his *Ṣaḥīḥ*, *Bāb al-Īmān*, vol. 1, p. 163.
47 Muḥammad Saʿīd Ramaḍān al-Būṭī, *Ḍawābiṭ al-Maṣlaḥa fī al-Sharīʿa al-Islāmiyya*, 1st edition (Damascus: al-Dār al-Muttaḥida, 1412 AH/1992), p. 73.
48 Narrated by al-Bukhārī in his *Ṣaḥīḥ*, *Bāb al-Ṣulḥ*, vol. 3, p. 170.
49 Al-Āmidī, *Al-Iḥkām fī Uṣūl al-Aḥkām*, vol. 3, p. 54.
50 Al-Ṭūfī, *Al-Taʿyīn fī Sharḥ al-Arbaʿīn*, p. 244.
51 For his profile, see Ibn Khallikān, *Wafayāt al-Aʿyān*, vol. 4, p. 135.
52 Muḥammad b. Aḥmad b. ʿAbd al-ʿAzīz Ibn al-Najjār, *Sharḥ al-Kawkab al-Munīr*, (alias) *Mukhtaṣar al-Taḥrīr* or *Al-Mukhtabar al-Mubtakar fī Uṣūl al-Fiqh al-Islāmi*, 1st edition (Riyadh: Maktabat al-ʿUbaykān, n.d.), vol. 1, pp. 313–14.
53 Al-Lakhmī, *Al-Taʿlīl bi al-Maṣlaḥa ʿinda al-Uṣūliyyīn*, p. 54.

54 ʿUthmān b. Ibrāhīm b. Murshid al-Murshid, *Al-Maqāṣid min Aḥkām al-Shāriʿ wa Atharuhā fī al-ʿUqūd*, unpublished research, Umm Al-Qurā University, 1402 AH/1982, p. 44; Al-Lakhmī, *Al-Taʿlīl bi al-Maṣlaḥa*, p. 55.

55 Al-Lakhmī, *Al-Taʿlīl bi al-Maṣlaḥa*, p. 8.

56 Al-Murshid, *Al-Maqāṣid min Aḥkām al-Shāriʿ*, p. 14.

57 Muṣṭafā Zayd, *Al-Maṣlaḥa fī al-Tashrīʿ al-Islāmī wa Najm al-Dīn al-Ṭūfī*, 2nd edition (Cairo: Dār al-Fikr al-ʿArabī, 1964), p. 143.

58 Q. 28:77.

59 Yūsuf Ḥāmid al-ʿĀlim, *Al-Maqāṣid al-ʿĀmma li al-Sharīʿa al-Islāmiyya*, 2nd edition (Riyadh: al-Dār al-ʿĀlamiyya li al-Kitāb wa al-Sunna, 1414 AH/1994), p. 46.

60 Al-Qarāfī, *Al-Furūq*, vol. 1, p. 317.

61 Al-Buṭī, *Ḍawābiṭ al-Maṣlaḥa fī al-Sharīʿa al-Islāmiyya*, p. 89.

62 Ibn ʿAbd al-Salām, *Mukhtaṣar al-Fawāʾid fī Aḥkām al-Maqāṣid*, p. 119.

63 Al-Buṭi, *Ḍawābiṭ al-Maṣlaḥa fī al-Sharīʿa al-Islāmiyya*, p. 47.

64 Al-Shāṭibī, *Al-Muwāfaqāt*, vol. 2, p. 63.

65 Q. 11:15–16.

66 Q. 18:104.

67 Q. 2:200.

68 Al-ʿĀlim, *Al-Maqāṣid al-ʿĀmma li al-Sharīʿa al-Islāmiyya*, pp. 325–6.

69 Ibn ʿAbd al-Salām, *Al-Qawāʾid al-Kubrā*, vol. 1, p. 7.

70 Abū Ḥāmid al-Ghazālī, *Maʿārij al-Quds fī Madārij al-Nafs*, 2nd edition (Beirut: Dār al-Āfāq al-Jadīda, 1975), p. 57.

71 Q. 24:35.

72 Al-Rāghib al-Aṣfahānī, *Tafṣīl al-Nashʾatayn wa Taḥṣīl al-Saʿādatayn*, ed. ʿAbd al-Majīd al-Najjār, 1st edition (Beirut: Dār al-Gharb al-Islāmī, 1408 AH/1988), pp. 140–3. That this statement is quoted by al-Ghazālī from al-Aṣfahānī's work can be proven by numerous indications. First, al-Aṣfahānī lived before al-Ghazālī and died in the early fifth century AH. Most of al-Aṣfahānī's biographers mentioned that he died in the early sixth century (502 AH). However, thorough investigation proves that he died in the early fifth century. Having edited al-Aṣfahānīs *Mufradāt Alfāẓ al-Qurʾān*, Dāwūdī provided an extensive biography of al-Aṣfahānī and used numerous evidences and proofs to show that al-Aṣfahānī died in approximately 425 AH. See Ṣafwān Dāwūdī (ed.), *Mufradāt Alfāẓ al-Qurʾān*, pp. 24–7. Al-Ghazālī died in the early sixth century AH. Second,

al-Ghazālī admired al-Aṣfahānī's works, notably his book *Al-Dharī'ah ilā Makārim al-Sharī'a*, which he is said to have carried with him all the time.

73 Ibn ʿAbd al-Salām, *Al-Qawāʾid al-Kubrā* (Beirut: Dār al-Kutub al-ʿIlmiyya), vol. 2, p. 189.

74 Ibn ʿAbd al-Salām, *Al-Qawāʾid al-Kubrā*, vol. 1, p. 13.

75 Al-ʿĀlim, *Al-Maqāṣid al-ʿĀmma li al-Sharīʿa al-Islāmiyya*, pp. 344–5.

76 Ibn ʿAbd al-Salām, *Al-Qawāʾid al-Kubrā*, vol. 1, p. 16.

77 ʿĪsā Manūn, *Nibrās al-ʿUqūl fī Taḥqīq al-Qiyās ʿinda ʿUlamāʾ al-Uṣūl*, 1st edition (Egypt: Maṭbaʿat al-Taḍāmun al-Akhawī, 1345 AH), pp. 92–113.

78 Abū Ḥāmid al-Ghazālī, *Al-Mustaṣfā min ʿIlm al-Uṣūl*, 3rd edition (Beirut: Dār Iḥyā' al-Turāth al-ʿArabī, 1414 AH/1993), vol. 1, p. 6.

79 Al-Shāṭibī, *Al-Muwāfaqāt*, vol. 1, p. 125.

80 Al-Shāṭibī, *Al-Muwāfaqāt*, vol. 1, p. 125; Ṣiddīq Khān, *Al-Dīn al-Khāliṣ*, 1st edition (Cairo: Maktabat Dār al-Turāth, n.d.), vol. 1, p. 143; Al-ʿĀlim, *Al-Maqāṣid al-Sharʿiyya*, p. 347.

81 Ibn Taymiyya, *Majmūʿ al-Fatāwā*, vol. 3, p. 338.

82 Ibn Taymiyya, *Majmūʿ al-Fatāwā*, vol. 19, p. 288.

83 Ibn Taymiyya, *Majmūʿ al-Fatāwā*, vol. 9, p. 279. 'Clear' here means evident and unmixed with any troubling element.

84 Ibn Taymiyya, *Majmūʿ al-Fatāwā*, vol. 9, p. 227.

85 Ibn Taymiyya, *Majmūʿ al-Fatāwā*, vol. 9, p. 228.

86 Q. 3:66.

87 Q. 16:74.

Chapter Two: Types of *Maṣlaḥa*

1 Ramaḍān 'Abd al-Wadūd al-Lakhmī, *Al-Taʿlīl bi al-Maṣlaḥa ʿinda al-Uṣūliyyīn*, 1st edition (Cairo: Dār al-Hudā li al-Ṭibāʿa, 1407 AH/1987), pp. 150–1.

2 ʿAbd al-Raḥman b. ʿAbd Allāh al-ʿAbd al-Karīm al-Darwīsh, *Al-Maṣāliḥ al-Mursala fī al-Sharīʿa al-Islāmiyya* (Riyadh: al-Maʿhad al-ʿĀlī li al-Qaḍāʾ, Imām Muḥammad b. Saud Islamic University, 1389 AH/1968), p. 15.

3 Aḥmad b. ʿAbd al-Ḥalīm b. Taymiyya, *Ziyārat al-Qubūr wa al-Istinjād bi al-Maqbūr*, 1st edition (Ṭanṭa: Dār al-Ṣaḥāba li al-Turāth, n.d.), p. 53.

4 Al-Lakhmī, *Al-Ta'līl bi al-Maṣlaḥa*, pp. 155–6.
5 Al-Shāṭibī, *al-Muwāfaqāt*, vol. 2, p. 15.
6 Al-Darwīsh, *Al-Maṣāliḥ al-Mursala*, p. 15.
7 'Uthman b. 'Umar b. Abū Bakr b. al-Ḥājib, *Mukhtaṣar al-Muntahā bi Sharḥ al-'Aḍud* (Bulāq, 1316 AH), vol. 2, p. 339; 'Alī b. Muḥammad al-Āmidī, *Al-Iḥkām fī Uṣūl al-Aḥkām*, 1st edition (Beirut: al-Maktab al-Islāmī, 1402 AH/1982), vol. 1, p. 270.
8 Al-Darwīsh, *Al-Maṣāliḥ al-Mursala*, p. 19.
9 This is according to Ibn al-Subkī who considers the strange *munāsib* the same as the nullified *munāsib*. This differs from what is followed in this study where the strange *maṣlaḥa* is used to express the strange *munāsib*, not the nullified *munāsib*, as shall be explained later.
10 Al-Darwīsh, *Al-Maṣāliḥ al-Mursala*, p. 19.
11 Fahd b. Sa'd al-Zāydī al-Juhanī, *Al-Qiyās 'inda al-Imām al-Shāfi'ī: Dirāsa Ta'ṣīliyya*, 1st edition (Riyadh: Imām Muḥammad b. Saud Islamic University, 1424 AH/2003), vol. 1, p. 484.
12 Najm al-Dīn b. Sulaymān b.'Abd al-Karīm al-Ṭūfī, *Sharḥ Mukhtaṣar al-Rawḍa*, ed. 'Abd Allāh 'Abd al-Muḥsin al-Turkī, 1st edition (Beirut: Mu'assasat al-Risāla, 1408 AH/1988), vol. 3, pp. 382–5.
13 Al-Ṭūfī, *Sharḥ Mukhtaṣar al-Rawḍa*, vol. 3, p. 382.
14 Al-Ṭūfī, *Sharḥ Mukhtaṣar al-Rawḍa*, vol. 3, p. 384.
15 Al-Ṭūfī, *Sharḥ Mukhtaṣar al-Rawḍa*, vol. 3, p. 384.
16 Al-Ṭūfī, *Sharḥ Mukhtaṣar al-Rawḍa*, vol. 3, p. 385.
17 Al-Ṭūfī, *Sharḥ Mukhtaṣar al-Rawḍa*, vol. 3, pp. 382–5.
18 Al-Husaynī, *Ṭabaqāt al-Shāfi'īyya*, p. 241; Al-Ziriklī, *Al-A'lām*, vol. 6, p. 60; Kaḥḥāla, *Mu'jam al-Mu'allifīn*, vol. 9, p. 121.
19 Al-Ḥusaynī, *Ṭabaqāt al-Shāfi'īyya*, p. 174.
20 Shawkānī quoting al-Khawarizmī, al-Ghazālī and Ibn Burhān. See Muḥammad Ali Shawkānī, *Irshād al-Fuḥūl ilā Taḥqīq alḥaq min 'ilm al-Uṣūl*, revised by Abu Ḥafṣ Sami ibn Arab al-Atharī, 1st edition (Riyadh Dār al-Faḍilah, 2000), vol. 2, p. 990.
21 Muḥammad b. Bahādir b. 'Abd Allāh al-Zarkashī, *Al-Baḥr al-Muḥīṭ fī Uṣūl al-Fiqh*, eds. 'Abd al-Sattār Abū Ghudda and 'Abd al-Qādir 'Abd Allāh al-'Ānī, 2nd edition (Kuwait: Ministry of Endowments and Islamic Affairs, 1413 AH/1992), vol. 4, p. 377.
22 Al-Shāṭibī, *Al-Muwāfaqāt*, vol. 3, p. 41.
23 Al-Shāṭibī, *Al-Muwāfaqāt*, vol. 3, p. 74.
24 'Abd Allāh b. Aḥmad b. Muḥammad Ibn Qudāma, *Rawḍat al-Nāẓir wa*

Junnat al-Munāẓir, ed. ʿAbd al-ʿAzīz ʿAbd al-Raḥmān al-Saʿīd, 2nd edition (Riyadh: Imām Muḥammad b. Saud Islamic University, 1399 AH), p. 304; ʿAli b. Muḥammad al-Āmidī, *Al-Iḥkām fī Uṣūl al-Aḥkām*, ed. Sayyid al-Jumaylī, 1st edition (Beirut: Dār al-Kitāb al-ʿArabī, 1404 AH), vol. 3, p. 313; Najm al-Dīn al-Ṭūfī, *Sharḥ Mukhtaṣar al-Rawḍa*, ed. ʿAbd Allāh b. ʿAbd al-Muḥsin al-Turkī, 4th edition (Beirut: Muʾassasat al-Risāla, 1424 AH/2003), vol. 3, p. 394; Muḥammad b. ʿUmar b. al-Ḥusayn al-Rāzī, *Al-Maḥṣūl fī ʿIlm al-Uṣūl*, ed. Ṭāha Jābir al-ʿAlwānī, 1st edition (Riyadh: Imām Muḥammad b. Saud Islamic University, 1400 AH), vol. 5, p. 232; ʿAbd al-Wahhāb b. ʿAli b. ʿAbd al-Kāfī b. al-Subkī, *Al-Jawāmiʿ: Nuskhat Ḥāshiyat al-ʿAṭṭār ʿalā Sharḥ al-Jalāl al-Maḥallī ʿalā al-Jawāmiʿ li Ḥasan b. Muḥammad b. Maḥmūd al-ʿAṭṭār al-Shāfiʿī* (Beirut: Dār al-Kutub al-ʿIlmiyya, n.d.), vol. 2, p. 327; ʿAbd Allāḥ b. al-Ḥājj Ibrāhīm al-Shanqīṭī, *Marāqī al-Suʿūd li Mubtaghī al-Ruqiyy wa al-Ṣuʿūd: Nuskhat Nathr al-Wurūd ʿalā Marāqī al-Suʿūd li Muḥammad al-Amīn b. Muḥammad al-Mukhtār al-Shanqīṭī*, 1st edition (Beirut: al-Maṭbaʿa al-ʿAṣriyya, 1425 AH/2004), p. 338.

25 Al-Shāīṭibī, *Al-Iʿtiṣām*, ed. ʿAbd al-Razzāq al-Mahdī (Beirut: Dār al-Kitāb al-ʿArabī, 1416 AH/1996), vol. 2, pp. 96–8.

26 Abū Ḥāmid Muḥammad b. Muḥammad b. Muḥammad al-Ghazālī, *Shifāʾ al-Ghalīl fī Bayān al-Shabah wa al-Makhīl wa Masālik al-Taʿlīl*, ed. Ḥamad al-Kubaysī, 1st edition (Baghdad: Maṭbaʿat al-Irshād, 1390 AH/ 1971), p. 189.

27 Al-Ghazālī, *Al-Mustaṣfā min ʿIlm al Uṣūl*, vol. 1, pp. 195–6; Al-Lakhmī, *Al-Taʿlīl bi al-Maṣlaḥa*, p. 174.

28 Al-Shāṭibī, *Al-Muwāfaqāt*, vol. 2, p. 31.

29 Al-Shāṭibī, *Al-Muwāfaqāt*, vol. 4, p. 14.

30 Al-Shāṭibī, *A-Iʿtiṣām*, vol. 2, p. 115.

31 Al-Lakhmī, *Al-Taʿlīl bi al-Maṣlaḥa*, pp. 177–9.

32 Al-Dhahabī, *Tadhkirat al-Ḥuffāẓ*, vol. 1, p. 168; Ibn Khallikān, *Wafayāt al-Aʿyān*, vol. 5, p. 405; Al-Ziriklī, *Al-Aʿlām*, vol. 8, p. 36.

33 Ibn Abū Yaʿlā, *Ṭabaqāt al-Ḥanābila*, vol. 1, p. 8; Al-Ziriklī, *Al-Aʿlām*, vol. 1, p. 203.

34 See ʿAbd al-Malik b. ʿAbd Allāh Abū al-Maʿālī al-Juwaynī, *Al-Burhān fī Uṣūl al-Fiqh*, ed. ʿAbd al-ʿAẓīm Maḥmūd al-Dīb, 4th edition (Al-Manuṣūra, Egypt: Dār al-Wafāʾ, 1418 AH), vol. 2, p. 722; Al-Ghazālī, *Al-Mustaṣfā*, 1st edition (Beirut: Dār al-Kutub al-ʿIlmiyya, 1431 AH/1993), p. 180; Al-Rāzī, *Al-Maḥṣūl fī ʿIlm al-Uṣūl*, ed. Ṭāḥa Jābir al-ʿAlwānī, 1st

edition (Riyadh: Imām Muḥammad b. Saud Islamic University, 1400 AH), vol. 6, p. 222; Taqī al-Dīn Abū al-Baqā' al-Ḥanbalī al-Futūḥī, *Sharḥ al-Kawkab al-Munīr* (Maṭbaʿat al-Sunna al-Muḥammadiyya, n.d.), p. 596.

35 Al-Zarkashī, *Al-Baḥr al-Muḥīt* (Dār Alkitbi, 1414 AH/1994), vol. 8, p. 84.

36 Al-Ziriklī, *Al-Aʿlām*, vol. 4, p. 110.

37 This disagreement is documented by al-Zarkashī in *al-Baḥr al-Muḥīṭ*, vol. 4, pp. 377–9.

38 Al-Shāṭibī says, 'The Unrestricted *maṣlaḥa* was acted upon by the righteous predecessors of the Companions and those who came after them. So, it is, according to the scholars of *uṣūl*, one of the approved juristic sources. Though there is some disagreement regarding this, this does not nullify what we are talking about.' Al-Shāṭibī, *Al-Iʿtiṣām*, vol. 1, p. 185. He also said, 'If the aforementioned disagreement of scholars about the unrestricted *maṣlaḥa* is used as a counter argument on the basis that the ruling is incorrect according to some *uṣūlīs*, then the evidence against such a claim would be the consensus of the Companions regarding [the collection of] the Qur'an in one book (*muṣḥaf*) and to refer to it. Once this is established in one instance, it is also established in all [similar] cases. This renders irrelevant any (considerable) disagreement among scholars except in sub-issues or details.' Al-Shāṭibī, *Al-Iʿtiṣām*, vol. 1, p. 187. See also Al-Lakhmī, *Al-Taʿlīl bi al-Maṣlaḥa*, p. 221.

39 Al-Darwīsh, *Al-Maṣāliḥ al-Mursala*, p. 17.

40 Al-Darwīsh, *Al-Maṣāliḥ al-Mursala*, p. 17.

41 Al-Darwīsh, *Al-Maṣāliḥ al-Mursala*, p. 17.

42 Al-Darwīsh, *Al-Maṣāliḥ al-Mursala*, p. 17.

43 Al-Ghazālī, *Al-Mustaṣfā*, vol. 2, p. 414.

44 Al-Juhanī, *Al-Qiyās ʿinda al-Shāfiʿī*, p. 564.

45 Al-Darwīsh, *Al-Maṣāliḥ al-Mursala*, p. 23.

46 Al-Lakhmī, *Al-Taʿlīl bi al-Maṣlaḥa*, p. 343.

47 Aḥmad b. Idrīs b. Abd al-Raḥmān Al-Qarāfī, *Nafā'is al-Uṣūl fī Sharḥ al-Maḥṣūl*, ed. Ali Muḥammad Muawwaḍ and ʿĀdil Aḥmad ʿAbd al-Mawjūd, 3rd edition (Beirut: Al-Maktaba al-ʿAṣriyya, 1419 AH/1999), vol. 3, p. 202.

48 See footnote no. 4, p. 38 in Al-Shāṭibī, *Al-Muwāfaqāt*, ed. Ibrahīm Ramaḍan, with comments by ʿAbd Allāh Draz, 4th edition (Beirut: Dār al-Maʿrifa, 1420 AH/1999).

49 Al-Shāṭibī, *Al-Muwāfaqāt*, vol. 1, p. 196; Al-Lakhmī, *Al-Taʿlīl bi al-Maṣlaḥa*, p. 344.

50 See al-Darwīsh, *Al-Maṣāliḥ al-Mursala*, p. 33.
51 Al-Shāṭibī, *Al-I'tiṣām*, p. 134.

Chapter Three: *Maṣlaḥa* Regulators: Function and Types

1 Al-Shāṭibī, *Al-Muwāfaqāt*, vol. 5, p. 42.
2 'Abd al-Malik b. 'Abd Allāh, Abū al-Ma'ālī al-Juwaynī, *Al-Burhān fī Uṣūl al-Fiqh*, 1st edition (Al-Manṣūra, Egypt: Dār al-Wafā', 1412 AH/1992), vol. 2, p. 1221.
3 Abū Ḥāmid Muḥammad b. Muḥammad al-Ghazālī, *Iḥyā' 'Ulūm al-Dīn* (Cairo: Maktabat Miṣr, n.d.), vol. 2, p. 332.
4 Ibn Manẓūr, *Lisān al-'Arab*, vol. 8, pp. 16–17.
5 Abū al-Ḥasan Aḥmad b. Fāris b. Zakariyya b. Fāris, *Mu'jam Maqāyīs al-Lugha*, ed. 'Abd al-Salām Muḥammad Hārūn, 2nd edition (Cairo: Maktabat Muṣṭafā al-Bābī al-Ḥalabī, n.d.) vol. 3, p. 386.
6 Abū al-Baqā' Ayyūb b. Mūsā al-Ḥusaynī al-Kafawī, *Al-Kuliyyāt: Mu'jam fī al-Muṣṭalaḥāt wal-Furūq al-Lughawiyya* (Beirut: Mu'assasat al-Risāla, 1418 AH/1998), p. 728.
7 Ibn 'Āshūr, *Maqāṣid al-Sharī'a*, p. 52.
8 Muḥammad Sa'd b. Aḥmad b. Mas'ūd al-Yūbī, *Maqāṣid al-Sharī'a al-Islāmiyya wa 'Ilāqatuha bi al-Adilla al-Shar'iyya*, 1st edition (Riyadh: Dār al-Hijra, 1419 AH/1998), p. 442.
9 Al-Shāṭibī, *Al-Muwāfaqāt*, vol. 2, p. 163.
10 Al-Shāṭibī, *Al-Muwāfaqāt*, vol. 1, pp. 308–9.
11 Al-Yūbī, *Maqāṣid al-Sharī'a al-Islāmiyya*, p. 438.
12 Ḥusayn Ḥāmid Ḥassān, *Naẓariyyat al-Maṣlaḥa fī al-Fiqh al-Islāmī*, 1st edition (Cairo: Maktabat al-Muthannā, 1401 AH/1981), pp. 40–1.
13 Muḥammad b. Idrīs al-Shāfi'ī, *Al-Risāla*, ed. Aḥmad Muḥammad Shākir, 1st edition (Beirut: Dār al-Kutub al-'Ilmiyya, n.d.), p. 20.
14 Muḥammad Sa'īd Ramaḍān al-Būṭī, *Ḍawābiṭ al-Maṣlaḥa fī al-Sharī'a al-Islāmiyya*, 1st edition (Damascus: al-Dār al-Muttaḥida, 1412 AH/1992), p. 109.
15 Ibn Taymiyya, *Majmū' al-Fatāwā*, vol. 3, p. 381.
16 Muḥammad Rashīd Riḍā, *Tafsīr al-Qur'ān al-Ḥakīm* (more famous as *Tafsīr al-Manār*), edited and explained by Ibrāhīm Shams al-Dīn, 1st edition (Beirut: Dār al-Kutub al-'Ilmiyya, 1420 AH/1999), vol. 2, p. 4.

17 Related by al-Bukhārī in the chapter *Al-Riqāq*. Related also by Ibn Mājah under *Al-Zuhd.*

18 Ibn Taymiyya, *Majmūʿ al-Fatāwā*, vol. 11, p. 342.

19 Ibn Taymiyya, *Majmūʿ al-Fatāwā*, p. 344.

20 Muḥammad b. Abū Bakr b. al-Qayyim, *Al-Ṭuruq al-Ḥukmiyya fī al-Siyāsa al-Sharʿiyya: Al-Firāsa al-Marḍiyya fī Aḥkām al-Siyāsa al-Sharʿiyya*, ed. Muḥammad Ḥāmid Fiqī, 1st edition (Beirut: Dār al-Kutub al-ʿIlmiyya, 1373 AH/1953), p. 13.

21 Kaḥḥāla, *Muʿjam al-Muʾallifīn*, vol. 3, p. 46; Al-Ziriklī, *Al-Aʿlām*, vol. 2, p. 55.

22 Al-Dhahabī, *Siyar Aʿlām al-Nubalāʾ*, vol. 9, p. 402.

23 Ibn Taymiyya, *Majmūʿ al-Fatāwā*, vol. 19, p. 271.

24 It seems from analysing scholars' statements that they take a lack of knowledge of dissent to be a reliable source of evidence. They use expressions such as 'We do not know of any dispute over this' and 'We do not know of any view that is at variance with this'. This can also be noticed in books of *fiqh*. See, for example, ʿAbd Allāh b. Aḥmad Ibn Qudāma, *Al-Mughnī*, ed. ʿAbd Allāh b. ʿAbd al-Muḥsin al-Turkī and ʿAbd al-Fattāh Muḥammad al-Ḥulw, 4th edition (Cairo: Dār Ālam al-Kutub, 1419 AH/1999), vol. 2, p. 271; vol. 12, p. 115.

25 Ibn Taymiyya, *Majmūʿ al-Fatāwā*, vol. 6, pp. 66–7.

26 ʿAbd al-ʿAzīz b. ʿAbd al-Salām b. Abū al-Qāsim, *Shajarat al-Maʿārif wal-Aḥwāl wa Ṣāliḥ al-Aqwāl wal-Aʿmāl*, 1st edition (Jeddah: Dār Mājid ʿUsayrī, 1400 AH/2000), p. 411.

27 Related by al-Bukhārī in the chapter entitled *Al-Iʿtiṣām bil-Kitāb wal-Sunna*; by Muslim in the chapters of *Al-Ḥajj* and *Al-Faḍāʾil*; by al-Tirmidhī in the chapter of *Al-ʿIlm*; by al-Nasāʾī in the chapter *of Manāsik al-Ḥajj*; by Ibn Mājah in his Introduction and by Aḥmad in *Bāqī Musnad al-Mukthirīn*.

28 Robin M. Hogarth, *Judgement and Choice*, 2nd edition (Singapore: Kim-hup lee printing, n.d.), pp. 72–139.

29 Herbert A. Simon, *Administrative Behaviour*, 4th edition (New York: The Free Press, 1997), pp. 22–139.

30 Ibn ʿAbd al-Salām, *Al-Qawāʾid al-Kubrā*, vol. 1, p. 75.

31 Ibn ʿAbd al-Salām, *Al-Qawāʾid al-Kubrā*, vol. 7, p. 219.

32 Saʿd al-Dīn b. Masʿūd al-Taftāzānī, *Al-Talwīh Sharḥ al-Tawḍīḥ fī Kashf Ḥaqāʾiq al-Tanqīḥ*, with comments by Muḥammad ʿAdnān, 1st edition (Beirut: Dār al-Arqam, 1418 AH/1998), p. 271.

33 Ibn Taymiyya, *Majmūʿ al-Fatāwā*, vol. 19, p. 270.

34 Related by al-Bukhārī under *Al-Iʿtiṣām bi al-Kitāb wa al-Sunna*, in the chapter entitled *Al-Iqtidāʾ bi Sunan Rasūlillāh Ṣallallāhu ʿAlayhi Wasallam*, vol. 8, p. 142.

35 For his biography, see Al-Mawlā Aḥmad b. Muṣṭafā Tāsh Kubrī Zada, *Miftāḥ al-Saʿāda wa Miṣbāḥ al-Siyāda*, 1st edition (Hyderabad al-Dakan: Maṭbaʿat Dāʾirat al-Maʿārif al-ʿUthmāniyya, n.d.), vol. 2, p. 54; Kaḥḥāla, *Muʿjam al-Muʾallifīn*, vol. 8, p. 239; Al-Ziriklī, *Al-Aʿlām*, vol. 5, p. 315.

36 Abū Bakr Muḥammad b. Aḥmad b. Sahl al-Sarakhsī, *Al-Mabsūṭ*, 1st edition (Al-Khubar: Dār Ibn ʿAffān, 1409 AH/1989), vol. 1, p. 64.

37 Muḥammad Sidqī b. Aḥmad al-Burnū, *Mawsūʿat al-Qawāʾid al-Fiqhiyya*, 2nd edition (Riyadh: Maktabat al-Tawba, 1417 AH/1997), vol. 2, p. 254.

38 Chapter 1 of ʿAbd al-Majīd Jumʿa al-Jazāʾirī, *Al-Qawāʾid al-Fiqhiyya al-Mustakhraja min Kitāb Iʿlām al-Muwaqqiʿīn li Ibn Qayyim al-Jawzjiyya*, 1st edition (Al-Dammām: Dār Ibn al-Qayyim, Dār Ibn ʿAffān for Publishing and Distribution, 1411 AH/1991).

39 See Muḥammad b. Abū Bakr b. Qayyim al-Jawziyya, *Iʿlām al-Muwaqqiʿīn ʿan Rabb al-ʿĀlamīn*, vol. 1, p. 161; *Al-Qawāʾid al-Fiqhiyya al-Mustakhraja min Kitāb Iʿlām al-Muwaqqiʿīn*, p. 435; Al-Burnū, *Mawsūʿat al-Qawāʾid al-Fiqhiyya*, vol. 1, p. 92.

40 Al-Burnū, *Mawsūʿat al-Qawāʾid al-Fiqhiyya*, vol. 1, p. 209.

41 Al-Sarakhsī, *Al-Mabṣūṭ*, vol. 1, p. 32; vol. 7, p. 87.

42 Ibn Taymiyya, *Majmūʿ al-Fatāwā*, vol. 25, pp. 125, 354; Al-Jazāʾirī, *Al-Qawāʾid al-Fiqhiyya al-Mustakhraja min Kitāb Iʿlām al-Muwaqqiʿīn*, p. 435.

43 Al-Sarakhsī, *Al-Mabṣūṭ*, vol. 26, p. 136; Al-Burnū, *Mawsūʿat al-Qawāʾid al-Fiqhiyya*, vol. 4, p. 425.

44 Al-Sarakhsī, *Al-Mabṣūṭ*, vol. 35, p. 135; Al-Burnū, *Mawsūʿat al-Qawāʾid al-Fiqhiyya*, vol. 4, p. 427.

45 Al-Burnū, *Mawsūʿat al-Qawāʾid al-Fiqhiyy*a, vol. 2, p. 65.

46 Al-Sarakhsī, *Al-Mabṣūṭ*, vol. 26, p. 137.

47 Abū al-Faḍl Jalāl al-Dīn ʿAbd al-Raḥmān b. Abū Bakr al-Suyūṭī, *Al-Ashbāh wal-Naẓāʾir fi Qawāʾid wa Furūʿ Fiqh al-Shāfiʿiyya*, ed. Khālid ʿAbd al-Fattāh Shibl, 1st edition (Beirut: Muʾassasat al-Kutub al-Thaqāfiyya, 1414 AH/1994), pp. 536–7.

48 Ibn ʿAbd al-Salām, *Al-Qawāʾid al-Kubrā*, pp. 130–1.

49 Maḥmūd Ḥāmid ʿUthmān, *Qāʾidat Sadd al-Dharāʾiʿ wa Atharuhā fi al-Fiqh al-Islāmī*, 1st edition (Cairo: Dār al-Ḥadīth, 1417 AH/1996), p. 211.
50 Al-Shāṭibī, *Al-Muwāfaqāt*, vol. 5, pp. 177–8.
51 ʿUthmān, *Qāʾidat Sadd al-Dharāʾiʿ*, p. 247.
52 Zayn al-ʿĀbidīn b. Ibrāhīm Ibn Nujaym, *Al-Ashbāh wal-Naẓāʾir*, ed. Muḥammad Muṭīʿ al-Ḥāfiẓ (Damascus: Dār al-Fikr, 1406 AH/1986), p. 99.
53 Henry Mintzberg, *The Structure of Organization: A Synthesis of Research*, 1st edition (New Jersey: Prentice-Hall, Inc. Engle Cliffs, 1979).
54 Henry Mintzberg, *The Rise and Fall of Strategic Planning* (Simon & Schuster Inc: The Free Press, 1994), pp. 23–7.
55 What is meant by 'the outcome departs from the intended objective' is that the outcome does not always conform to what is intended. Sometimes it is different from what is expected, and this is known after a decision has been taken to achieve a particular outcome. When this happens a corrective measure should be taken to adjust the action so that it leads to the planned outcome. This takes the form of opening a means to rectify the resulting outcome and bring it back to the intended outcome, or this may mean blocking a means, as the case requires. Means, in this way, are a method or a policy used by the administration to correct the outcome.
56 Muḥammad Muṣṭafā Shalabī, *Taʿlīl al-Aḥkām: ʿArḍ wa Taḥlīl li Ṭarīqat al-Taʿlīl wa Taṭawwurātihā fi ʿAṣr al-Ijtihād wal Taqlīd*, 2nd edition (Dār al-Nahḍa al-ʿArabiyya, 1401 AH/1981), p. 382.

Chapter Four: *Maṣlaḥa* Preferability

1 Ibn Abd al-Salām, *Al-Qawāʾid al-Kubrā*, vol. 1, p. 79; pp. 52–3.
2 Abū al-Faḍl Jamāl al-Dīn Muḥammad b. Mukrim b. Manẓūr, *Lisān al-ʿArab*, 3rd edition (Beirut: Dār Ṣādir, 1414 AH/1994), vol. 11, p. 524.
3 ʿAlī b. Aḥmad b. Ḥazm, *Al-Faṣl fī al-Milal wa al-Ahwāʾ wa al-Niḥal*, 2nd edition (Beirut: Dār al-Kutub al-ʿIlmiyya, 1420 AH/1999), vol. 3, pp. 33–4.
4 Ibn Khallikān, *Wafayāt al-Aʿyān*, vol. 3, p. 284. Also Kaḥḥāla, *Muʿjam al-Muʾallifīn*, vol. 4, p. 38.
5 ʿAlī b. Aḥmad b. Ḥazm, *Al-Muḥallā bi al-Āthār*, ed. ʿAbd al-Ghaffār al-Bindārī, 1st edition (Beirut: Dār al-Kutub al-ʿIlmiyya, 1408 AH/1988), p. 44.

6 Muḥammad b. Abū Bakr Muḥammad ʿAbd al-Raḥmān al-Shaẓīfī, *Mabaḥith al-Mufāḍala fī al-ʿAqīda* (Al-Khubar, Saudi Arabia: Dār Ibn ʿAffān, 1998), p. 17.

7 Ibn Ḥazm, *Al-Faṣl fī al-Milal wa al-Ahwāʾ wa al-Niḥal*, vol. 3, pp. 33–4.

8 Al-Rāghib al-Aṣfahānī (d. 502 AH) is considered one of leading Sunni scholars. In his book *Al-Mufradāt fī Gharīb al-Qurʾān*, he follows the Sunni tradition and answers various non-Sunni schools such as *al-Muʿtazila*, *al-Jabriyya* and *al-Qadariyya*, critically evaluating their arguments with rational and textual proofs. He was well versed in the Arabic language. See Kaḥḥāla, *Muʿjam al-Muʾallifīn*, vol. 4, p. 59; Al-Ziriklī, *Al-Aʿlām*, vol. 2, p. 255.

9 Abū al-Qāsim Ḥusayn b. Muḥammad b. al-Mufaḍḍal al-Rāghib al-Aṣfahānī, *Al-Mufradāt fī Gharīb al-Qurʾān*, ed. Muḥammad Sayyid Kīlānī (Beirut: Dār al-Maʿrifa, n.d.), pp. 380–1.

10 In his commentary on the Qur'an, Ibn Kathīr asserts that this does not contradict what has been reported in the two *Ṣaḥīḥs* of al-Bukhārī and Muslim quoting the Prophet as saying, 'Do not draw distinction between prophets.' What is meant here, according to Ibn Kathīr, is to draw distinction on the basis of one's own preference or personal zeal, having no clear evidence in support. When there is clear evidence, it should be followed. Scholars are unanimous that messengers are more distinguished than all other prophets, and that those of the messengers described as *ulū al-ʿazm*, the ones endowed with firm resolve, are of a higher rank than the rest. These are five, mentioned by name in two Qur'anic verses in *sūra* al-Aḥzāb and al-Shūrā. Again scholars are unanimous that Prophet Muhammad is of a higher rank than the other four. Next comes Abraham, then Moses, then Jesus and finally Noah according to the majority of scholars. Ibn Kathīr, *Tafsīr al-Qurʾān al-Aẓīm*, vol. 3, p. 46.

11 Al-Qarāfī, *Al-Furūq*, vol. 2, p. 18.

12 Abū Bakr Muṣṭafā Baʿīra et al., *Al-Mawsūa al-Idāriyya: Muṣṭalaḥāt Idāriyya Mukhtāra*, 2nd edition (Benghazi: Qār Yūnis University, 1411 AH/1991), p. 50.

13 Yūsuf Karam, *Tārīkh al-Falsafa al-Ḥadītha* (Beirut: Dār al-Qalam, n.d.), p. 276.

14 Related by Abū Dāwūd in the *Malāḥim* section of his *Sunan*, vol. 4, p. 109. It is classified as authentic by al-Albānī in his *Silsilat al-Aḥādīth al-Ṣaḥīḥa*, p. 599.

15 Ibn Taymiyya, *Majmūʿ al-Fatāwā*, vol. 35, p. 31.

16 Aḥmad b. ʿAbd al-Halim b. Taymiyya, *Fuṣūl fī Uṣūl al-Fiqh*, ed. Abū al-Faḍl ʿAbd al-Salam b. Muḥammad b. ʿAbd al-Karīm, 2nd edition (Cairo: Al-Maktaba al-Islāmiyya, 1420 AH/2000), p. 116.
17 Ibn Taymiyya, *Majmūʿ al-Fatāwā*, vol. 22, pp. 344–5.
18 ʿAbd al-Azīz b. Saṭṭām Āl Suʿūd, *Al-Athār Ghayr al-Akādīmiyya li al-Marḥala al-Jāmiʿiyya*, 1st edition (Beirut: Dār al-ʿIlm li al-Malāyīn, 1420 AH/2000), p. 79.
19 Ibn Taymiyya, *Majmūʿ al-Fatāwā*, vol. 17, pp. 57–62.
20 Ibn Taymiyya, *Majmūʿ al-Fatāwā*, vol. 24, pp. 195–6.
21 Ibn Taymiyya, *Majmūʿ al-Fatāwā*, vol. 10, pp. 427–9.
22 Ibn Taymiyya, *Majmūʿ al-Fatāwā*, vol. 20, pp. 48–54.
23 Ibn Taymiyya, *Majmūʿ al-Fatāwā*, vol. 20, p. 105.
24 Ibn Taymiyya, *Majmūʿ al-Fatāwā*, vol. 20, pp. 85–8.
25 Ibn Taymiyya, *Majmūʿ al-Fatāwā*, vol. 24, pp. 195–6.
26 Ibn Taymiyya, *Majmūʿ al-Fatāwā*, vol. 24, pp. 245–51.
27 Ibn Taymiyya, *Majmūʿ al-Fatāwā*, vol. 22, pp. 346–7.
28 Ibn Taymiyya, *Majmūʿ al-Fatāwā*, vol. 6, pp. 455–6.
29 Ibn Taymiyya, *Majmūʿ al-Fatāwā*, vol. 22, pp. 308–9.
30 Ibn Taymiyya, *Majmūʿ al-Fatāwā*, vol. 20, pp. 57–8.
31 Ibn Taymiyya, *Majmūʿ al-Fatāwā*, vol. 8, pp. 19–22.
32 Ibn Taymiyya, *Majmūʿ al-Fatāwā*, vol. 22, pp. 344–5.
33 Ibn Taymiyya, *Majmūʿ al-Fatāwā*, vol. 35, pp. 28–32.
34 Al-Shāṭibī, *Al-Muwāfaqāt*, vol. 1, p. 377.
35 Ibn Taymiyya, *Majmūʿ al-Fatāwā*, vol. 35, p. 31.
36 Ibn Taymiyya, *Majmūʿ al-Fatāwā*, vol. 20, pp. 57–8.
37 Ibn Taymiyya, *Majmūʿ al-Fatāwā*, vol. 24, pp. 245–51.
38 Ibn Taymiyya, *Majmūʿ al-Fatāwā*, vol. 10, pp. 511–14.
39 Ibn Taymiyya, *Majmūʿ al-Fatāwā*, vol. 6, pp. 41–2.
40 Ibn Taymiyya, *Majmūʿ al-Fatāwā*, vol. 22, p. 313.
41 Ibn Taymiyya, *Majmūʿ al-Fatāwā*, vol. 27, pp. 45–6.
42 Ibn Taymiyya, *Majmūʿ al-Fatāwā*, vol. 6, pp. 41–2.
43 This sign ($\cap$) indicates a correlation between two things, that is, what is better for an individual is contingent upon being more obedient to God. That means here that the greater the interdependence between the two, the better the action.
44 Ibn Taymiyya, *Majmūʿ al-Fatāwā*, vol. 10, pp. 427–9.
45 Ibn Taymiyya, *Majmūʿ al-Fatāwā*, vol. 13, p. 414.
46 Ibn Taymiyya, *Majmūʿ al-Fatāwā*, vol. 20, p. 172.

47 Ibn Taymiyya, *Majmūʿ al-Fatāwā*, vol. 5, pp. 132–41.
48 Ibn Taymiyya, *Majmūʿ al-Fatāwā*, vol. 20, p. 172.
49 Ibn Taymiyya, *Majmūʿ al-Fatāwā*, vol. 14, pp. 433–4.
50 Shalabī, *Taʿlīl al-Aḥkām*, p. 280.

Chapter Five: Types of *Maṣlaḥa* Preferability

1 Related by Muslim, vol. 4, no. 1994.
2 Ibn Taymiyya, *Majmūʿ al-Fatāwā*, vol. 24, pp. 251–2.
3 Related by al-Tirmidhī, vol. 5, p. 467; Abū Dāwūd, vol. 4, p. 316; and Ibn Mājah, vol. 1, p. 246.
4 Related by al-Bukhārī, vol. 7, p. 162.
5 Aḥmad b. ʿAlī al-Manjūr, *Sharḥ al-Manhaj al-Muntakhab ilā Qawāʿid al-Madhhab*, ed. Muḥammad al-Shaykh Muḥammad al-Amīn, 1st edition (Cairo: Dār Iḥyā' al-Kutub al-ʿArabiyya, n.d.), pp. 501–8.
6 Al-Manjūr, *Sharḥ al-Manhaj*, p. 726.
7 Al-Shāṭibī, *Al-Muwāfaqāt*, vol. 2, p. 67.
8 Al-Shāṭibī, *Al-Muwāfaqāt*, vol. 3, p. 53.
9 Al-Shāṭibī, *Al-Muwāfaqāt*, vol. 5, p. 351.
10 Muḥammad b. Abū Bakr b. Qayyim al-Jawziyya, *Zād al-Maʿād fī Hady Khayr al-ʿIbād* (Beirut: Muʾassasat al-Risāla, 1991), vol. 3, p. 486.
11 Al-Shāṭibī, *Al-Muwāfaqāt*, vol. 1, p. 319.
12 Mutual contradiction occurs when two factors mutually exclude each other in one situation. See al-Kafawī, *Al-Kulliyyāt*, p. 311.
13 Muḥammad b. Abū Bakr b. Qayyim al-Jawziyya, *Miftāḥ Dār al-Saʿāda wa Manshūr al-ʿIlm wa al-Irāda*, 2nd edition (Beirut: Dār al-Kutub al-ʿIlmiyya, 1422 AH/2002), pp. 400–1.
14 Abū Zayd al-Dabbūsī, *Taʾsīs al-Naẓar*, 2nd edition (Cairo: Maktabat al-Khānjī, 1414 AH/1994), p. 150; Al-Burnū, *Mawsūʿat al-Qawāʾid al-Fiqhiyya*, vol. 1, p. 526. For a biographical note on al-Dabbūsī, see Abū al-ʿAbbas Shams al-Dīn Aḥmad b. Muḥammad b. Abū Bakr b. Khallikān, *Wafayāt al-Aʿyān wa Anbāʾ Abnāʾ al-Zamān*, ed. Yūsuf al-Ṭawīl, 1st edition (Beirut: Dār al-Kutub al-ʿIlmiyya, 1419 AH/1998), vol. 3, p. 36.
15 Zayn al-ʿĀbidīn b. Ibrāhīm Ibn Nujaym, *Al-Ashbāh wal-Naẓāʾir*, ed. Muḥammad Muṭīʿ al-Ḥāfiẓ (Damascus: Dār al-Fikr, 1406 AH/1986), p. 99.

16 ʿAbd Allāh b. ʿAbd al-Raḥmān al-Bassām, *Nayl al-Maʾārib fī Tahdhīb Sharḥ ʿUmdat al-Ṭālib wa maʿahu al-Ikhtiyārāt al-Jaliyya fī al-Masāʾil al-Khilāfiyya*, 2nd edition (Mecca: Maktabat wa Maṭbaʿat al-Nahḍa al-Ḥadītha, n.d.), vol. 1, p. 183.

17 Al-Qarāfī, *Al-Furūq*, vol. 2, p. 150.

18 ʿAbd al-Salām al-ʿAsarī, *Naẓariyyat al-Akhdh bimā Jarā bihi al-ʿAmal fī al-Maghrib* (Rabat: Wizārat al-Awqāf wa al-Shuʾūn al-Islāmiyya, 1416 AH/1996), p. 62.

19 Ibn Khallikān, *Wafayāt al-ʿAyān*, vol. 3, p. 153.

20 Abū ʿĪsa Sīdī al-Mahdī al-Wazzānī, *Al-Nawāzil al-Jadīda al-Kubrā fīma li Ahl Fās wa Ghayrihim mina al-Badw wa al-Qurā* (Rabat: Wizārat al-Awqāf wa al-Shuʾūn al-Islāmiyya, 1966), vol. 9, p. 151.

21 Al-Wazzani, *Al-Nawāzil al-Jadīda al-Kubrā*, vol. 9, p. 101; Al-ʿAsarī, *Naẓariyyat al-Akhdh bimā Jarā bihi al-ʿAmal fī al-Maghrib*, p. 62.

22 Kaḥḥāla, *Muʿjam al-Muʾallifīn*, vol. 10, p. 116; Al-Ziriklī, *Al-Aʿlām*, vol. 6, p. 181.

23 Al-ʿAsarī, *Naẓariyyat al-Akhdh bimā Jarā bihi al-ʿAmal fī al-Maghrib*, p. 62.

24 Kaḥḥāla, *Muʿjam al-Muʾallifīn*, vol. 9, p. 77; Al-Zirikli, *Al-Aʿlām*, vol. 6, p. 42.

25 Muḥammad Amīn b. ʿUmar b. ʿĀbidīn, *Hāshiyat Ibn ʿĀbidīn*, 2nd edition (Beirut: Dār Iḥyaʾ al-Turāth al-ʿArabī, 1407 AH/1987), vol. 6, pp. 64–5.

26 See Ibn ʿAbd al-Salām, *Al-Qawāʾid al-Kubrā*, vol. 2, p. 101.

27 Ibn ʿAbd al-Salām, *Al-Qawāʾid al-Kubrā*, vol. 1, p. 8.

28 Ibn ʿAbd al-Salām, *Al-Qawāʾid al-Kubrā*, vol. 2, p. 102.

29 Ibn ʿAbd al-Salām, *Al-Qawāʾid al-Kubrā*, vol. 2, p. 87.

30 Ibn Nujaym, *Al-Ashbāh wa al-Naẓāʾir*, p. 99.

31 Ibn Nujaym, *Al-Ashbāh wa al-Naẓāʾir*, p. 85; Al-Suyūṭī, *Al-Ashbāh wa al-Naẓāʾir*, p. 83.

32 ʿAlī Haydar, *Durar al-Hukkām Sharḥ Majallat al-Aḥkām*, translated by Fahmī al-Husaynī, 1st edition (Beirut: Dār al-Kutub al-ʿIlmiyya, n.d.), vol. 1, p. 41; Al-Zarqā, Aḥmad b. Muḥammad, *Sharḥ al-Qawāʾid Al-Fiqhiyya*, ed. Muṣṭafā Aḥmad al-Zarqā, 2nd edition (Damascus: Dār al-Qalam, 1409 AH/1989), p. 201.

33 Muḥammad b. Muḥammad al-Muqqrī, *Al-Qawāʾid*, ed. Aḥmad b. ʿAbd Allāh b. Ḥumayd, 1st edition (Mecca: Umm Al-Qurā University, n.d.), vol. 1, p. 294.

34 Ibn Taymiyya, *Majmūʿ al-Fatāwā*, vol. 24, pp. 199–200.
35 Ibn ʿAbd al-Salām, *Al-Qawāʾid al-Kubrā*, vol. 1, p. 294.

Chapter Six: Criteria of *Maṣlaḥa* Preferability

1 Muḥammad Muṣṭafā Shalabī, *Taʿlīl al-Aḥkām: ʿArḍ wa Taḥlīl li Ṭarīqat al-Taʿlīl wa Taṭawwurātihā fi ʿAṣr al-Ijtihād wal Taqlīd*, 2nd edition (Dār al-Nahḍa al-ʿArabiyya, 1401 AH/1981), p. 140.
2 Al-Shāṭibī, *Al-Muwāfaqāt*, vol. 2, pp. 17–19; vol. 3, p. 171; vol. 5, p. 351.
3 Scott Plous, *The Psychology of Judgement and Decision Making* (New York: McGraw Hill, 1993), p. 104.
4 Al-Shāṭibī, *Al-Muwāfaqāt*, vol. 2, p. 31.
5 Al-Shāṭibī, *Al-Muwāfaqāt*, vol. 2, p. 31.
6 ʿAlī Aḥmad al-Nadwī, *Al-Qawāʾid al-Fiqhiyyā: Mafhūmuhā, Nashʾatuhā wa Taṭawwuruhā*, 2nd edition (Damascus: Dār al-Qalam, 1412 AH/1991), p. 123.
7 Zayn al-ʿĀbidīn b. Ibrāhīm Ibn Nujaym, *Al-Ashbāh wal-Naẓāʾir*, ed. Muḥammad Muṭīʿ al-Ḥāfiẓ (Damascus: Dār al-Fikr, 1406 AH/1986), p. 101.
8 See ʿAbd al-Salām al-ʿAsarī, *Naẓariyyat al-Akhdh bimā Jarā bihi al-ʿAmal fī al-Maghrib* (Rabat: Wizārat al-Awqāf wa al-Shuʾūn al-Islāmiyya, 1416 AH/1996), p. 69.
9 Yaʿqūb b. ʿAbd al-Wahhāb Al-Bāḥusayn, *Ṭuruq al-Istidlāl wa Muqaddimātuhā ʿinda al-Manāṭiqa wa al-Uṣūliyyīn* (Riyadh: Maktabat al-Rushd, 1421 AH/2001), p. 36.
10 Quṭb al-Dīn al-Rāzī, *Taḥrīr al-Qawāʾid al-Manṭiqiyya Sharḥ al-Risāla al-Shamsiyya* (Egypt: Dār Iḥyāʾ al-Kutub al-ʿArabiyya, n.d.), pp. 166–7; Al-Ghazālī, *Al-Mustaṣfā*, vol. 1, p. 43; Al-Bāḥusayn, *Ṭuruq al-Istidlāl wa Muqaddimātuhā*, pp. 36–7.
11 Al-Bāhusayn, *Ṭuruq al-Istidlāl wa Muqaddimātuhā*, p. 39.
12 Muhyī al-Dīn b. Sharaf al-Dīn al-Nawawī, *Al-Majmūʿ: Sharḥ al-Muhadhdhab*, 1st edition, ed. Maḥmūd Maṭarjī (Beirut: Dār al-Fikr, 1421 AH/2000), vol. 1, p. 187.
13 ʿAli b. Muḥammad al-Jurjānī, *Al-Taʿrīfāt: Qāmūs lughawī Fiqhī* (Egypt: Maṭbaʿat Muṣṭafā al-Bābī al-Ḥalibī, 1357 AH/1938), p. 17; Muḥammad b. ʿAlī al-Tahānawī, *Kashshāf Iṣṭilāḥāt al-Funūn* (Istanbul: Dār Qahramān, 1414 AH/1984), vol. 2, p. 600.

14 Al-Manāwī al-Ḥaddādī, *Al-Tawqīf ʿalā Muhimmāt al-Taʿārīf: Taʿārīf al-Alfāẓ al-Mutadāwala fī al-ʿUlūm al-Islāmiyya*, ed. Muḥammad Raḍwān al-Dāya, 1st edition (Damascus: Dār al-Fikr, 1990), p. 260.
15 Al-Bāḥusayn, *Ṭuruq al-Istidlāl*, p. 43.
16 Aḥmad b. Fāris b. Zakariyyā' al-Qazwīnī al-Rāzī, nicknamed Abū al-Ḥusayn, a top scholar of language and literature, who wrote several books including *Maqāyīs al-Lugha* and *al-Mujmal fī al-Lugha*. See Kaḥḥāla, *Muʿjam al-Muʾallifīn*, vol. 2, p. 40.
17 Al-Bāḥusayn, *Ṭuruq al-Istidlāl*, p. 23; Ibn Fāris, *Muʿjam Maqāyīs al-Lugha*, vol. 3, p. 462.
18 Al-Kafawī, *Al-Kulliyyāt*, p. 588.
19 Related by al-Bukhāri in the chapter of *Al-Nikāḥ*, vol. 6, p. 136.
20 See Ibn Manẓūr, *Lisān al-ʿArab*; Aḥmad b. Muḥammad b. ʿAlī al-Ḥamawī al-Fayyūmī, *Al-Miṣbāḥ al-Munīr fī Gharīb al-Sharḥ al-Kabīr li al-Rāfiʿī*, 2nd edition (Cairo: Niẓārat al-Maʿārif al-ʿUmūmiyya, 1909), '*ẓanna*'.
21 Al-Jurjānī, *Al-Tarīfāt*, p. 125; Al-Bāḥusayn, *Ṭuruq al-Istidlāl*, p. 44.
22 Muḥammad al-Ḥasan Ibn Abū Yaʿlā, *Al-ʿUdda fī Uṣūl al-Fiqh*, ed. Aḥmad b. ʿAlī Sayr al-Mubārākī, 2nd edition (Riyadh: Al-Mubārakī, 1420 AH/1990), p. 83; Al-Zarkashī, *Al-Baḥr al-Muḥīṭ*, vol. 1, p. 74.
23 Ibn Nujaym, *Al-Ashbāh wa al-Naẓāʾir*, p. 73.
24 Al-Kafawī, *Al-Kulliyyāt*, pp. 528, 583.
25 Kaḥḥāla, *Muʿjam al-Muʾallifīn*, vol. 3, p. 31; Al-Ziriklī, *Al-Aʿlām*, vol. 2, p. 38.
26 Al-Kafawī, *Al-Kulliyyāt*; Al-Tahānawī, *Kashāf Iṣṭilāḥāt al-Funūn*, vol. 2, p. 939.
27 Saʿd al-Dīn Al-Taftāzānī, *Sharḥ al-Talwīḥ ʿalā al-Tawḍīḥ li Matn al-Tanqīḥ* (Beirut, n.d.), vol. 2, p. 4.
28 Al-Bāḥusayn, *Ṭuruq al-Istidlāl*, p. 45.
29 Al-Bāḥusayn, *Ṭuruq al-Istidlāl*, p. 48.
30 Ibn Fāris, *Muʿjam Maqāyīs al-Lughah*, vol. 3, p. 173.
31 Ibn Abī Yaʿlā, *Al-ʿUdda*, vol. 1, p. 83; Abū al-Walīd Sulaymān b. Khalaf al-Bājī, *Al-Ḥudūd fī al-Uṣūl*, ed. Nazīh Ḥammād, 1st edition (Beirut: Mu'assasat al-Zughbī li al-Ṭibāʿa wa al-Nashr, 1392 AH/1973), p. 29.
32 Al-Jurjānī, *Al-Taʿrīfāt*, p. 113; Zayn al-Dīn b. Ibrāhīm b. Nujaym, *Ghamz ʿUyūn al-Baṣāʾir: Sharḥ Kitāb al-Ashbāh wa al-Naẓāʾir ʿalā Madhhab Abī Ḥanīfa*, ed. Aḥmad Muḥammad al-Ḥamawī, 1st edition (Beirut: Dār al-Kutub al-ʿIlmiyya, n.d.), vol. 1, p. 193.
33 Al-Bāḥusayn, *Ṭuruq al-Istidlāl*, p. 48.

34 See al-Kafawī, *Al-Kulliyyāt*, p. 528; Al-Tahānawī, *Kashāf Iṣṭilāḥāt al-Funūn*, vol. 2, p. 780.

35 See Muhyī al-Dīn b. Sharaf al-Dīn al-Nawawi, *Al-Majmū' Sharḥ al-Muhadhdhab*, ed. Muḥammad Najīb al-Muṭī'ī, 1st edition (Cairo: Maktabat Dār al-Turāth, n.d.), vol. 1, p. 166; Al-Nawawī, *Taḥrīr Alfāẓ al-Tanbīh*, ed. 'Abd al-Ghanī al-Daqr, 1st edition (Damascus: Dār al-Qalam, 1408 AH/1988), p. 36.

36 Muḥammad b. Abū Bakr b. Qayyim al-Jawziyya, *Badā'i' al-Fawā'id*, ed. Muḥammad al-Iskandarānī, 1st edition (Beirut: Dār al-Kitāb al-'Arabī), 1999, vol. 4, p. 26.

37 Al-Zarkashī, *Al-Baḥr al-Muḥīṭ*, vol. 1, p. 81.

38 Muḥammad Bahādir b. 'Abd Allāh al-Zarkashī, *Al-Manthūr fī al-Qawā'id*, ed. Fā'iq Aḥmad Maḥmūd (Kuwait: Wizārat al-Awqāf wa al-Shu'ūn al-Islāmiyya, 1402 AH/1982), vol. 2, pp. 284–5.

39 Ibn Fāris, *Mu'jam Maqāyīs al-Lugha*, vol. 6, p. 149.

40 Al-Zarkashī, *Al-Baḥr al-Muhīṭ*, vol. 1, p. 80; Ibn al-Najjār, *Sharḥ al-Kawkab al-Munīr*, vol. 1, p. 74.

41 Al-Kafawī, *Al-Kulliyyāt*, p. 943.

42 Al-Tahānawī, *Kashf Iṣṭilāḥāt al-Funūn*, vol. 3, p. 1513.

43 Shalabī, *Ta'līl al-Aḥkām*, p. 233.

44 Ibn 'Abd al-Salām, *Al-Qawā'id al-Kubrā*, vol. 2, p. 189.

45 Related by al-Bukhārī in the chapter of *Al-Ādāb*, vol. 7, p. 101; and by Muslim in the chapter of *Al-Faḍā'il*, vol. 4, p. 1813.

46 Ibn 'Abd al-Salām, *Al-Qawā'id al-Kubrā*, vol. 1, p. 132.

47 Al-Ghazālī, *Shifā' al-Ghalīl*, p. 260.

48 Al-Shāṭibī, *Al-Muwāfaqāt*, vol. 3, p. 257.

49 Muḥammad al-Ḥasan Muṣṭafā al-Bughā, *Dar' al-Mafsada fī al-Sharī'a al-Islāmiyya: Uṣūl wa Ḍawābiṭ wa Taṭbīqāt* (Damascus: Dār al-'Ulūm al-Insāniyya, 1417 AH/1997), p. 214.

50 See Ibn 'Abd al-Salām, *Al-Qawā'id al-Kubrā*, vol. 1, p. 246.

51 See Ibn 'Abd al-Salām, *Al-Qawā'id al-Kubrā*, vol. 1, p. 51.

52 'Abd al-Fattāḥ Abū Ghudda, *Qīmat al-Zamān 'Inda al-'Ulamā'*, 7th edition (Aleppo: Maktabat al-Maṭbū'āt al-Islāmiyya, 1417 AH/1996), p. 27.

53 Muḥammad b. Abū Bakr b. Qayyim al-Jawziyya, *Al-Jawāb al-Kāfī liman Sa'ala 'an al-Dawā' al-Shāfī*, 4th edition (Mecca: Maktabat Muṣṭafā al-Bāz, 2001), pp. 208–9.

54 Al-Shāṭibī, *Al-Muwāfaqāt*, vol. 2, p. 242.

55 Ibn ʿAbd al-Salām, *Al-Qawāʾid al-Kubrā*, vol. 1, pp. 124, 126.

56 Ibn ʿAbd al-Salām, *Al-Qawāʾid al-Kubrā*, vol. 1, p. 54.

57 Ibn Qayyim al-Jawziyya, *Zād al-Maʿad*, vol. 5, p. 826; Aḥmad b. ʿAbd al-Ḥalīm b. Taymiyya, *Al-Qawāʾid al-Nūrāniyya al-Fiqhiyya*, 2nd edition (Riyadh: Maktabat al-Maʿārif, 1403 AH/1983), p. 171.

58 Related by al-Bukhārī in his *Saḥīḥ*, in the chapter of *Al-Nikāḥ*, vol. 6, p. 123.

59 See Scott Plouse, *The Psychology of Judgement and Decision Making*, pp. 102–4.

60 See, for example: George M. Marakas, *Decision Support Systems in the 21st Century*, 1st edition (Upper Saddle River, NJ: Prentice Hall, 2003); Peter Kischka et al., *Models, Methods and Decision Support for Management*, 1st edition (New York: Physica-Verlag Heidelberg Company, 2001); Lawrence L. Lapin, *Statistics for Modern Business Decisions*, 5th edition (San Diego, CA: Harcourt Brace Jovanovich Publisher, 1990); Ralph L. Keeney, *Decision with Multiple Objectives: Preferences and Value Tradeoffs*, 4th edition (Cambridge: Cambridge University Press, 1990); George Wright and Paul Goodwin, *Forecasting with Judgement*, 1st edition (Chichester, West Sussex: John Wiley and Son's Ltd, 1998).

61 Related by al-Bukhārī in his *Ṣaḥīḥ*, in the chapter of *Al-Nikāḥ*, vol. 6, p. 123.

62 Al-Shāṭibī emphasizes the importance of ascertaining (*taḥqīq al-manāṭ*) that an effective cause behind an original ruling is proper (*munāsib*) to be used in other new cases. He clarifies that the effective cause of the original case may have been decided on the basis of 'definitive' knowledge, as there are multiple textual evidences indicating the suitability of such a meaning to be an effective cause behind the ruling in question. However, to ascertain that it exists in other similar cases is of an assumptive nature. Al-Shāṭibī, *Al-Muwāfaqāt*, vol. 1, p. 41. Al-Shāṭibī also looks at the compatibility of *maṣlaḥa* with the dictates of religion. He says that this is not determined on the basis of one piece of evidence or one text; it is determined on the basis of several items of evidence and several texts that together give a definitive conclusion. Al-Shāṭibī, *Al-Muwāfaqāt*, vol. 2, p. 39. Hassān indicates that such agreement is of a factual or theoretical definitive import. Hassān, *Naẓariyyat al-Maṣlaḥa*, pp. 54, 61. Also see Mohammad Kamali, *Principles of Islamic Jurisprudence* (Cambridge: The Islamic Texts Society, 2003), pp. 282–4 for the concept of *taḥqīq al-manāṭ*.

BIBLIOGRAPHY

Abū Ghudda, ʿAbd al-Fattāḥ, *Qīmat al-Zamān ʿInda al-ʿUlamāʾ*, 7th edition (Aleppo: Maktabat al-Maṭbūʿāt al-Islāmiyya, 1417 AH/1996).

Āl Suʿūd, ʿAbd al-Azīz b. Saṭṭām, *Al-Athār Ghayr al-Akādīmiyya li al-Marḥala al-Jāmiʿiyya*, 1st edition (Beirut: Dār al-ʿIlm li al-Malāyīn, 1420 AH/2000).

al-ʿĀlim, Yūsuf Ḥāmid, *Al-Maqāṣid al-ʿĀmma li al-Sharīʿa al-Islāmiyya*, 2nd edition (Riyadh: Al-Dār al-ʿĀlamiyya li al-Kitāb wa al-Sunna, 1414 AH/1994).

al-Āmidī, ʿAli b. Muḥammad, *Al-Iḥkām fī Uṣūl al-Aḥkām*, ed. Sayyid al-Jumaylī, 1st edition (Beirut: Dār al-Kitāb al-ʿArabī, 1404 AH).

——— *Al-Iḥkām fī Uṣūl al-Aḥkām*, 1st edition (Beirut: Al-Maktab al-Islāmī, 1402 AH/1982).

al-ʿAsarī, ʿAbd al-Salām, *Naẓariyyat al-Akhdh bimā Jarā bihi al-ʿAmal fī al-Maghrib* (Rabat: Wizārat al-Awqāf wa al-Shuʾūn al-Islāmiyya, 1416 AH/1996).

al-Bāḥusayn, Yaʿqūb b. ʿAbd al-Wahhāb, *Ṭuruq al-Istidlāl wa Muqaddimātuhā ʿinda al-Manāṭiqa wa al-Uṣūliyyīn* (Riyadh: Maktabat al-Rushd, 1421 AH/2001).

Baʿīra, Abū Bakr Muṣṭafā et al., *Al-Mawsūʿa al-Idāriyya: Muṣṭalaḥāt Idāriyya Mukhtāra*, 2nd edition (Benghazi: Qār Yūnis University, 1411 AH/1991).

al-Bājī, Abū al-Walīd Sulaymān b. Khalaf, *Al-Ḥudūd fī al-Uṣūl*, ed. Nazīh Ḥammād, 1st edition (Beirut: Muʾassasat al-Zughbī li al-Ṭibāʿa wa al-Nashr, 1392 AH/1973).

al-Bassām, ʿAbd Allāh b. ʿAbd al-Raḥmān, *Nayl al-Maʾārib fī Tahdhīb Sharḥ ʿUmdat al-Ṭālib wa maʿahu al-Ikhtiyārāt al-Jaliyya fī al-Masāʾil al-Khilāfiyya*, 2nd edition (Mecca: Maktabat wa Maṭbaʿat al-Nahḍa al-Ḥadītha, n.d.).

al-Bughā, Muḥammad al-Ḥasan Muṣṭafā, *Darʾ al-Mafsada fī al-Sharīʿa al-Islāmiyya: Uṣūl wa Ḍawābiṭ wa Taṭbīqāt* (Damascus: Dār al-ʿUlūm al-Insāniyya, 1417 AH/1997).

al-Burnū, Muḥammad Sidqī b. Aḥmad, *Mawsūʿat al-Qawāʾid al-Fiqhiyya*, 2nd edition (Riyadh: Maktabat al-Tawba, 1417 AH/1997).

al-Būṭī, Muḥammad Saʿīd Ramaḍān, *Ḍawābiṭ al-Maṣlaḥa fī al-Sharīʿa al-Islāmiyya*, 1st edition (Damascus: Al-Dār al-Muttaḥida, 1412 AH/1992).

al-Dabbūsī, Abū Zayd, *Taʾsīs al-Naẓar*, 2nd edition (Cairo: Maktabat al-Khānjī, 1414 AH/1994).

al-Darwīsh, ʿAbd al-Raḥman b. ʿAbd Allāh al-ʿAbd al-Karīm, *Al-Maṣāliḥ al-Mursala fī al-Sharīʿa al-Islāmiyya* (Riyadh: Al-Maʿhad al-ʿĀlī li al-Qaḍāʾ, Imām Muḥammad b. Saud Islamic University, 1389 AH/1968).

al-Dhahabī, Muhammad, *Siyar Aʿlām al-Nubalāʾ*, 2nd edition (Beirut: Muʾassasat al-Risāla, 1402 AH/1982).

al-Fayrūzabādī, Majd al-Dīn Muḥammad b. Yaʿqūb, *Al-Qāmūs al-Muḥīṭ*, 1st edition (Beirut: Dār Iḥyāʾ al-Turāth al-ʿArabī, 1417 AH/1997).

al-Fayyūmī, Aḥmad b. Muḥammad b. ʿAlī al-Ḥamawī, *Al-Miṣbāḥ al-Munīr fī Gharīb al-Sharḥ al-Kabīr li al-Rāfiʿī*, 2nd edition (Cairo: Niẓārat al-Maʿārif al-ʿUmūmiyya, 1909).

al-Futūḥī, Taqī al-Dīn Abū al-Baqāʾ al-Ḥanbalī, *Sharḥ al-Kawkab al-Munīr* (Maṭbaʿat al-Sunna al-Muḥammadiyya, n.d.).

al-Ghazālī, Abū Ḥāmid Muḥammad b. Muḥammad, *Al-Mustaṣfā min ʿIlm al-Uṣūl*, 1st edition (Beirut: Dār al-Kutub al-ʿIlmiyya, 1414 AH/1993).

——— *Al-Mustaṣfā min ʿIlm al-Uṣūl*, 3rd edition (Beirut: Dār Iḥyāʾ al-Turāth al-ʿArabī, 1414 AH/1993).

——— *Maʿārij al-Quds fī Madārij al-Nafs*, 2nd edition (Beirut: Dār al-Āfāq al-Jadīda, 1975).

——— *Shifāʾ al-Ghalīl fī Bayān al-Shabah wa al-Makhīl wa Masālik al-Taʿlīl*, ed. Ḥamad al-Kubaysī, 1st edition (Baghdad: Maṭbaʿat al-Irshād, 1390 AH/1971).

——— *Al-Mustaṣfā min ʿIlm al-Uṣūl*, ed. Ḥamza Zuhayr Ḥāfiẓ, 1st edition (Medina: Sharikat al-Madīna al-Munawwara li al-Ṭibāʿa wa al-Nashr, n.d.).

——— *Iḥyāʾ ʿUlūm al-Dīn* (Cairo: Maktabat Miṣr, n.d.).

al-Ḥaddādī, al-Manāwī, *Al-Tawqīf ʿalā Muhimmāt al-Taʿārīf: Taʿārīf al-Alfāẓ al-Mutadāwala fī al-ʿUlūm al-Islāmiyya*, ed. Muḥammad Raḍwān al-Dāya, 1st edition (Damascus: Dār al-Fikr, 1990).

Ḥassān, Ḥusayn Ḥāmid, *Naẓariyyat al-Maṣlaḥa fī al-Fiqh al-Islāmī*, 1st edition (Cairo: Maktabat al-Muthannā, 1401 AH/1981).

Haydar, ʿAlī, *Durar al-Hukkām Sharḥ Majallat al-Aḥkām*, translated by Fahmī al-Husaynī, 1st edition (Beirut: Dār al-Kutub al-ʿIlmiyya, n.d.).

——— *The Structure of Organization: A Synthesis of Research*, 1st edition (New Jersey: Prentice-Hall, Inc. Engle Cliffs, 1979).

Hogarth, Robin M., *Judgement and Choice*, 2nd edition (Singapore: Kim-hup Lee Printing, n.d.).

al-Husaynī, Abū Bakr b. Hidāyat Allāh, *Ṭabaqāt al-Shāfiʿiyya*, ed. ʿĀdil Nuwayhiḍ, 2nd edition (Dār al-Āfāq, 1399 AH/1997).

Ibn ʿAbd al-Salām, ʿAbd al-ʿAzīz b. ʿAbd al-Salām b. Abū al-Qāsim, *Al-Qawāʿid al-Kubrā*, (alias) *Qawāʿid al-Aḥkām fī Iṣlāḥ al-Anām*, ed. Nazīh Ḥammād and ʿUthmān Ḍamīriyya, 1st edition (Damascus: Dār al-Qalam, 1421 AH/2000).

——— *Shajarat al-Maʿārif wa al-Aḥwāl wa Ṣāliḥ al-Aqwāl wal-Aʿmāl*, 1st edition (Jeddah: Dār Mājid ʿAsyrī, 1400 AH/2000).

——— *Mukhtaṣar al-Fawā'id fī Aḥkām al-Maqāṣid*, (alias) *Al-Qawāʾid al-Ṣughra*, ed. Ṣāliḥ b. ʿAbd al-ʿAzīz al-Manṣūr, 1st edition (Riyadh: Dār al-Furqān, 1417 AH/1997).

Ibn ʿĀbidīn, Muḥammad Amīn b. ʿUmar, *Hāshiyat Ibn ʿĀbidīn*, 2nd edition (Beirut: Dār Iḥyaʾ al-Turāth al-ʿArabī, 1407 AH/1987).

Ibn Abū Yaʿlā, Muḥammad al-Ḥasan, *Ṭabaqāt al-Ḥanābila*, ed. ʿAbd al-Raḥmān al- ʿUthaymīn (n.p.: 1419 AH/1999).

——— *Al-ʿUdda fī Uṣūl al-Fiqh*, ed. Aḥmad b. ʿAlī Sīr al-Mubārākī, 2nd edition (Riyadh: Al-Mubārakī, 1420 AH/1990).

Ibn ʿĀshūr, Muḥammad, *Maqāṣid al-Sharīʿa al-Islāmiyya*, revised by Mohammed Tahar Almisawī, 2nd edition (Amman: Dār Al-Nafāʾis, 1421 AH/2001).

Ibn Fāris, Abū al-Ḥasan Aḥmad b. Fāris b. Zakariyya, *Muʿjam Maqāyīs al-Lugha*, ed. ʿAbd al-Salām Muḥammad Hārūn, 2nd edition (Cairo: Maktabat Muṣṭafā al-Bābī al-Ḥalabī, n.d.).

Ibn al-Ḥājib, ʿUthman b.ʿUmar b. Abū Bakr, *Mukhtaṣar al-Muntahā bi Sharḥ al-ʿAḍud* (Bulāq, 1316 AH).

Ibn Ḥazm, ʿAli b. Aḥmad, *Al-Faṣl fī al-Milal wa al-Ahwaʾ wa al-Niḥal*, 2nd edition (Beirut: Dār al-Kutub al-ʿIlmiyya, 1420 AH/1999).

——— *Al-Muḥallā bi al-Āthār*, ed. ʿAbd al-Ghaffār al-Bindārī, 1st edition (Beirut: Dār al-Kutub al-ʿIlmiyya, 1408 AH/1988).

Ibn Khallikān, Abū al-ʿAbbas Shams al-Dīn Aḥmad b. Muḥammad b. Abū Bakr, *Wafayāt al-Aʿyān wa Anbāʾ Abnāʾ al-Zamān*, ed. Yūsuf al-Ṭawīl, 1st edition (Beirut: Dār al-Kutub al-ʿIlmiyya, 1419 AH/1998).

Ibn Manẓūr, Abū al-Faḍl Jamāl al-Dīn Muḥammad b. Makram, *Lisān al-ʿArab*, 3rd edition (Beirut: Dār Ṣādir, 1414 AH/1994).

——— *Lisān al-ʿArab*, ed. ʿAlī Shīrī, 1st edition (Beirut: Dār Iḥyāʾ al-Turāth al-ʿArabī, 1408 AH/1988).

Ibn al-Najjār, Muḥammad b. Aḥmad b. ʿAbd al-ʿAzīz, *Sharḥ al-Kawkab al-Munīr*, (alias) *Mukhtaṣar al-Taḥrīr* or *Al-Mukhtabar al-Mubtakar fī Uṣūl al-Fiqh al-Islāmī*, 1st edition (Riyadh: Maktabat Al-ʿUbaykān, n.d.).

Ibn Nujaym, Zayn al-ʿĀbidīn b. Ibrāhīm, *Al-Ashbāh wa al-Naẓāʾir*, ed. Muḥammad Muṭīʿ al-Ḥāfiẓ (Damascus: Dār al-Fikr, 1406 AH/1986).

——— *Ghamz ʿUyūn al-Baṣāʾir: Sharḥ Kitāb al-Ashbāh wa al-Naẓāʾir ʿalā Madhhab Abī Ḥanīfa*, ed. Aḥmad Muḥammad al-Ḥamawī, 1st edition (Beirut: Dār al-Kutub al-ʿIlmiyya, n.d.).

Ibn al-Qayyim, Muḥammad b. Abū Bakr, *Iʿlām al-Muwaqqiʿīn ʿan Rabb al-ʿĀlamīn*, 1st edition (Beirut: Al-Maktaba al-ʿAṣriyya, 1407 AH/1987).

——— *Al-Ṭuruq al-Ḥukmiyya fī al-Siyāsa al-Sharʿiyya: Al-Firāsa al-Marḍiyya fī Aḥkām al-Siyāsa al-Sharʿiyya*, ed. Muḥammad Ḥāmid Fiqī, 1st edition (Beirut: Dār al-Kutub al-ʿIlmiyya, 1373 AH/1953).

Ibn Qayyim al-Jawziyya, Muḥammad b. Abū Bakr, *Miftāḥ Dār al-Saʿāda wa Manshūr al-ʿIlm wa al-Irāda*, 2nd edition (Beirut: Dār al-Kutub al-ʿIlmiyya, 1422 AH/2002).

——— *Al-Jawāb al-Kāfī li man Saʾala ʿan al-Dawāʾ al-Shāfī*, 4th edition (Mecca: Maktabat Muṣṭafā al-Bāz, 2001).

——— *Badāʾiʿ al-Fawāʾid*, ed. Muḥammad al-Iskandarānī, 1st edition (Beirut: Dār al-Kitāb al-ʿArabī, 1999).

——— *Zād al-Maʿād fī Hady Khayr al-ʿIbād* (Beirut: Mu'assast al-Risāla, 1991).

Ibn Qudāma, ʿAbd Allāh b. Aḥmad b. Muḥammad, *Al-Mughnī*, ed. ʿAbd Allāh b. ʿAbd al-Muḥsin al-Turkī and ʿAbd al-Fattāh Muḥammad al-Ḥulw, 4th edition (Cairo: Dār ʿĀlam al-Kutub, 1419 AH/1999).

——— *Rawḍat al-Nāẓir wa Junnat al-Munāẓir*, ed. ʿAbd al-ʿAzīz ʿAbd al-Raḥmān al-Saʿīd, 2nd edition (Riyadh: Imām Muḥammad b. Saud Islamic University, 1399 AH).

Ibn al-Subkī, ʿAbd al-Wahhāb b. ʿAli b. ʿAbd al-Kāfī, *Al-Jawāmiʿ: Nuskhat Ḥāshiyat al-ʿAṭṭār ʿalā Sharḥ al-Jalāl al-Maḥallī ʿalā al-Jawāmiʿ li Ḥasan b. Muḥammad b. Maḥmūd al-ʿAṭṭār al-Shāfiʿī* (Beirut: Dār al-Kutub al-ʿIlmiyya, n.d.).

Ibn Taymiyya, Aḥmad b. ʿAbd al-Ḥalīm, *Fuṣūl fī Uṣūl al-Fiqh*, ed. Abū al-Faḍl ʿAbd al-Salam b. Muḥammad b. ʿAbd al-Karīm, 2nd edition (Cairo: Al-Maktaba al-Islāmiyya, 1420 AH/2000).

——— *Al-Qawāʿid al-Nūrāniyya al-Fiqhiyya*, 2nd edition (Riyadh: Maktabat al-Maʿārif, 1403 AH/1983).

——— *Ziyārat al-Qubūr wa al-Istinjād bi al-Maqbūr*, 1st edition (Ṭanṭa: Dār al-Ṣaḥāba li al-Turāth, n.d.).

al-Jazā'irī, 'Abd al-Majīd Jum'a, *Al-Qawā'id al-Fiqhiyya al-Mustakhraja min Kitāb I'lām al-Muwaqqi'īn li Ibn Qayyim al-Jawziyya*, 1st edition (Al-Dammām: Dār Ibn al-Qayyim; Dār Ibn 'Affān for Publishing and Distribution, 1411 AH/1991).

al-Juhanī, Fahd b. Sa'd al-Zāydī, *Al-Qiyās 'inda al-Imām al-Shāfi'ī: Dirāsa Ta'ṣīliyya*, 1st edition (Riyadh: Imām Muḥammad b. Saud Islamic University, 1424 AH/2003).

al-Jurjānī, 'Ali b. Muḥammad, *Al-Ta'rīfāt: Qāmūs lughawī Fiqhī* (Egypt: Maṭba'at Muṣṭafā al-Bābī al-Ḥalibī, 1357 AH/1938).

al-Juwaynī, 'Abd al-Malik b. 'Abd Allāh Abū al-Ma'ālī, *Al-Burhān fī Uṣūl al-Fiqh*, ed. 'Abd al-'Aẓīm Maḥmūd al-Dīb, 4th edition (Al-Manuṣūra, Egypt: Dār al-Wafā', 1418 AH).

——— *Al-Burhān fī Uṣūl al-Fiqh*, 1st edition (Al-Manṣūra, Egypt: Dār al-Wafā', 1412 AH/1992).

al-Kafawī, Abū al-Baqā' Ayyūb b. Mūsā al-Ḥusaynī, *Al-Kuliyyāt: Mu'jam fī al-Muṣṭalaḥāt wal-Furūq al-Lughawiyya* (Beirut: Mu'assasat al-Risāla, 1418 AH/1998).

Kaḥḥāla, 'Umar, *Mu'jam al-Mu'allifīn* (Damascus: Al-Taraqī Press, 1376 AH/1957).

Kamali, Mohammad, *Principles of Islamic Jurisprudence* (Cambridge: The Islamic Texts Society, 2003).

Karam, Yūsuf, *Tārīkh al-Falsafa al-Ḥadītha* (Beirut: Dār al-Qalam, n.d.).

Keeney, Ralph L., *Decision with Multiple Objectives: Preferences and Value Tradeoffs*, 4th edition (Cambridge: Cambridge University Press, 1990).

Khān, Ṣiddīq, *Al-Dīn al-Khāliṣ*, 1st edition (Cairo: Maktabat Dār al-Turāth, n.d.).

Kischka, Peter, et al., *Models, Methods and Decision Support for Management*, 1st edition (New York: Physica-Verlag Heidelberg Company, 2001).

al-Lakhmī, Ramaḍān 'Abd al-Wadūd, *Al-Ta'līl bi al-Maṣlaḥa 'inda al-Uṣūliyyīn*, 1st edition (Cairo: Dār al-Hudā li al-Ṭibā'a, 1407 AH/1987).

Lapin, Lawrence L., *Statistics for Modern Business Decisions*, 5th edition (San Diego, CA: Harcourt Brace Jovanovich Publisher, 1990).

al-Manjūr, Aḥmad b. 'Alī, *Sharḥ al-Manhaj al-Muntakhab ilā Qawā'id al-Madhhab*, ed. Muḥammad al-Shaykh Muḥammad al-Amīn, 1st edition (Cairo: Dār Iḥyā' al-Kutub al-'Arabiyya, n.d.).

Manūn, ʿĪsā, *Nibrās al-ʿUqūl fī Taḥqīq al-Qiyās ʿinda ʿUlamāʾ al-Uṣūl*, 1st edition (Egypt: Maṭbaʿat al-Taḍāmun al-Akhawī, 1345 AH).

Marakas, George M., *Decision Support Systems in the 21st Century*, 1st edition (Upper Saddle River, NJ: Prentice Hall, 2003).

Mintzberg, Henry, *The Rise and Fall of Strategic Planning* (Simon & Schuster Inc. The Free Press, 1994).

al-Muqqrī, Muḥammad b. Muḥammad, *Al-Qawāʾid*, ed. Aḥmad b. ʿAbd Allāh b. Ḥumayd, 1st edition (Mecca: Umm Al-Qurā University, n.d.).

al-Murshid, ʿUthmān b. Ibrāhīm b. Murshid, *Al-Maqāṣid min Aḥkām al-Shāriʿ wa Atharuhā fī al-ʿUqūd*, unpublished research (Umm Al-Qurā University, 1402 AH/1982).

al-Nadwī, ʿAlī Aḥmad, *Al-Qawāʾid al-Fiqhiyyā: Mafhūmuhā, Nashʾatuhā wa Taṭawwuruhā*, 2nd edition (Damascus: Dār al-Qalam, 1412 AH/1991).

al-Nawawi, Muhyī al-Dīn b. Sharaf al-Dīn, *Al-Majmūʿ Sharḥ al-Muhadhdhab*, ed. Maḥmūd Maṭarjī (Beirut: Dār al-Fikr, 1421 AH/2000).

——— *Taḥrīr Alfāẓ al-Tanbīh*, ed. ʿAbd al-Ghanī al-Daqr, 1st edition (Damascus: Dār al-Qalam, 1408 AH/1988).

——— *Al-Majmūʿ: Sharḥ al-Muhadhdhab*, ed. Muḥammad Najīb al-Muṭīʿī, 1st edition (Cairo: Maktabat Dār al-Turāth, n.d.).

Plous, Scott, *The Psychology of Judgement and Decision Making* (New York: McGraw Hill, 1993).

al-Qarāfī, Aḥmad b. Idrīs b. ʿAbd al-Raḥmān, *Nafāʾis al-Uṣūl fī Sharḥ al-Maḥṣūl*, ed. ʿAli Muḥammad Mu'awwaḍ and ʿĀdil Aḥmad ʿAbd al-Mawjūd, 3rd edition (Beirut: Al-Maktaba al-ʿAṣriyya, 1419 AH/1999).

——— *Al-Furūq*, 1st edition (Beirut: Dār al-Kutub al-ʿIlmiyya, 1418 AH/1998).

al-Rāghib al-Aṣfahānī, Abū al-Qāsim Ḥusayn b. Muḥammad b. al-Mufaḍḍal, *Tafṣīl al-Nashʾatayn wa Taḥṣīl al-Saʿādatayn*, ed. ʿAbd al-Majīd al-Najjār, 1st edition (Beirut: Dār al-Gharb al-Islāmī, 1408 AH/1988).

——— *Al-Mufradāt fī Gharīb al-Qurʾān*, ed. Muḥammad Sayyid Kīlānī (Beirut: Dār al-Maʿrifa, n.d.).

al-Rāzī, Fakhr al-Dīn Muḥammad b. ʿUmar b. al-Ḥusayn, *Al-Maḥṣūl fī ʿIlm Uṣūl al-Fiqh*, ed. Jābir Fayyāḍ al-ʿAlwāni, 1st edition (Beirut: Dār al-Kutub al-'Ilmiyya, 1418 AH/1998).

——— *Al-Maḥṣūl fī ʿIlm al-Uṣūl*, ed. Ṭāḥa Jābir al-ʿAlwānī, 1st edition (Riyadh: Imām Muḥammad b. Saud Islamic University, 1400 AH).

al-Rāzī, Quṭb al-Dīn, *Taḥrīr al-Qawāʾid al-Manṭiqiyya Sharḥ al-Risāla al-Shamsiyya* (Egypt: Dār Iḥyāʾ al-Kutub al-ʿArabiyya, n.d.).

Riḍā, Muḥammad Rashīd, *Tafsīr al-Qur'ān al-Ḥakīm* (more famous as *Tafsīr al-Manār*), edited and explained by Ibrāhīm Shams al-Dīn, 1st edition (Beirut: Dār al-Kutub al-ʿIlmiyya, 1420 AH/1999).

al-Sarakhsī, Abū Bakr Muḥammad b. Aḥmad b. Sahl, *Al-Mabsūṭ*, 1st edition (Al-Khubar: Dār Ibn ʿAffān, 1409 AH/1989).

al-Shāfiʿī, Muḥammad b. Idrīs, *Al-Risāla*, ed. Aḥmad Muḥammad Shākir, 1st edition (Beirut: Dār al-Kutub al-ʿIlmiyya, n.d.).

Shalabī, Muḥammad Muṣṭafā, *Taʿlīl al-Aḥkām: ʿArḍ wa Taḥlīl li Ṭarīqat al-Taʿlīl wa Taṭawwurātihā fi ʿAṣr al-Ijtihād wal Taqlīd*, 2nd edition (Dār al-Nahḍa al-ʿArabiyya, 1401 AH/1981).

al-Shanqīṭī, ʿAbd Allāḥ b. al-Ḥājj Ibrāhīm al-Shanqīṭī, *Marāqī al-Suʿūd li Mubtaghī al-Ruqiyy wa al-Ṣuʿūd: Nuskhat Nathr al-Wurūd ʿalā Marāqī al-Suʿūd li Muḥammad al-Amīn b. Muḥammad al-Mukhtār al-Shanqīṭī*, 1st edition (Beirut: Al-Maṭbaʿa al-ʿAṣriyya, 1425 AH/2004).

al-Shanqīṭī, Muḥammad al-Amīn b. Muḥammad al-Mukhtār, *Aḍwā' al-Bayān* (Beirut: Dār al-Fikr, 1415 AH/1995).

al-Shāṭibī, Ibrāhīm b. Mūsā b. Muḥammad, *Al-Iʿtiṣām*, 2nd edition (Amman: Al-Dār al-Athariyya, 1428 AH/2007).

——— *Al-Muwāfaqāt*, ed. Ibrahīm Ramaḍan, with comments by ʿAbd Allāh Draz, 4th edition (Beirut: Dār al-Maʿrifa, 1420 AH/1999).

——— *Al-Muwāfaqāt*, 1st edition (KSA, Al-Khubar: Dār Ibn ʿAffān, 1417 AH/1997).

——— *Al-Iʿtiṣām*, ed. ʿAbd al-Razzāq al-Mahdī (Beirut: Dār al-Kitāb al-ʿArabī, 1416 AH/1996).

Shawkānī, Muḥammad Ali, *Irshād al-Fuḥūl ilā Taḥqīq alḥaq min ʿilm al-Uṣūl*, revised by Abu Ḥafṣ Sami ibn Arab al-Atharī, 1st edition (Riyadh: Dār al-Faḍilah, 2000).

al-Shaẓīfī, Muḥammad b. Abū Bakr Muḥammad ʿAbd al-Raḥmān, *Mabāḥith al-Mufāḍala fī al-ʿAqīda* (Al-Khubar, Saudi Arabia: Dār Ibn ʿAffān, 1998).

Simon, Herbert A., *Administrative Behaviour*, 4th edition (New York: The Free Press, 1997).

al-Suyūṭī, Abū al-Faḍl Jalāl al-Dīn ʿAbd al-Raḥmān b. Abū Bakr, *Al-Ashbāh wa al-Naẓā'ir fi Qawā'id wa Furūʿ Fiqh al-Shāfiʿiyya*, ed. Khālid ʿAbd al-Fattāh Shibl, 1st edition (Beirut: Mu'assasat al-Kutub al-Thaqāfiyya, 1414 AH/1994).

al-Taftāzānī, Saʿd al-Dīn b. Masʿūd, *Al-Talwīḥ Sharḥ al-Tawḍīḥ fī Kashf Ḥaqā'iq al-Tanqīḥ*, with comments by Muḥammad ʿAdnān, 1st edition (Beirut: Dār al-Arqam, 1418 AH/1998).

al-Tahānawī, Muḥammad b. ʿAlī, *Kashshāf Iṣṭilāḥāt al-Funūn* (Istanbul: Dār Qahramān, 1414 AH/1984).

Tāsh Kubrī Zada, Al-Mawla Aḥmad b. Muṣṭafā, *Miftāḥ al-Saʿāda wa Miṣbāḥ al-Siyāda*, 1st edition (Hyderabad al-Dakan: Maṭbaʿat Dāʾirat al-Maʿārif al-ʿUthmāniyya, n.d.).

al-Ṭūfī, Najm al-Dīn, *Sharḥ Mukhtaṣar al-Rawḍa*, ed. ʿAbd Allāh b. ʿAbd al-Muḥsin al-Turkī, 4th edition (Beirut: Mu'assasat al-Risāla, 1424 AH/2003).

——— *Kitāb al-Taʿyīn fī Sharḥ al-Arbaʿīn*, ed. Aḥmad Ḥājj 'Uthmān, 1st edition (Beirut: Mu'assasat al-Rayyān, 1419 AH/1998).

al-Ṭūfī, Najm al-Dīn b. Sulaymān b. ʿAbd al-Karīm, *Sharḥ Mukhtaṣar al-Rawḍa*, ed. ʿAbd Allāh ʿAbd al-Muḥsin al-Turkī, 1st edition (Beirut: Muʾassasat al-Risāla, 1408 AH/1988).

ʿUthmān, Maḥmūd Ḥāmid, *Qāʾidat Sadd al-Dharāʾiʿ wa Atharuhā fi al-Fiqh al-Islāmī*, 1st edition (Cairo: Dār al-Ḥadīth, 1417 AH/1996).

al-Wazzānī, Abū ʿĪsa Sīdī al-Mahdī, *Al-Nawāzil al-Jadīda al-Kubrā fīma li Ahl Fās wa Ghayrihim mina al-Badw wa al-Qurā* (Rabat: Wizārat al-Awqāf wa al-Shuʾūn al-Islāmiyya, 1966).

Wright, George and Paul Goodwin, *Forecasting with Judgement*, 1st edition (West Sussex: John Wiley and Son's Ltd, 1998).

al-Yūbī, Muḥammad Saʿd b. Aḥmad b. Masʿūd, *Maqāṣid al-Sharīʿa al-Islāmiyya wa ʿIlāqatuha bil-adilla al-Sharʿiyya*, 1st edition (Riyadh: Dār al-Hijra, 1419 AH/1998).

al-Zarkashī, Muḥammad Bahādir b. ʿAbd Allāh, *Al-Baḥr al-Muḥīt*, 1st edition (Dār Alkitbi, 1414 AH/1994).

——— *Al-Baḥr al-Muḥīṭ fī Uṣūl al-Fiqh*, eds ʿAbd al-Sattār Abū Ghudda and ʿAbd al-Qādir ʿAbd Allāh al-ʿĀnī, 2nd edition (Kuwait: Ministry of Endowments and Islamic Affairs, 1413 AH/1992).

——— *Al-Manthūr fī al-Qawāʾid*, ed. Fāʾiq Aḥmad Maḥmūd (Kuwait: Wizārat al-Awqāf wa al-Shuʾūn al-Islāmiyya, 1402 AH/1982).

al-Zarqā, Aḥmad b. Muḥammad, *Sharḥ al-Qawāʾid al-Fiqhiyya*, ed. Muṣṭafā Aḥmad al-Zarqā, 2nd edition (Damascus: Dār al-Qalam, 1409 AH/1989).

Zayd, Muṣṭafā, *Al-Maṣlaḥa fī al-Tashrīʿ al-Islāmī wa Najm al-Dīn al-Ṭūfī*, 2nd edition (Cairo: Dār al-Fikr al-ʿArabī).

al-Ziriklī, Khayr al-Dīn, *Al-Aʿlām*, 6th edition (Beirut: Dār al-ʿIlm li al-Malāyīn, 1404 AH/1984).

INDEX